Walt —
Thanks for putting me on the right track at Canisius. Best, always, and beware the Tiger!

Jack

BITTEN by the TIGER

BITTEN by the TIGER

THE TRUE STORY OF IMPEACHMENT, THE GOVERNOR & TAMMANY HALL

Jack O'Donnell

CHAPEL HILL
PRESS, INC.

Copyright © 2013 John F. O'Donnell

All rights reserved. No part of this book may be used, reproduced or transmitted in any form or by any means, electronic or mechanical, including photograph, recording, or any information storage or retrieval system, without the express written permission of the author, except where permitted by law.

First Printing

Publisher's Cataloging-In-Publication Data (Prepared by The Donohue Group, Inc.)
O'Donnell, Jack, 1974-
    Bitten by the tiger : the true story of impeachment, the Governor & Tammany Hall / Jack O'Donnell.
    p. : ill. ; cm.
    Includes bibliographical references.
    ISBN: 978-1-59715-096-5
    1. Sulzer, William, 1863-1941. 2. Sulzer, William, 1863-1941—Impeachment. 3. Tammany Hall—History. 4. Governors—New York (State)—Biography. 5. Impeachments—New York (State)—History—20th century. 6. New York (State)—Politics and government—1865-1950. I. Title.
F124 .O366 2013
974.7/041/092 B   2013948338

The book is dedicated to my father, John O'Donnell. He inspired my love of history and politics and I enjoy ~~arguing~~ discussing both with him.

It is dedicated also to my grandfather Thomas J. O'Donnell, with whom I truly wish I could have talked about William Sulzer and Al Smith and Charles Murphy.

Finally, to my wife, Marina O'Donnell, you encourage and inspire me, you tolerate and support me, and you continue to take my breath away. I would be lost without you. Love, always and forever. Desayuna!

CONTENTS

Foreword..xiii

PART ONE

Chapter One: A Reformer Is Born...............................3
Chapter Two: Empire State Politics and Tammany Hall...............9
Chapter Three: William Sulzer's Political Beginnings................15
Chapter Four: Onward to Congress..............................23
Chapter Five: Mayor William Gaynor............................31
Chapter Six: The Campaign of 1910.............................37
Chapter Seven: The Election of 1912............................49

PART TWO

Chapter Eight: Governor William Sulzer..........................67
Chapter Nine: Legislative Program..............................81
Chapter Ten: Reformer.......................................85
Chapter Eleven: The Commission on Inquiry......................93
Chapter Twelve: "Gaffney or War!"............................101

Chapter Thirteen: Jobs, Jobs, and More Jobs 109
Chapter Fourteen: Direct Primaries. 113
Chapter Fifteen: The Scandals. 139

PART THREE

Chapter Sixteen: The Frawley Committee. 147
Chapter Seventeen: The Sulzer Campaign Fund. 153
Chapter Eighteen: Impeachment. 161
Chapter Nineteen: The Fallout 175
Chapter Twenty: Governor Glynn? 185

PART FOUR

Chapter Twenty-One: Court of Impeachment 191
Chapter Twenty-Two: The Verdict 229

PART FIVE

Chapter Twenty-Three: Aftermath 239
Chapter Twenty-Four: The Campaign of 1917. 251
Chapter Twenty-Five: A Ghost Before He Died 259

Acknowledgments 263
Notes 265
Bibliography 277

I want no glory — no credit for doing my duty — no future preferment — and when the office the People gave me goes back to the People — to whom it belongs — to give to some other man — I say again, and I say advisedly — I want to retire from the misrepresentations and the disappointments of political life — to a little farm, by the side of the road, and be the friend of man.[1]

—WILLIAM SULZER

I would not be alive today without the family of my organ donor. They made a wonderful choice during a very difficult time, giving me the Gift of Life. I am forever grateful.

In appreciation, any proceeds from this book will be donated to the Transplant Miracles Foundation, which is dedicated to furthering organ transplant research, supporting the treatment and care of transplant recipients, and promoting organ donation. More information is available at www.TransplantMiracles.org.

FOREWORD

William Sulzer is remembered by history as a wronged man. He was a reformer destroyed by the corrupt system he was elected to challenge and that he tried to change. As a politician, Sulzer was extremely ambitious and very successful. Under his governorship, New York led the nation in progressive legislation, from workers' rights (especially protections for women and children) to food safety and the protection of natural resources. From there he became the first—and thus far last—governor of New York to be impeached. Immediately afterward he was returned to Albany after being elected by an overwhelming majority to the Assembly.

A polarizing figure, Sulzer provoked strong emotions throughout his career. His supporters pointed to his accomplishments while his detractors doubted his motives, his tactics, and his choice of allies. Nonetheless, as we shall see, the heavy-handed nature of his impeachment caused a backlash, and Sulzer is remembered in a positive light—when he is remembered at all. As one writer said, "To this day the name William Sulzer evokes in the public mind the memory of an independent governor 'railroaded' out of office by a revengeful boss, of an altruistic and devoted friend of the people and champion of good government frustrated by a corrupt and vindictive machine."[1]

Although defunct and defanged by the 1930s, Tammany Hall still today evokes the corrupt organizations of a bygone era of political bosses, smoke-filled rooms, and stolen elections.

Tammany was constantly criticized by reformers and good-government groups while periodic investigations exposed graft and corruption, resulting in various prosecutions. However, to millions of immigrants, Tammany Hall was their guide to American culture and citizenship. To the mostly Irish and German immigrants, Tammany provided food, shelter, and jobs; the political organization provided the social safety net that helped them survive. To Tammany, they gave their loyalty along with the numerous and reliable votes that kept Tammany in power.

Over time, reputations change. In fact, time and events change both men and history. Political scientist (and later president) Woodrow Wilson saw President Andrew Johnson as a hero,[2] but in his time Johnson left office in disgrace; again today, historians consistently rank his presidency as among the worst in history.[3] Dwight Eisenhower, once perceived as a duffer, has seen a recent upsurge in popularity. So, too, have the reputations of Presidents John Adams and Harry Truman been improved.[4] Seen beyond their own time—and in the context of other times—different values are recognized and appreciated, and the full range of actions can be measured. This book is an examination of Sulzer's historical legacy.

The greatest thing about history is that, much like beauty itself, it is in the eye of the beholder. As such, Sulzer's story is complex and confusing. The facts have been clouded by heliographs, propaganda, mistakes, half-truths, and straight-out lies, until the truth itself is difficult to determine.

The author of one of the only objective histories of the events surrounding William Sulzer, Jacob Alexis Friedman, writing in 1939, found that "Despite the importance of the case and the widespread interest it arouses, there is a surprising paucity of reliable material and the facts recorded are of only fragmentary nature." Friedman continued, "The few accounts published are frankly partisan, being almost wholly anti-Tammany, and are incomplete and distorted. Indignant and denunciatory, almost all writers accept unquestioningly Sulzer's version of the incidents that led to his break with Sulzer's nemesis, the Tammany Hall Leader Charles Francis Murphy and the legislative leaders and base their narratives almost solely on the statements issued by him after the trial."⁵ History, once corrupted, is hard to set straight again.

In this case, the nature of the protagonists served to further distort the record. Sulzer himself spoke regularly and voluminously to the press (except during his impeachment) although his veracity was questionable, while Murphy was nicknamed "Silent Charlie" because of his reticence.

Sulzer's story reaches its crescendo in 1912. In that year, New York was truly the Empire State and the major player in national politics. A New Yorker was on the national ticket as either a presidential or vice presidential candidate ten out of the eleven campaigns from 1868 through 1908, and in 1904 both presidential candidates were from New York.⁶ The 1910 population of the state was 9,113,614—more than 25 percent of the entire republic.⁷ The Statute of Liberty was only twenty-six years old in 1912 and still served as a beacon of welcome for millions of immigrants. These immigrants were the men and women who have made America—and New York City—great. They also created the New York City of William Sulzer and Tammany Hall, a city divided by class. These newcomers were the fuel that powered the Tammany machine.

The cast of characters in the story of Sulzer's governorship and subsequent impeachment is as rich and varied as the state in which it takes place. These characters include:

- WILLIAM SULZER. A longtime member of Congress and former speaker of the New York State Assembly, he liked to be called "Plain Bill." In the Assembly he outlawed imprisonment for debt. As a congressman he was national leader as chair of the Committee on Foreign Relations. His gregariousness endeared him to Tammany leaders, who rewarded him and supported him in his campaigns for Assembly, Congress, and governor. His work on Jewish issues in Washington gave him an important political edge and landed him as head of the Democratic ticket in New York in 1912.
- CHARLES FRANCIS MURPHY. A saloonkeeper, Murphy rose from district

leader in the Gas Light District to become the undisputed head of Tammany Hall in 1902 until his death in 1924. Unlike earlier bosses, Murphy was a taciturn teetotaler who pushed progressive policies to reward the immigrants who voted for Tammany but also to distance the organization from its past, especially his predecessor, "Boss" William Tweed.*

- AL SMITH. Elected Speaker of the New York Assembly the same year Sulzer was elected governor, Smith was another politician who had risen through the ranks of Tammany Hall. Close to Murphy he was promoted above several other more experienced legislators to become Speaker. Later president of the New York City Board of Aldermen, Smith was elected four times as governor and was the first Catholic candidate of a major political party for president. He also was president of the Empire State Building Company.
- ROBERT F. WAGNER. Wagner became president pro tem of the New York State Senate in the same landslide that elected Sulzer as governor and Smith as Speaker. Wagner served in the state senate through 1918, when he was elected a Justice of the Supreme Court and, later, four terms as a U.S. senator. Wagner was a member of Franklin Roosevelt's Brain Trust and the author of groundbreaking legislation especially in the area of labor protections.
- WOODROW WILSON. Wilson's improbable rise from university president to president of the United States in just two years inspired

---

* The Tweed Ring, infamous for corruption, was exposed in part by the political cartoons of Thomas Nast. Elected to the U.S. House of Representatives, the New York State Senate, and the New York County Board of Supervisors, Tweed himself was the third largest landowner in New York City; a director of the Erie Railroad, the Tenth National Bank, and the New York Railroad; as well as the proprietor of the Metropolitan Hotel at the height of his influence. A committee of aldermen estimated his malfeasance at between $25 million and $45 million, or roughly $1 billion to $1.8 billion in 2010 dollars. Convicted of corruption, Tweed died in the Ludlow Street Jail after a well-publicized flight from justice.

others, including Sulzer, who shared the ambition to follow in Wilson's boss-busting footsteps. Wilson was elected president in 1912, the same year Sulzer was elected governor.
- THEODORE ROOSEVELT. The former president's candidacy for president in 1912 split the Republican Party and created the Progressive Party. In New York the Progressives nominated Oscar Strauss, forcing the Democrats to turn to Sulzer to try to win. Roosevelt remained a force in New York politics for years to come.
- LOUIS SARECKY. The least known of the characters, his role as Sulzer's able lieutenant would be rewarded. He took responsibility for all of Sulzer's problems.
- ALTON PARKER. Former chief judge of the New York State Court of Appeals, he was the Democratic nominee for president in 1904. He would serve as one of the impeachment managers against Governor Sulzer.
- WILLIAM RANDOLPH HEARST. In 1902 he was elected congressman from the district neighboring Sulzer's district. They remained friends long after Sulzer left Albany. Hearst's desire to be elected to statewide office was a driving factor in much of the Sulzer story. A fierce rival of Smith's, Hearst's papers later published unsubstantiated rumors that Smith had bribed assemblymen during the impeachment vote.
- THURLOW WEED. Sulzer would try to get Weed, a Republican powerhouse, to help save his governorship. Weed served as secretary of war under Presidents William McKinley and Theodore Roosevelt and secretary of state under Roosevelt. A U.S. senator from 1909 through 1915, he received the Nobel Peace Prize in 1912 for his work to bring countries together in part through his position as chairman of the Carnegie Endowment for International Peace.
- HENRY MORGENTHAU SR. Chairman of the Finance Committee of the Democratic National Committee and later ambassador to the Ottoman Empire, his contributions to Sulzer and testimony in the

impeachment trial would play a major role in deciding Sulzer's fate. His son would serve as secretary of the treasury under President Franklin Roosevelt.

It is easy to agree on the characters. Beyond that, the story becomes murky. To those who are pro–good government and anti–Tammany Hall, Sulzer is Paul, the tax collector who finds religion. They see Sulzer as the sinner turned saint, an important cog in the Tammany machine who discovered good government and was martyred for joining its forces. Others see Sulzer as a selfish, ambitious politician—one who talked loudly of reform in order to conceal his own power grab and was brought down by his former friends to save the state (or at least the party) and whose own personal greed sealed his downfall.

Who is right?

This book attempts to answer that question.

PART ONE

1

A REFORMER IS BORN

WILLIAM SULZER BECAME GOVERNOR of New York on New Year's Day in 1913. It was a cold but clear day in Albany as the new governor exhibited the folksy style that endeared him to many of his new constituents. Dismissing the below-freezing weather and breaking with generations of precedent, Sulzer dispensed with the traditional military parade that had escorted all previous governors to their inaugurations. In keeping with his democratic ideals and playing to his followers, Sulzer walked from the Executive Mansion—which he had renamed the "People's House"—to the state capitol. This walk sent the crowds into a frenzy, with shouts of "Hurrah!" echoing over and over as they signaled their support by accompanying Sulzer along his way. According to the New York Times, "When the crowd realized that Mr. Sulzer really was to give what it seemed to regard as the greatest exhibition of Jeffersonian simplicity its imagination could conjure, [the crowds] became jubilant and flocked boisterously in the wake of the procession."[1]

By October, everything had changed. A mere ten months after his triumphant march to the capitol, Sulzer was leaving Albany in disgrace as the first—and so far only—governor of New York to be impeached. The cold, clear weather from January had given way to a fierce late-fall thunderstorm, the lightning in the sky as electric as the mood in this capital city.

Despite the storm, a crowd gathered to show their support for William Sulzer, now impeached and removed as governor. A Sulzer loyalist described his hero's exit in an extremely biased account of the impeachment. Nonetheless, the account is striking for the contrast with Sulzer's entrance into Albany.

> MR. SULZER: "My friends, this is a stormy night. It is certainly very good of you to come here to bid Mrs. Sulzer and me good-bye."
> A VOICE FROM THE CROWD: "You will come back, Bill, next year."
> MR. SULZER: "You know why we are going away."
> A VOICE: "Because you were too honest."
> MR. SULZER: "I impeach the criminal conspirators, these looters and grafters, for stealing the taxpayers' money. That is what I never did."
> FROM THE CROWD: Cheers.
> MR. SULZER: "Yes my friends, I know that the court of public opinion before long will reverse the judgment of Murphy's 'court of infamy.'"
> FROM THE CROWD: Cheers.
> MR. SULZER: "Posterity will do me justice. Time sets all things right. I shall be patient."
> CROWD: Cheers.
>
> THOMAS, *BOSS, OR THE GOVERNOR*, 3

Although Sulzer briefly returned to Albany as a member of the Assembly, elected as an independent candidate, this exit from Albany was the true end to his political power and the close of a titanic struggle between Sulzer and the party machine that enabled him to reach his pinnacle.

This exchange, apocryphal as it may be, does not tell the whole story. Did Sulzer truly expect he would be vindicated and returned to power? Did he believe he was being punished for speaking the truth or for trying to increase his own power at the expense of his former allies? Could he honestly have believed he was innocent? Or more likely, did he feel that the punishment did not fit the crime? *Which was the bigger loss to this man with mysterious motives: No longer having the ability to bring change and reform to the people or losing his political power, personal stature, and hopes of higher office?*

It may help to know William Sulzer's personal story.

Sulzer was born, according to his official biography, "in an old brick house" on Liberty Street in Elizabeth, New Jersey, on March 18, 1863.[2] Originally called Elizabethtown, Elizabeth was founded in 1664 as the first permanent English settlement in the state, part of a 500,000-acre tract of land between the Raritan and Passaic Rivers. Three English settlers purchased the land from the Staten Island Indians in a deal brokered by Colonel Richard Nicolls, governor of all the territories in North America. By the standards of the day, the purchase price was a princely sum: twenty fathoms of trading cloth, two coats, two guns, two kettles, ten bars of lead, twenty handfuls of powder, and 400 fathoms of white wampum, payable in one year after the territory was occupied. The settlement thrived, quickly growing to a population of 700, and became the first capital of New Jersey.

Elizabeth is and was a city rich in history. During the Revolutionary War, Elizabeth was constantly under attack by British forces, while off the city's coast the newly independent states sunk their first British warship. Alexander Hamilton lived there in his youth, and George Washington stopped en route to New York City to be sworn in as the first president of the United States in 1789.

By the time Sulzer was born, Elizabeth had become a thriving city and a hub for manufacturing. The Singer Sewing Machine Company built its first factory for mass production in town the same year Sulzer was born.

That factory eventually employed almost 2,000 people. Liberty Street itself was a solid, lower-middle-class neighborhood, home to some of the new professionals who worked in the Singer factory and other manufacturing concerns.

William Sulzer was the second son in a family of five boys and two girls.[3] His mother, Lydia Sulzer, was of Dutch and Scots-Irish ancestry. His father, Thomas Sulzer, was born in Germany. While a student at Heidelberg University, Thomas joined the Revolution of 1848, also known as the March Revolution. A popular uprising, the so-called Forty-Eighters were committed to liberal principles, including constitutional government as well as more far-reaching change for the working class. A split between the more moderate middle-class aims and radical working-class goals lead to the collapse of the revolution, defeated by the conservative aristocracy. Thomas Sulzer was captured and imprisoned for his role, eventually escaping to Switzerland and immigrating to New York City in 1851.

The ideals of the March Revolution—including belief in representative government and improved conditions for the working class—would be hallmarks of his son's political career.

William Sulzer's parents bought a farm in Wheatsheaf, a suburb of Elizabeth, and moved the family there while William was just a boy. The whole family pitched in on the farm and William spent time in the country school, but farming did not satisfy William's sense of adventure.

When William was twelve years old, he ran away from home, signing on as a cabin boy on a sailing ship that rounded Cape Horn, a perilous journey in 1875. Aside from visiting trading ports along the west coast of South America, little is known of Sulzer's trip. He rarely spoke of it.[4] Suffice it to say, he returned home nearly a year later and returned to his schooling.

In 1877 Sulzer graduated from grammar school. His parents hoped he would study for the ministry, but he traveled the short distance across the Arthur Kill to Staten Island and continued to the Lower East Side of Manhattan: the quintessential American melting pot. In the daytime Bill worked as a clerk in a wholesale grocer; in the evenings he continued his education with the free classes offered at Cooper Union. Sulzer became interested in the legal profession and entered Columbia College Law School.[5] He furthered his studies clerking with the firm of Parrish and Pendleton in Manhattan. At the age of twenty-one, William Sulzer was admitted to the practice of law.[6] The year was 1884.

In 1884 New York State was on the move. The year before, the New York and Brooklyn Bridge was opened to traffic in grand fashion. President Chester A. Arthur and New York mayor Franklin Edson crossed the bridge to meet Brooklyn mayor Seth Low accompanied by a band, cannon fire, and fireworks. The bridge cost over $15.5 million to build and cost at least twenty-seven people their lives. A total of 1,800 vehicles and over 150,300 people crossed the bridge on that day, which was the first land passage between Manhattan and Brooklyn. P. T. Barnum, in an effort to prove the safe nature of the bridge, conducted a parade of twenty-one elephants over the bridge, led by the famous elephant "Jumbo."

That same year saw the cornerstone of the Statute of Liberty laid on Bedloe's Island. The New York Gothams, soon to be called the Giants, were a new baseball team. An eighty-five-unit apartment building called the Dakota opened on Central Park West. Dow Jones, the editor of a young newspaper called the *Wall Street Journal*, published the first stock averages. George Eastman patented paper strip photographic film.

The same year, Alaska became a territory of the United States and William Sherman refused the Republican presidential nomination with the famous declaration, "I will not accept if nominated and will not serve if elected." The Ringling Brothers circus premiered. The Washington Monument, begun in 1848, was finally completed. Nikola Tesla, inventor of alternating current, moved to New York City from Yugoslavia, entering through Castle Clinton at the base of Manhattan (Ellis Island would not open for another eight years). The year 1884 saw Theodore Roosevelt flee New York State for the Badlands and ranch life in the Dakotas following the death of his mother, Martha Bulloch Roosevelt, and wife, Alice Hathaway Lee Roosevelt, in the same house within hours of each other. His distant cousin Eleanor Roosevelt was born in October 1884.

On Third Avenue near Fifty-Fifth Street, P.J. Clarke's eponymous saloon was founded. The same year, a new craze swept New York City: skates on wheels. Ice skating had been popular since midcentury but by 1884, residents were roller-skating on streets or in newly built roller rinks like the Cosmopolitan on Broadway in Midtown. Throughout the 1880s and much of the 1890s, roller-skating was the principal pastime of citizens of every age and condition—businessmen went to work on skates, and skating parties were much in vogue among the fashionable.[7]

That was New York in 1884, the world where William Sulzer was going to try to make his name and fortune.

2

EMPIRE STATE POLITICS AND TAMMANY HALL

SINCE THE SETTLEMENT OF NORTH AMERICA by Europeans, the colony and later state of New York played an outsized role. Henry Hudson claimed the area for the Dutch in 1609, and Dutch settlers founded Fort Nassau in 1614, which gave way to Fort Orange in 1624—a settlement that grew into the city of Albany. New Amsterdam was founded as a trading post in 1625. It was the site of present-day New York City. Together with other settlements along the Hudson River, these made up the colony of New Netherland. In 1664 the Dutch ceded New Netherland to the British at the conclusion of the Third Anglo-Dutch War.

New York City became a hotbed of political activity. The Sons of Liberty were organized there in the 1760s while the Stamp Act Congress, with representatives from all thirteen colonies and a forerunner of the Continental Congress, met in the city in 1765 and issued the Declaration of Rights and Grievances, which declared many of the same rights later espoused by the Declaration of Independence. During the Revolutionary War, more battles were fought in New York State than anywhere else; they included the Battle of Fort Ticonderoga (which provided the artillery that relieved the siege of Boston), the Battle of Brooklyn (the largest battle of the war), and the Battle of Saratoga (where the American victory provided the impetus for France to ally with the Americans).

Following independence, New York served as the national capital under the Articles of Confederation, and New York played a major role in the debate and subsequent ratification of the Constitution. In fact, the Federalist Papers were published in New York newspapers to advocate for ratification, and two of the three authors, Alexander Hamilton and John Jay, were New Yorkers. New York remained the national capital following ratification, and George Washington was inaugurated there.

New York was governed under a royal colonial charter until 1777, when the first state constitution was written by a convention in White Plains. Written primarily by John Jay, the constitution was passed with only one dissenting vote. The new state government created a bicameral legislature with a senate and assembly. That form remains today as it was in William Sulzer's time. The same convention also chose Kingston as the capital of New York.* In 1797 Albany became the permanent state capital.

The same political currents that led to the creation of the Sons of Liberty, steeped as they were in independence fervor and enthusiasm for America, led to the creation of the Society of St. Tammany. Founded in New York City in 1786 and incorporated on May 12, 1789, it was part of a wider network of Tammany Societies, the first formed in Philadelphia in 1772. The first leader, known as the grand sachem, was a Revolutionary War veteran named William Mooney, then an upholsterer living on Nassau Street. The association's name came from a chief of the Lenape or Delaware Indians known as Tammend or Tananend who was well respected both for helping European settlers and as a close friend of William Penn. The society was a fraternal organization made up mainly of Revolutionary War veterans whose primary activities were social.

---

* At the time, New York City was occupied by the British while Albany was under threat of attack. In fact, the British army was marching to attack Albany when they were defeated at Saratoga.

By 1798, however, the society's activities had grown increasingly politicized. Under Aaron Burr's leadership, Tammany emerged as a political force, organized as the central proponent of Jeffersonian policies in the city of New York. The group played a major role in delivering New York State's electoral votes to Thomas Jefferson and Burr himself in the election of 1800. Having voted for John Adams in 1796, New York's electoral votes were the difference four years later, electing Jefferson as president.

Throughout the early nineteenth century the association between Tammany and the Democratic Party continued to grow, and with Andrew Jackson's presidential victory in 1828, the society emerged as the controlling power in New York City elections. Throughout the 1830s and 1840s, Tammany expanded its political control even further by earning the loyalty of the city's ever-expanding immigrant community, a task that was accomplished by helping newly arrived foreigners obtain jobs, a place to live, and even citizenship, which allowed the grateful new Americans to vote for Tammany's candidates in city and state elections. Tammany was the intermediary between the poor—particularly the immigrant poor—and American society. The poor gave Tammany their votes. In return, Tammany provided jobs and handouts.

Moreover, Tammany opponents were often more interested in cutting the cost of government rather than bettering the lives of the common people. They regularly tried to impose Protestant morality, with rigid observance of Sunday closing laws (which, in the context of a six-day week, meant workers had no fun at all) among other "decency" mores. In contrast, Tammany winked at Sunday openings and distributed free turkeys at Christmas, coal for heating during the winter, ice during the summer, and many other comforts and necessities unavailable to the very poor. More importantly, Tammany scrupulously maintained the personal contacts with the poor to know when a new niece or nephew would arrive from the old country and when a family displaced by a fire or other tragedy needed support. Tammany always provided the necessary support.

This symbiotic relationship continued to flourish, fostering a culture where political candidates supported public spending to benefit the immigrant community in order to win votes from that community. In 1830 the Society of St. Tammany established a headquarters on East Fourteenth Street, and forever after, the society and its new Tammany Hall were synonymous.

By 1854, all these factors combined to make Tammany the dominant political force in New York City, culminating in the election of Fernando Wood as mayor. These electoral successes concentrated enormous political power in the hands of Tammany Hall's bosses, many of whom enriched themselves and their associates through corruption and administrative abuse. During the early nineteenth century, Tammanyites such as Samuel Swartout, U.S. collector of customs and embezzler, literally grabbed the money and ran. William M. "Boss" Tweed's infamously corrupt reign—exposed in part by the political cartoons of Thomas Nash that communicated the boss's nefarious ways directly to the still mostly illiterate immigrant population—was enough to bring an attempt at reform in the early 1870s. Still later, Boss Croker extorted bribes from whorehouses, gambling halls, and illegal bars in exchange for protection from law enforcement. Tammany continued to function and thrive in spite of regular efforts at reform; the flow of money, patronage, and votes continued into the early 1930s.

Ultimately the social and cultural revolution brought by the Great Depression caught up to even Tammany Hall. In 1932 the machine suffered serious setbacks when Mayor James Walker was forced from office and Franklin Roosevelt was elected president. Roosevelt's New Deal altered the demographic landscape of New York by restricting immigration and providing serious social reform that reduced the electorate's dependency on Tammany for jobs and assistance. Simultaneously the election of Fiorello LaGuardia removed City Hall and municipal patronage from Tammany's immediate control.

Despite these setbacks Tammany Hall enjoyed a revival in the 1950s under the leadership of Carmine DeSapio, who engineered the elections of

"THE TAMMANY TIGER LOOSE"
This Thomas Nast cartoon appeared in Harper's Weekly *on November 11, 1871. The vicious Tammany tiger has beaten Columbia symbolizing the Republic while the emperor, Tammany Boss William Tweed, looks on. Nast challenges the reader with the caption: What are you going to do about it?*

Robert Wagner Jr. in 1953 and Averell Harriman in 1954, while also defeating candidates who had not curried his favor—including, most notably, Franklin D. Roosevelt Jr., whose defeat in the 1954 race for New York attorney general was related to DeSapio's downstate mobilization against his election. DeSapio's short-term success contributed to his long-term defeat, since Eleanor Roosevelt held DeSapio responsible for her son's loss and grew into a determined enemy through the rest of the 1950s. She would join with her old friends Herbert Lehman and Thomas Finletter, forming the New York Committee for Democratic Voters, a group dedicated to enhancing the democratic process by opposing DeSapio's reincarnated Tammany. Eventually their efforts succeeded. By 1961 DeSapio was removed from power. The once mighty Tammany political machine, without leadership, faded from political importance and by the mid-1960s had ceased to exist.

Corruption in New York State was not, of course, the sole providence of Tammany Hall. For decades in the late nineteenth century, the Black Horse Cavalry, a bipartisan group of legislators, held sway in Albany. In the language of the contemporary press, they would launch regular raids to strike at various industries or corporations, introducing "strike bills" to lower prices below the fixed costs for a specific corporation or to introduce competition ending another company's monopoly. The various legislation would cause destruction or ruin to their intended targets if it passed, but for a generous consideration ($5,000 per legislator was the usual price) the sponsors would allow the bills to die.

Other urban areas had their own political machines—controlled at various times by Democrats, Whigs, and Republicans. In fact, the Albany Regency was one of the first political machines in the country, wielding power from the 1820s through 1838. The stories are too numerous to tell, but none challenged Tammany Hall for the time of its dominance nor for sheer scope of its ambitions or its scope.

In 1884, when William Sulzer joined Tammany Hall, John Kelly was the grand sachem. Kelly had replaced the scandalous Tweed and rebuilt Tammany's structure and political power. Upon Kelly's death in 1886, his estate was valued at $500,000—an enormous sum for the time, to be sure, but several contemporary sources thought the amount small for someone who held control of a great city for so long and praised Kelly for his moderation.[1]

3

WILLIAM SULZER'S POLITICAL BEGINNINGS

STANDING OVER SIX FEET, Sulzer was a tall man, especially for his times. He had sandy-colored hair while his lanky frame and controlled movements gave him the air of a trained athlete, but his distinguishing feature was his piercing blue eyes; his intense gaze could dominate a room. Sulzer's eyes led constituents to believe in his deep sincerity, but on different occasions they would flash with anger and turn into cold, hard steel to intimidate opponents.

Sulzer's description of himself in his official biography is also significant: "[Sulzer] resorts to no political arts or personal pretenses. He is just a plain, common, every-day plodding, good-natured citizen, sincere, square, and loyal in every fiber of his manhood. He does not command support by subtle influence, trickery, hypocrisy, self-advertising and the command of wealth, like some others, but succeeds solely through his brains, his intrepidity and his fidelity to friends and to principles."[1] The lengths Sulzer goes to show himself as "Plain Old Bill" are quite significant in terms of later events, while the unctuousness of the self-portrait seems striving even by political standards.

Sulzer was also a thirty-second degree Mason and years before had become a life member. He was a member of the Lloyd Aspinall Post, Grand Army of the Republic (a post–Civil War veterans' association to provide support for soldiers and their families); the Army and Navy Union; the Eagles; the Pioneers of Alaska; Arctic Brotherhood; the National-Democratic Club; the Manhattan Club; the Press Club; and the Masonic Club. A Presbyterian, Sulzer offered this advice to young men: "Work hard, cultivate good habits, have a motive in life and a positive determination to succeed."[2] He once summed up his approach to government with this quote, "You remember Mark Twain once said, 'When in doubt take a drink.' My policy is a little different — when in doubt I shall confide in the People."[3]

While serving in Congress, William Sulzer married Miss Clara Rodelheim of Philadelphia. His official biography had this to say about her: "Mrs. Sulzer is as Democratic and as popular with the people as her distinguished husband."[4] In a way familiar to modern politicians, though Sulzer's family could be a distraction. His brother-in-law, William Rodelheim, was charged on one occasion with embezzling over $13,000 from a publishing company he was associated with; on another with embezzling from a "paper concern"; and went through a very public bankruptcy, owing between $160,000 and $170,000.[5]

Charles August Sulzer, William's younger brother, also served in Congress. Born in 1879 Charles attended the U.S. Military Academy at West Point and served with the Fourth Regiment of the New Jersey Volunteer Infantry during the Spanish-American War; two other brothers, a captain and a lieutenant, died in military service during the war. In either 1901 or 1902 Charles Sulzer dropped out of West Point and moved to Alaska. There he explored and developed mines for the Alaska Industrial Company. Most productively, Charles developed mines, bunkers, and an 8,500-foot-long aerial tramway 1,500 above ground to work the "Jumbo" copper mine. Charles increased production from 1,000 tons to more than 2,500 tons of high-grade ore, making it the second-largest producer of copper in southeast Alaska in operation through 1918.[6] Charles became a member of the

Alaska Territorial Senate in 1914. He was a delegate to Congress from 1917 through his death in 1919 in Sulzer, Alaska.[7]

Much of this was still to come for William Sulzer. In 1884 the young man was newly arrived in Manhattan and anxious to begin his life as a lawyer, the profession that he would call "his life work."[8] The same urgency that drew Sulzer to New York and the same impulse that led him to hop a boat to South America combined with liberal principles instilled in him by his revolutionary father to push him toward politics. He had a flair for campaigns and for campaigning.

While participating in a debating society at Cooper Union, Sulzer attracted the attention of the Tammany leader of the Fourteenth Assembly District, John Reilly. Reilly was impressed enough to appoint Sulzer as a member of the Tammany Hall General Committee and send him out to speak on behalf of candidates. Loquacious and engaging, Sulzer became known as "Reilly's boy spellbinder."[9] Sulzer worked tirelessly on behalf of Tammany's candidates, impressing the society's leaders enough that in 1889 Tammany Hall endorsed Sulzer for New York State Assembly.

"Plain Bill" Sulzer styled himself a "Jeffersonian Democrat" and ran on a populist platform chiefly devoted to preventing a monopoly for the Broadway railway franchise.[10] He won by just about 800 votes, but he worked hard, campaigning throughout the district. Sulzer's strength was connecting directly with voters, using his searching gaze and powerful blue eyes to forge a bond with his constituents. As a result, he was reelected by progressively larger margins in 1890, 1891, 1892, 1893, and 1894.

Part of that electoral success was based on his work in Albany. Sulzer was an extremely active and successful legislator, known in the assembly chamber as "Henry Clay Sulzer."[11] The nickname came as much from a physical resemblance to Clay as to Sulzer's exaggerated attempts to consciously imitate that great statesman. In fact, journalist Henry F. Pringle, a Pulitzer Prize–winning author, remarked that newspaper reporters looked upon Sulzer as "very much of an ass."[12] Nonetheless, he clearly cultivated his image as a man of the people.

Sulzer made an impression on many people. One was Henry Morgenthau—a lawyer, businessman, and U.S. ambassador, most famously as ambassador to the Ottoman Empire during World War I and the most prominent American to speak out against the Armenian genocide. Having made a substantial fortune in real estate, Morgenthau became a leader in New York City's Jewish Reform movement and a major donor to Democratic causes, beginning with Woodrow Wilson's campaign for president in 1912. Morgenthau's son Henry would be secretary of the treasury under Franklin Roosevelt, and his grandson served as New York County district attorney for thirty-five years.

Morgenthau did not seriously participate in politics until he was fifty-six, but his contributions as a fund-raiser were so significant that he was named finance chairman of the Democratic National Committee that same year. Morgenthau was well known for his quick and penetrating intelligence. He gave the following description of Sulzer as Sulzer appeared to Morgenthau one day during a later campaign: "His coat was of one pattern, and his vest of another. His baggy trousers were of a third. The gray sombrero was rather dingy; his linen just a trifle soiled. Familiar as I was with Sulzer's poses, through our acquaintance, I mentally noted the skill of the morning's costume, in dressing the part of 'a friend of the people.'"[13] To others he was simply "a vain and empty demagogue, a cheap, professional politician."[14]

Throughout his career, Sulzer would engender very strong but often contradictory opinions. This difference in perceptions was based primarily on individual assessments of Sulzer's sincerity. Sulzer went to great lengths to present himself as a friend and supporter of everyone and everything. To many, this attitude combined with his striving and affected behavior made him seem insincere and a little too inclined to say or do anything to get elected. To others, Sulzer shared their values and admired Sulzer's hard work and appreciated his successes. These varying opinions had less to do with what Sulzer said as much as with his motives, or why he would say such things, and significantly, if he believed them himself.

These divergent views did not matter. Sulzer was succeeding

professionally. He served as counsel in several significant legal proceedings, often appearing alongside or as an adversary to quite prominent attorneys.[15] He also continued to impress the people who mattered most in his career, the leadership of the Society of St. Tammany. They were impressed by the activeness of his campaigning—for himself and other Tammany candidates—as well as the effectiveness of this campaigning as his vote totals continued to grow. In Albany he was also proving valuable as a Tammany soldier, following orders on votes and toeing the party line. As a reward, he was made a member of the influential Assembly Committee on General Laws, a prize granted through the influence of Tammany Hall.[16]

Newly empowered in Albany, Sulzer authored significant legislation and used his influence to pass the bills. Sulzer's work resulted in abolishing sweatshops, ending imprisonment for debt, forcing the weekly payment of workers' wages, establishing a women's reformatory, creating an epileptic colony, abolishing corporal punishment in prisons, and, ironically, for the punishment of corrupt election practices. Sulzer also wrote a freedom-of-worship law that allowed anyone in state institutions to worship according to their conscience, a state care act that put hospitals under the charge of the state government and provided for free care for "insane whose relatives are poor," and a Saturday "half-holiday" act that gave workers time off.

Sulzer was allied with—and a leader of—social, political, and economic reform. These were the same causes for which his father had fought in 1848 and for which he had been imprisoned; the son's support was only natural. But these reforms were also the ones that mattered to his constituents, and supporting them was certainly politically expedient, like much of Tammany's legislative program. In other words, Sulzer's role as a reformer provided fodder for his supporters as well as his detractors.

Regardless of his motives, the breadth and measure of Sulzer's accomplishments was prodigious by any standard, although some credit must go to the rapid change brought about by industrialization and a changing society.

Additionally, Sulzer was involved in codifying the state statutes for the first time; opening Stuyvesant Park and the Metropolitan Museum of Art to the public; establishing a prevailing wage regulation; creating the first state forest park; authorizing legislation to protect the Adirondack forest and the Hudson watershed; securing funds to complete the state capitol,[*] enlarging the state canals, including the Erie Canal; creating an aquarium in New York City; establishing the New York City Public Library (with funds provided by former governor Samuel Tilden); and providing for both the Bronx and Van Cortland parks.

In the state capitol, these were the days of the Black Horse Cavalry. As mentioned earlier, this bipartisan group of legislators was notorious for extorting campaign contributions and outright bribes through the use of so-called strike bills. These bills were introduced and threatened to do great damage to industries or individual companies, which would then pay to have the legislation killed or tabled. Theodore Roosevelt entered the assembly in 1882 and frequently referred to these practices as driving his reforming instincts. Significantly, Sulzer offered no similar reservations.

Sulzer's colleagues recognized his work, and with strong support from Tammany Hall he was elected Speaker in 1893 unanimously and in 1894 he was minority leader.[17] As Speaker he "reduced the usual representation of the minority on the committees, almost all of which he put under the control of Tammany Hall and Kings County Democrats."[18] Sulzer took

---

* The current capitol was constructed between 1867 and 1899. Three teams of architects worked on the design of the capitol during the thirty-two years of its construction. The teams were managed by Thomas Fuller (1867–75), Leopold Eidlitz and Henry Hobson Richardson (1875–83), and Isaac G. Perry (1883–99).

The ground floor was built in the Classical/Romanesque style. Lieutenant Governor William Dorsheimer then dismissed Fuller in favor of Eidlitz and Richardson, who built the next two floors in a Renaissance Classical style. The increasing construction costs became an ongoing source of conflict in the legislature, and it was difficult to secure the necessary funding.

Upon his election as governor, Grover Cleveland dismissed Eidlitz and Richardson in view of the ever escalating costs of construction. He hired Perry to complete the project. The legislative chambers, the fourth floor, and roof work were all finished in Victorian-modified Romanesque that was distinctively Richardson's design.

Spanning four decades, the final cost of construction was a staggering $25 million. Adjusted for inflation, the cost would be more than $500 million in 2013 dollars.

great pride in his tenure as Speaker. His official biography said, "As Speaker of the Assembly he gave the people one of the cleanest, one of the most economical and one of the shortest sessions of the Legislature in years. He was one of the fairest and most impartial presiding officers in the history of the State."[19] Of course, not everyone agreed. It was no coincidence that following his tenure as Speaker, the Democrats would not take control of that chamber for another twenty years—when a Democratic landslide with Sulzer at the top of the ticket would sweep the state.

One of Sulzer's big causes was passing legislation that provided for the state to support mentally ill people who could not afford their own care. The *New York Times* announced passage of this bill as "a victory for humanity":

> It has had nothing behind it but sentiment. It has had everything before it to obstruct, to threaten, and to kill it that brutal selfishness, cupidity, and malignancy could devise, invent and practice. The barnyard politicians were its most savage opponents, the men who have controlled the county poorhouses and the local Board of Supervisors, who have enjoyed all the powers that pigmies in politics can attain, who have grown wealthy and callous, and who saw in the passage of the bill a loss to them in political prestige and, still more painful, a diminution in their annual profits.[20]

On another issue, the *Times* captured the paradox of William Sulzer. Concerning a bridge that the legislature wanted built between Manhattan and Brooklyn, the *Times* called the legislation a "big steal." "Mr. Sulzer of New-York was the only outspoken opponent of the bill," reported the paper, "but his utterances were so extravagant in part that Judge Greene [the assemblyman sponsoring the 'steal'] speedily recognized their value to his project and requested that the time of Mr. Sulzer might be extended. The force of this remark was lost upon the young New Yorker, who discussed the bill fully a half hour."[21]

According to one of the few impartial sources on Sulzer, "The Legislature of that year is reported to have been most scandalously partisan and its effect was to end the Democrat party's rule in Albany until 1910."[22] A more scathing analysis—of the time and of Sulzer specifically—comes from the *New York Evening Post*:

> The session of 1893 was remarkable for the number of pet measures that were rushed through, for incompetent committees, for "snap" hearings, for strangled measures, for the surreptitious, tricky, jamming of "ripper bills" with graft as the goal, and with Speaker Sulzer frankly, naively, and unquestioningly obeying every nod and beck of the Croker-Sheehan-Murphy [Tammany leaders] triumvirate.... The Legislature represented a small group of political bosses, and it served the machine they constructed.[23]

The *New York World* agreed and tied Sulzer more securely to Tammany Hall: "[The legislature] was machine-ridden.... The Legislature has done the will of the bosses with a shameful but by no means unprecedented servility."[24]

Sulzer admitted as much, telling the *World*, "All legislation came from Tammany Hall and was dictated by that great statesman, Richard Croker."[25] However, in a pattern that was to continue through this entire saga, different people saw very different things in William Sulzer. *Cosmopolitan Magazine* wrote, "Under [Sulzer's] speakership, New York enjoyed the lowest tax rate and the most economical budget in 47 years and the cleanest and the shortest session of the Legislature in 51 years."[26] The idea that Sulzer was in the eye of the beholder was not unusual. One Albany reporter wrote, "William Sulzer is an enigma. The more you study him at close range the less apparently you can define his thoughts, fathom his motives and comprehend the purport of his sayings."[27]

4

ONWARD TO CONGRESS

ONE OF THE OLDEST NEIGHBORHOODS in the city, the Lower East Side has everything that makes a neighborhood quintessentially Manhattan—streets at inexplicable angles, buildings from every time period, and borders that shift regularly.

The core of the Lower East Side is a combination of two pre–Revolutionary era farms: the Delancey and Rutgers estates. A Tory, Delancey's family's property was confiscated in 1787, broken up, and sold at auction. Rutgers hosted clandestine meetings of the Sons of Liberty and, as a patriot, kept his land.

By the 1820s the Lower East Side had become home to much of New York City's social elite. When the Marquis de La Fayette, who helped win the revolution and was nearly as well loved as George Washington, returned to New York City in 1824, one of the grandest receptions in the city's history was held at Colonel Rutgers's mansion, then the center of high society.

The city's commercial center was still in lower Manhattan, but a nascent commercial community was fostered, up on the Bowery, on the Lower East Side. Brooks Brothers (1818) and Lord and Taylor (1826) opened their first stores here.

Between 1820 and 1840 the population of Manhattan grew from 123,000 to over 310,000 due to the country's first wave of immigration. Mostly English, German (including German Jews), and Irish came to America for their own reasons, poverty being the most common. Two things would bring the Irish in huge numbers before the potato famines: the work to build the Erie Canal beginning in 1817 and increased transportation. The same year, the Black Ball Line began running packet ships between Liverpool and New York on a regular schedule, not waiting for a full load before disembarking, and with reasonable fares.

Even before these newcomers arrived, many Germans who fought as British mercenaries stayed in New York City after the Revolution, often to be joined by their families.

The Lower East Side was also a prime destination for immigrants in the second wave: the Irish came with the potato famines of 1845–49; the Germans (like William Sulzer's father) came after the Central European revolutions in 1848; the Chinese came at the end of the Gold Rush and the completion of the Transcontinental Railroad, after rampant discrimination out west in the 1870s; the Italians came following natural disasters and economic depression in southern Italy in the 1870s; and the Russian, Polish, and Eastern Europeans, mostly Jewish, came as a result of pogroms and rampant discrimination starting in the 1880s.

Between the 1880s and 1920s, Italian and Eastern European immigration had the effect of turning previous immigrations almost into historical footnotes. The Russian, Polish, and Eastern European Jewish history with which the Lower East Side is closely associated creating the neighborhoods of Kleindeutschland (Little Germany) as well as Irish, Italian, Polish, Ukrainian, and others. These voters were the base of Sulzer's political support. Seeing the opportunity, especially with his popularity among these German immigrants, in 1894 Sulzer declined renomination to the assembly, choosing instead to run for Congress.

Sulzer's congressional district encompassed much of Manhattan's Lower East Side, including the neighborhoods along the East River from about the Williamsburg Bridge or Clinton Street in the South, meandering northwest from First Avenue at Houston Street, Second Avenue up to St. Marks Place, and then Third Avenue up to Fourteenth Street, the northern district. Today, the area encompasses the neighborhoods of the East Village, Alphabet City, Bowery, and Little Italy.

The Tenth District was one of the most cosmopolitan places in the United States.[1] Republicans held the seat, and 1894 was a good year for the GOP. North of the Mason/Dixon line, only five Democrats were elected that year. In New York City, only three won. One was Sulzer. He won by just over 800 votes, although the Democratic candidate for governor, David Hill, lost the district by 11,000 votes. Two years later, the Democratic candidate for president, William Jennings Bryan, lost the district by over 17,000 votes while Sulzer was reelected by a plurality of 2,400. Sulzer continued to drive up his margin of victory and in 1906 won with 75 percent of the votes. This ability to outpoll the top of the ticket was a testament to Sulzer's popularity and especially to the strength of his political abilities.

In eighteen years in Congress, Sulzer authored twenty-five major bills that would become law. Some of this legislation was symbolic, such as acts to raise the battleship *Maine* and to provide a light for the torch of the Statue of Liberty. Other legislation was more substantial including raising the pay of letter carriers, providing for the victims of the *General Slocum* steamboat disaster, a pension law for orphans and widows of Union Army veterans, reviving the merchant marine service, creating postal savings banks, forcing all ships sailing from U.S. ports to have safety devices, and providing federal aid for railroads that met certain prescribed standards. Among the most significant legislation sponsored or cosponsored by Sulzer was a new Bureau of Corporations (which became the basis for much of the enforcement of antitrust laws), legislation to regulate interstate commerce on the railroads, a federal Department of Transportation, and reduction of the tariff on American manufactures as well as the addition of meat, wood, coal, lumber, and paper to a list exempt from the tariff.[2] Throughout his time in Congress Sulzer was also known for his support of the movement for conservation of natural resources.[3]

Sulzer's bombast, reputation, and nature followed him to Washington. His colleagues called him "Seltzer" because of the effervescence of his speech or the "Siphon of Debate" for his long-windedness.[4] A reporter described trying to get to know the new congressman thus: "William Sulzer, the man, is hard to reach. To get at the real Sulzer you have to wade through, not a mass of red tape or ceremony or a retinue of lackeys, but an exasperating bog of bombast and 'hifalutin' oratory, best summed up in the effective slang word 'bunk.'"[5]

For example, on his bill to keep the Statue of Liberty lit every night, Sulzer bloviated,

> Why is it that after all this time this light must go out? Is liberty dead? I hope not. I am a friend of liberty here and everywhere. As a citizen of this Republic, I take a just pride in the grandeur of Liberty Enlightening the World and for all it typifies here and symbolizes to people in other lands. I would not darken its effulgent light, but I would make it burn brighter and brighter as the years come and go. It stands at the gates of America, a magnificent altar to man's faith in liberty, whose light should penetrate the darkness of tyranny throughout the world and guide men from oppression to our hospitable shores of freedom.[6]

For all the criticism, Sulzer was a forceful debater who by most accounts took a close interest in the proceedings on the floor of the House.[7]

Sulzer's most significant accomplishment in Washington was advocating for a Department of Labor with Cabinet rank. Sulzer reintroduced this legislation year after year and continued to fight for passage. Originally dismissed as "preposterous" when Sulzer introduced it in 1904, the measure gained support every year, in large part due to Sulzer's relentless advocacy. The congressman argued,

> My bill for a department of labor is a meritorious measure and it should be law. It is the first bill ever introduced in Congress

to create a Department of Labor. It is the first attempt to systematically classify labor in an intelligent way that has ever been presented in a bill in Congress, and its enactment into law will evidence a disposition on the part of the Government to see to it that labor gets full recognition, the dignity of having a voice in the councils of State, and the opportunity to have its claims dispassionately discussed. Give labor this book and the "labor question" will be reduced to the minimum.

The bill, he argued, should be supported by both business and labor:

Capital as well as labor should favor this Department of Labor, because it will go far to solve the labor problem and bring about industrial peace. For years this legislation has been advocated by the wage-earners of the country. The bill meets with their approbation and has the approval of the best thought in our land. It has been indorsed by some of the ablest thinkers, some of the wisest political economists, and many of our leading newspapers. The time is ripe, it seems to be to me, for a creation of a Department of Labor with a secretary having a seat in the Cabinet, with all the rights and powers conferred by this bill. It will bring labor and capital closer together, and one is dependent on the other. They should be friends—not enemies—and walk hand in hand in the march along the paths of mutual prosperity.

In 1912, having gained support across the country, the legislation was discharged out of committee and passed the House of Representatives without opposition. As governor-elect of New York, Sulzer traveled to Washington, spending three weeks lobbying for the legislation in the Senate and personally lobbying President Taft. Finally, in his last official act as president, William Howard Taft signed William Sulzer's legislation to create a cabinet-level Department of Labor.[8]

In addition to giving the labor secretary cabinet rank, the legislation also created a Bureau of Statistics, which would report once a year on "conditions of labor," especially unemployment, and a Board of Arbitration and Board of Conciliation to improve worker/employer relations and prevent strikes. Sulzer also successfully lobbied incoming president Woodrow Wilson to appoint his friend, Congressman William B. Wilson, as the first secretary of labor. This legislation had long been a goal of Progressive activists and helped to improve the conditions of working men and women throughout the country.

Sulzer made his mark beyond legislation itself with the time-honored tradition of resolutions, professing to be the friend of all humanity and champion of universal liberty: supporting Cuban "patriots" in their fight for freedom, "the liberty-loving and patriotic Boers of South Africa" (he also tried to stop the sale of arms to England for use in South Africa), in solidarity with oppressed Russian Jews, celebrating and commemorating Columbus Day on October 12, congratulating the Chinese people on establishing a republic, and many more. Other Sulzer resolutions had more substance, such as calling for an investigation of the New York Customs House and supporting constitutional amendments for both the direct election of senators and the creation of an income tax. Most productively, Sulzer introduced resolutions that led to the development of a parcel post.

In his final term in Congress, Sulzer's seniority enabled him to became chairman of the House Committee on Foreign Affairs. No less an authority than Woodrow Wilson said Sulzer handled his chairmanship with "capacity and discretion of a very fine sort."[9] As chairman, he forcefully opposed any American involvement in Mexico and supported independence and sovereignty for Latin American countries. In that vein he convened hearings to investigate the U.S. acquisition of the Panama Canal.

When Russia refused to honor American passports held by Jews, Sulzer led an effort to abrogate the 1832 Treaty governing relations between the United States and Russia. A resolution to that end passed the House by the vote of 300-1. Coupled with his strong condemnation of various pogroms and other attacks, Sulzer became a national leader on behalf of the Jewish people, in and outside America. This stand was strong and idealistic, but it was also very good politics in New York City. His leadership on these issues positioned him to be the Democratic candidate for governor.

Sulzer's advocacy was not limited to policy issues during his time in Washington. Throughout each of William Jennings Bryan's national campaigns (1896, 1900, and 1908) Sulzer was a fierce advocate—some called his actions agitating—for the "Great Commoner." Bryan was the embodiment of the populist movement of which Sulzer considered himself a part. Bryan stood for the working class against big business and for radical reform. (Bryan's famous speech to the 1896 Democratic National Convention ended with the line, "You shall not press down upon the brow of labor this crown of thorns; you shall not crucify mankind upon a cross of gold.") Sulzer declared Bryan a "bulwark against the centralization of wealth and power."[10]

Despite all his accomplishments in Congress—or maybe because of them—Sulzer never silenced all his skeptics. His detractors saw in Sulzer's battles the pandering of a politician long on political skills and short on principles. However, even his fiercest critics admitted that whatever his motivations, Plain Bill was popular with voters. *Harper's Weekly* summed up both attitudes succinctly when they described Sulzer's career in Congress:

> He never stood up for his opinion against his immediate advantage. He never relied upon reason, but placed his trust in pose and rhetoric. He had no element of superiority, and yet the people trusted him. He posed and screamed. And the people took him at his word.... Sulzer has never done an unpopular thing that I know of. He never had any morality except to seek cheap success at any cost.[11]

5

MAYOR WILLIAM GAYNOR

THE PREVAILING WISDOM IN 1910 was that New York City mayor William J. Gaynor would be the Democratic candidate for governor when the convention gathered in September. In August, Gaynor decided on a well-deserved vacation and booked passage to Europe on the *Kaiser Wilhelm der Grosse*. After embarking, Gaynor was visiting with well-wishers and posing for photographs (a fellow passenger was the president of Chile) when an unkempt man rushed at the mayor, shouting, "You have taken away my bread and butter!" The man placed a .38-caliber pistol to the back of the mayor's neck and fired. It was the first attempted assassination of a New York City mayor. "Tell the people good-bye for me," Gaynor gasped, believing that he was mortally wounded.

The shooter was an Irish immigrant named James J. Gallagher. A city employee, Gallagher believed he was the victim of a conspiracy when he was dismissed from his 25-cents-an-hour job as a night watchman on the East River piers. Gallagher wrote to the mayor and tried to meet with him only to be rejected with the terse reply, the mayor "can do nothing in the matter of which you write."[1]

Gaynor's path to City Hall and potential governor is fascinating. Born in 1849 on a farm in Oriskany in Upstate New York, he was educated at local public schools. Becoming a novitiate of the Christian Brothers he took the name Brother Adrian Denys, but because of his youth he never took vows and, after four years of study, dropped out (he would later renounce Catholicism). Gaynor became a reporter for the *Brooklyn Argus* and then a lawyer. Reading the law at the Law Firm of Horatio and John Seymour, Gaynor was inspired by Horatio Seymour's political career as New York's governor and Democratic Party nominee for president. Gaynor was elected a justice of the New York State Supreme Court in 1893 and elevated to the Appellate Division, Second Department in 1905.[*]

By 1909 Boss Charlie Murphy was searching for a way to keep Tammany's hold on the New York city hall. Murphy had held effective control there since George McClellan Jr. had defeated Independent/Fusion mayor Seth Loew in 1903. Murphy endorsed Gaynor, a

---

[*] Known as a bon vivant with an explosive temper, two anecdotes as reported in the *New York Press* are worth sharing:

If a reporter caught him on a good day, as did a reporter from the *World* who met him at his Long Island summer home, he would murmur, "Well, if you have to interview me, let's step inside and go to work on it like mechanics." There he took out two tumblers and uncorked the "Old Senator" [a contemporary whiskey].

He loved dining with friends over a bottle of champagne, talking about history, politics, literature, the law and whatever came to mind. His capacity for spirits was bottomless and seemed only to sharpen his tongue. Ira Bamberger, a lawyer and friend, once spent the evening at dinner with the judge... their talk lasted well into the night, and more than one cork was popped. Bamberger had a case on Gaynor's calendar the next morning. Bamberger missed the first call.

He staggered late into court, evidencing the kind of hangover in which the growth of one's hair is an agony. Judge Gaynor called Bamberger up to the bench and rebuked him for his lateness, concluding, "From your appearance, you would seem to have fallen among bad companions." (William Bryk, "Mayor William J. Gaynor, Primitive American," *New York Press*, December 26, 2000)

well-respected and anticorruption jurist, in large part to block publisher William Randolph Hearst from winning the mayoralty.

Murphy chose Gaynor, somehow believing he could be controlled or influenced. This was a mistake. The Republicans nominated Otto Bannard, a wealthy, colorless banker, and a strong ticket with him. Then William Randolph Hearst, the publisher—who had unsuccessfully run for president in 1904, mayor in 1905, and governor in 1906—announced his independent candidacy. Gaynor found his thirty years' public service meant nothing. Only the *World* and the *New York Press* endorsed him. The *Times* called his nomination "a scandal." Gaynor's opponents called him "a symbol for everything that is indecent and disgusting," "a poor, I will go further and say a bad, judge," "a hypocrite," a "learned fraud," "mentally cross-eyed," and "incapable of telling the truth."

On Election Day, Gaynor polled 43 percent of the vote; Bannard, 30 percent; and Hearst, 27 percent. Hearst never forgave him. Of course, Gaynor had said, "Hearst's face almost makes me want to puke."

Gaynor's marriage with Tammany was short-lived, and he appointed qualified officials regardless of party ties. Without patronage, Tammany was on a starvation diet. "What do we have for Charlie Murphy?" a colleague once asked. "A few kind words," the mayor replied.

Upon his election, Gaynor walked to city hall from his home in Brooklyn's Park Slope: it was the first time he had ever visited that building.

Gaynor's legacy is larger than one would expect for his short time in office. A memorial stands in Brooklyn's Cadman Plaza, near the Brooklyn Bridge, and after his death Astoria Park was renamed in his honor, although a group of Tammany aldermen later rescinded that designation. Beyond honest government, Gaynor's largest legacy was abolishing East River bridge tolls (driving across the bridge at the time cost a dime, cyclists paid a nickel, and horse riders three cents). Gaynor saw removing the tolls as a way of knitting together the newly unified city of New York, which had been formed only thirteen years earlier.* He also fought police use of excessive force and corruption and championed mass transit.

Yet that was all in doubt on the deck of the *Kaiser Wilhelm der Grosse* as Gaynor's life hung in the balance. A photographer from the New York *World* captured a picture of Gaynor in his pain and agony only seconds after the shot. According to the mayor's own account, he could not see, was unable to breathe, and heard a "metallic roar" coming and going in his head. He was taken to St. Mary's Hospital in Hoboken, New Jersey, where he spent several weeks recuperating. Gaynor recovered somewhat, although the bullet would remain lodged in his throat, and he would remain weakened and haggard throughout the rest of his term. The bullet had lodged in the vault of Gaynor's larynx and, on doctors' advice, was not removed. Nonetheless, it brought on frequent fits of exhausting coughing. The mayor became more difficult. He would even use the injury as a reason to get out of discussing delicate subjects, saying, "Sorry, can't

---

* During lulls in his office routine, Gaynor buzzed for a stenographer, took a basket of letters, and began dictating. Many correspondents received such letters as the following:
Dear Sir: I thank you very much for your kind and encouraging letter of March 31. Very truly yours, W. J. Gaynor, Mayor.
Others received more individual replies:
Dear Sir: I care nothing for common rumor, and I guess you made up the rumor in this case yourself. Very truly yours, W. J. Gaynor, Mayor.
* * *
Dear Sir: Your letter is at hand and I have read enough of it to see that you are a mere scamp. Nonetheless, I sometimes derive profit from the sayings and doings of scamps. Very truly yours, W. J. Gaynor, Mayor.
* * *
Dear Madam: I regret to say that I do not know anyone I can recommend to you as a husband. You can doubtless make a better selection than I can, as you know the kind of man you want. Of course, it may be very hard to find him, but no harder for you than for me. Very truly yours, W. J. Gaynor, Mayor.
* * *
Dear Sir: I am very glad to receive your letter and your poem. The poem is very fine but your advice is very bad. Very truly yours, W. J. Gaynor, Mayor.
* * *
Dear Sir: No, I do not want a bear. Very truly yours, W. J. Gaynor, Mayor.

talk today. This fish hook in my throat is bothering me." Gaynor was the first—and to date only—mayor of New York City to be the victim of an assassination attempt.*

While recovering, the mayor sent word he would decline any statewide nomination. "When a man has gone down into the Valley of the Shadow and looked the specter Death in the face, and said to it, 'I am ready,' nothing in this world looks very large to him," Gaynor wrote.

On September 4, 1913, an exhausted Gaynor left for a brief vacation in Europe. Just before sailing, Gaynor delivered a vituperative parting salvo at Tammany and planned his reelection campaign as an independent. In the meantime, he said, "I am going to spend two weeks on the ocean where nobody can get at me."

Somebody should have told Gaynor, however, that he should have avoided ocean liners. Eight days later, as the RMS *Baltic* approached Ireland, Gaynor's son walked up to his father, who was reclining in a deck chair, bent down, and realized death had preceded him. Curiously, Gaynor's would-be assassin, Gallagher, had died just a few months prior at an insane asylum in Trenton, New Jersey.[2]

Gaynor's exit from the race for governor opened up the nomination to other aspirants. The result was a free-for-all with many Democrats taking the covers off their gubernatorial ambitions.

---

* The following April, a seventy-one-year-old unemployed blacksmith fired at Gaynor's successor, John Purroy Mitchel, in City Hall Plaza, but missed, striking the city's corporation counsel in the cheek instead. In his defense, Mr. Mitchel drew his own revolver, which he had become accustomed to carrying.

6

THE CAMPAIGN OF 1910

WILLIAM SULZER WAS ONE OF THOSE DEMOCRATS waiting in the wings. This would not be the year he achieved his lofty ambition, but to understand Sulzer's eventual rise—and the underpinning of his stunning fall—we must examine earlier statewide campaigns.

Electing a governor is always important in U.S. politics. The top executive office is the most powerful in the state, and the success of the top of the party ticket usually also means victory in the state legislature and in local municipal offices (the so-called coattails effect)—especially in an era when most voters cast one ballot for an entire ticket. All these reasons made gubernatorial races the most closely watched; the fact that the governor held thousands of patronage jobs in his gift made these campaigns the most fiercely fought of their era. Patronage jobs were available in every corner of the state and in scores of different agencies, and they paid well with little heavy lifting. Although former New Yorker Chester A. Arthur signed legislation that required federal hiring by merit (the Pendleton Civil Service Act of 1883), that law did not apply in New York State. While the state had a

Civil Service Commission, it was notoriously weak and ineffectual. In fact, these were halcyon days for the spoils system in New York.*

By 1910, Republicans had been winning these battles on a regular basis—eight elections in a row—controlling the New York Governor's Mansion for sixteen years and distributing patronage across the state.

As their losses mounted, Democrats were dejected and divided. For a couple of elections the party even deferred to outsiders, nominating gubernatorial candidates favored by the Independence League, including William Randolph Hearst in 1906 and Lewis Stuyvesant Chanler in 1908. Republican Charles Evans Hughes, a reformer unafraid to challenge Republican political bosses, soundly defeated both candidates. In addition to ideological differences, these losses especially contributed to a growing conflict between factions known as "Reform" or "Independent Democrats" on the one side and "Organization Democrats" on the other. The Tammany Democrats were firmly in this latter group.

Organization Democrats, as the name implies, controlled the internal machinery of the Democratic Party. Unable to dislodge them, the reformers formed their own group, the Democratic League. The league's goals were reform of the party organization and a platform committed to "strict construction, resistance to Federal encroachment, tariff for revenue only, popular election of Senators, anti-imperialism and an income tax."[1] The league was not friendly to Tammany Hall and was vehemently opposed to Tammany's chief, Charlie Murphy, but the league had a bigger target in state chairman William J. Conners of Buffalo.

Connors, known as "Fingy" because he lost the thumb on his left hand, was a character.** Called a "dock walloper" or street fighter even by his friends, he made a fortune contracting out dock labor from his saloons,

---

* A former governor of New York, William Learned Marcy, defending President Andrew Jackson's nomination of another New Yorker, Martin Van Buren, as minister to Great Britain, used the phrase "to the victor belong the spoils"—the common origin of the term "spoils system."

** One story has Connors losing his thumb after daring a pal to cut it off. Another story had him as the model for the character Jiggs in the influential comic strip *Bringing Up Father*, also called *Maggie and Jiggs*, created by George McManus in 1913.

financed originally from the accidental deaths of four family members in an unlikely order that left him as heir. He ran company stores where his workers were forced to shop at unreasonable prices and eventually expanded to running his own grain-handling business. He also owned the *Buffalo Enquirer* and *Morning Courier*.

Murphy's once friendly relationship with Connors had deteriorated by 1910, and Murphy saw in the Democratic League a diabolical opportunity. Pointing to the splintering party and pinning the blame on Connors for recent electoral defeats, Murphy was able to drive Fingy Connors out of office, and used votes from his own bloc and his broad influence to elect as state chairman one of the Democratic League leaders, John Alden Dix.[2] In one fell swoop, Murphy had weakened a rival, ingratiated himself with the reformers, and named a state chair who could not survive without Murphy's support. This skullduggery was the brilliant political strategy typical of the Tammany leader.

John Alden Dix was forty-nine years old in 1910. Born to a wealthy family in Glens Falls, Dix attended Cornell University and went into business in Washington and Albany Counties. He parlayed his family connections—his uncle John Adams Dix[*] had been a famous Civil War general and governor of New York—into success as a lumber merchant, banker, marble dealer, and paper manufacturer. Tall and thin like his uncle, Dix was fastidious, planting a tree for every single one he cut down.

Dix considered himself a crusader for personal freedom and an advocate of economic conservatism and tariff revision, and he supported the abolition of protection for gigantic "infant industries."[3] Dix was a statewide

---

[*] John Adams Dix was also president of the Union Pacific Railroad and the Erie Railroad, secretary of the treasury under President James Buchanan, minister to France, and as a major general during the Civil War sent a telegram to Louisiana that was opened and read to say, "If anyone attempts to haul down the American flag, shoot him on the spot." During the war he was also part of Major General George McClellan's Department of the Potomac and was responsible for arresting the Maryland Legislature, thereby preventing the secession of Maryland from the Union. He lost his campaign for reelection to Samuel Tilden and a race for mayor of New York City at the age of seventy-eight (Morgan Dix, *Memoirs of John Adams Dix*, and John Adams Dix, *Speeches and Occasional Addresses*).

figure by this time, having been the Democratic candidate for lieutenant governor in 1908. Dix's wife, Gertrude Alden Thomson, was also from a prominent New York family; she was a direct descendant of Roger Sherman, a signer of the Declaration of Independence.[4]

In the early twentieth century, political conventions were significant happenings, central to the functioning of the state and national parties and in fact essential to shaping those political parties. This was the era of smoke-filled back rooms filled with cigar-chomping bosses handpicking candidates—a time when delegates would engage in epic battles over their party platforms and spectacular floor fights would choose candidates, sometimes after days and days of voting. These conventions, at least in New York State, were also the only way for a candidate to get on the statewide ballot; state law did not provide for a petition process, making the convention necessary for anyone who wanted to be governor or hold another state office.

The 1910 New York State Democratic Convention was just such an occasion. The party faithful gathered in Rochester on September 29 with Dix as the leader but with Tammany's Charles Murphy as the true power. Dix's position as state chair and the apparent ascendency of the reformers inspired high hopes in many Independent Democrats and drew them to the convention. However, Boss Murphy and the Organization Democrats were not about to relinquish their power without a fight. That contest came on the first piece of business, choosing a temporary chair of the convention. Contemporary conventions feature any number of temporary chairpersons in largely ceremonial roles, but in 1910 the temporary chair was a very powerful position, with the ability to recognize delegates to speak and to determine the rules and the order of business, among other powers.

Murphy and the Organization Democrats quite quickly shattered the hopes of the reformers, installing Alton Parker as temporary chair. Parker, the former chief judge of the Court of Appeals and nominee of the Democratic National Committee for president in 1904, was Murphy's chum and his choice. Tammany's power led to an atmosphere of distrust and suspicion that would pervade the entire convention.[5]

Conventional wisdom had placed Mayor Gaynor as the front-runner until the would-be-assassin's bullet derailed his plans. First off the block to replace Gaynor were a number of reformers. No matter how much support they garnered, Murphy quietly shot each down. Newspaper publisher—and leader of the reform-minded Democratic League—William Randolph Hearst continued to advance candidate after candidate to the assembled party faithful (including William Sulzer, albeit briefly) before settling on Martin H. Glynn, a newspaper publisher from Albany.

Murphy continued his strategy of dividing to conquer and eventually convinced Dix to become a candidate. This was a conscious and strategic decision to reject Hearst and to reject support from Hearst's army of newspapers. It also meant not having to share control or power with Hearst.

True to his reputation as a reformer, Dix did not want to be seen abusing his position as chairman of the state party, so he would only agree to run for governor as long as the other candidates withdrew from consideration. All the other candidates complied, except for William Sulzer, but without support from Boss Murphy and Tammany Hall, Sulzer had no chance. Dix was nominated by a vote of 434-16.

The rest of the convention went according to script. The platform declared, "The party pledges itself anew to the old nationalism embodied in the Constitution."[6] It also denounced the tariff revision, complained of Republican extravagance, and dwelt on the corruption revealed by state investigations. The convention favored a statewide direct primary, an income tax amendment, and the direct election of U.S. senators.

For Republicans, 1910 foreshadowed the divisive split to come in 1912 with conservatives and radicals fighting each other. Theodore Roosevelt was gone from the national scene, and Taft was in charge. As Roscoe C. E. Brown says in his *History of the State of New York*, "The tide, which since 1894 had stood so strongly in favor of the Republicans, had turned throughout the country."[7] Dix won, receiving 689,700 votes, winning by a margin of 67,401 votes.[8] Election irregularities helped in "bringing about the election of a Democratic Governor."[9]

As governor, Dix's priorities were a revised tariff and fiscal restraint, or as his biography says, "an economical administration of the affairs of the State."¹⁰ Under Dix, the state passed a worker protection act known as the Fifty-Four-Hour Law and a food safety measure known as the Cold Storage Law, established a State Fire Marshal's Department, revised insurance laws, funded agricultural education, and established agricultural schools and colleges. Dix's administration tried to cut costs and reform government through a program of fiscal and electoral reforms. He favored the federal income tax amendment (disregarding the objections of former governor Charles Evans Hughes and successfully lobbying the legislature to pass it) and asked the legislature to pass a constitutional amendment for the direct election of senators.¹¹

A hallmark of Dix's tenure was an effort to abolish state commissions. The governor wanted to abolish commissions not just to save money but also to reassert executive control of the state government. This move was especially important to this administration because the board members of these state commissions had primarily been appointed by prior administrations—Republican administrations—and were hostile to Governor Dix and his programs. The result was a series of so-called Ripper bills. For example, the Highway Commission, with members appointed by Republicans, was replaced with a new board composed of the superintendent of highways, the superintendent of public works, and the state engineer, all appointed by Dix or—in the case of the state engineer—a Democrat elected along with Dix. A new Conservation Commission replaced the Forest, Fish and Game Department and the state Water Supply Commission, and several minor boards and a Board of Claims were replaced by a statewide Court of Claims.¹²

The result was streamlined executive control for Governor Dix. Another result was patronage for the Democratic Party, controlled almost exclusively by Charles Murphy. Dix lacked the inclination to prevent this exercise of the spoils system and may have lacked the energy to change what had been common practice in New York State government for generations. Besides, Dix owed his selection as Democratic candidate (and earlier as state Democratic chairman) directly to Murphy.

Dix's largesse to Charlie Murphy went even further. Dix signed a new election law that extended personal registration requirements to rural districts, strengthening the statewide Democratic Party.* The law also strengthened Democrats in New York City by including a provision preventing a candidate's name from appearing on a ballot more than once (handicapping so-called fusion tickets where Republicans and Independents banded together to win elections mostly in New York City). Despite Dix's best efforts to aid or level the playing field for the Democratic Party, both of the provisions were rejected by the Court of Appeals.[13]

Notwithstanding his goals and accomplishments, Dix's governorship was marred by trouble. A serious fire in the capitol on March 29 significantly delayed and impeded the operation of the legislature.[14] More significantly, different elements of the Democratic Party were at war: reformers versus Tammany Hall. The reformers knew that Murphy had handpicked Dix to run for governor, but they still expected him to deliver various reform measures.

As a founder of the Democratic League, Dix was a leading voice of reform within the Democratic Party. His predecessor as governor, Charles Evans Hughes, had set a high standard, signing into law reform measures in three areas: improving government operations, increasing state regulation of business, and increasing, albeit modestly, social welfare protections. Hughes also distinguished himself by standing up to GOP bosses in using the newly passed Moreland Act to fire corrupt municipal officials in different parts of the state. All these factors combined to increase the expectations that reformers had for their new governor.

Dix's administration tried to balance these two competing interests: the reformers or Independent Democrats, whose philosophy and goals

---

* Following the Civil War, many states, including New York, required men who lived in large cities to register periodically, often before each major election. The laws were justified as efforts to combat ballot fraud but had the added benefit of making it more difficult for lower-class, often immigrant voters, to participate in elections. This lowered turnout in New York City, a stronghold of Democratic voters. By extending this requirement to rural areas, which were Republican strongholds, Democrats were leveling the playing field.

Dix shared, versus the Organization Democrats, led by Tammany's chief, Charlie Murphy, whose support had been responsible for Dix's election. Dix's strategy was to try to balance both wings of the party. The first major test of this approach was the contest to select a U.S. senator to succeed Chauncey Depew. Depew was the personification of a nineteenth-century politician: a Yale-educated lawyer invited by "Commodore" Cornelius Vanderbilt to join the board of the New York Central Railroad, where he would rise to be chairman. He was a voluminous and well-respected public speaker, delivering the principal address at the dedication of the Statute of Liberty, the cornerstone laying of Grant's Tomb, and the dedication oratory at the Chicago World's Fair of 1892. Notorious for his girth, Depew was said to have remarked to equally rotund William Howard Taft, in reference to Taft's large belly, "I hope, if it is a girl, Mr. Taft will name it after his charming wife." Taft's reply was punishing, "If it is a girl, I shall, of course, name it for my lovely helpmate of a number of years. And if it is a boy, I shall claim the father's prerogative and name it Junior. But if, as I suspect, it is only a bag of wind, I shall name it Chauncey Depew." The senator's oratory and wit aside, Depew was a Republican and would be replaced by the Democratic majorities in both houses of the state legislature.

Prior to the ratification of the Seventeenth Amendment (officially adopted in 1913), U.S. Senators were chosen by state legislatures and not directly by voters. The wrangling, discord, and just out-and-out trouble appointing senators, along with pure democratic sentiments, were prime movers in the ratification of that amendment.*

The Independent Democrats, still with high hopes for Dix to support their cause, rallied around a reform candidate: Edward M. Shepard of

---

* For instance, in 1885 the Oregon Legislature went through sixty-eight ballots before finally selecting a senator. Throughout 1887 the West Virginia Legislature was unable to select a senator at all. Also unable to select a senator were Louisiana in 1892; Montana, Washington, and Wyoming in 1893; Kentucky in 1896; Oregon in 1897; California, Utah, and Pennsylvania in 1899; Rhode Island in 1907; and worst of all, Delaware went without any representation in the Senate from 1901 to 1903. All in all, there were seventy-one legislative deadlocks from 1885 through 1912.

Brooklyn—a leader in the reform movement (he was chairman of the Saratoga Conference where the Democratic League was formed) and particularly in regard to the tariff, ballot taxation, and civil service. In fact, Shepard authored New York State's original civil service reform bill and upon its passage in 1883 was named a member of the Brooklyn Civil Service Commission. He was a candidate for mayor of Brooklyn in 1895 and for mayor of New York City in 1901,* and was a serious candidate for governor at the Rochester convention that nominated Dix.

Boss Murphy opposed Shepard and had the votes to block him in the legislature. In a story on the senate vote, the *New York Times* put it this way: Tammany Boss Charles Murphy's "word seems to be law to a majority of the men who were elected to make laws for the people of the State of New York."[15] Murphy resisted Shepard in part because of the reformer's dedication to civil service reform, which would deprive Murphy's political machine of the patronage that fed it, but also because of Shepard's attitude toward Tammany; he had once called Tammany Hall the "most burning and disgraceful blot upon the municipal history of this country."

Months of political battling followed as the legislature's Organization Democrats nominated William F. Sheehan, also known as "Billie Blue Eyes."** A native of Buffalo, Sheehan had been Speaker of the state assembly, lieutenant governor, and partner in a prosperous New York City law firm with Alton Parker, a former chief judge of the New York State Court of Appeals

---

* Shepard's mayoral ambition was defeated by Seth Low, a Fusion candidate. Low's enthusiastic supporter Mark Twain, objecting strongly to Shepard accepting Tammany's support, characterized the race thus: "A Tammany banana is a strange thing. One end of it, or one part, here or there is perfectly white. The rest of it is rotten. Now, I have the greatest respect for Mr. Shepard personally, but nine-tenths of the rest of the bananas on that ticket are rotten. Mr. Shepard is the white part of the banana. The best we can do is throw the whole banana from us, for it is unfit. It will make us sick" (*New York Times*, October 30, 1901).

** Sheehan's brother, John Sheehan, had been comptroller of the city of Buffalo until Grover Cleveland, who thought Sheehan corrupt, refused to have him on his mayoral ticket in 1881.

and Democratic nominee for president of the United States in 1904. Sheehan was a close friend of Boss Murphy and an attorney for financier Thomas F. Ryan, a name that will play prominently in Sulzer's impeachment trial.[16]

Even though Sheehan was the nominee of the party caucus in the legislature, he needed votes from reformers to be elected. The refusal of these reformers to vote for Billie Blue Eyes effectively blocked his nomination. The longest deadlock in the history of the state resulted.

After thirty-four official ballots, Shepard withdrew from the race in late February and hoped, unsuccessfully, that Sheehan would do the same. On June 16, Shepard fell ill with a cold that rapidly developed into pneumonia, but as his obituary noted, "Before that, however, he had not been strong, due in great measure to his long fight with William F. Sheehan for the United States Senatorship from this State."[17] A month later he had died.

After seventy-four days of deadlock and sixty-two ballots, Murphy proposed James Aloysius O'Gorman Sr. O'Gorman was a loyal Tammany solider, but he had avoided most of the rough give-and-take of politics by being on the bench, first on the New York District Court and later as a justice of the Supreme Court. Dix, who saw his whole legislative program falling apart, pleaded with the insurgents to compromise. A few of them, led by Franklin D. Roosevelt, relented, and O'Gorman received 63 out of 101 votes in the caucus.

Eventually, on March 1, the Democrats offered a united front, and O'Gorman defeated Depew on a party-line vote of 112-80. The *New York Times* described the result as the "surrender of the insurgents" and said, "We have been told that the insurgents were fighting for a 'principle.' Mr. Murphy also was fighting for a 'principle,' the principle of Murphy rule. He has won his fight."[18]

The battle over the senate seat was more than simply a distraction. It caused real trouble for Governor Dix's legislative program and exacerbated philosophical differences in the Democratic coalition while also illustrating Dix's weak political and leadership skills.[19] Charlie Murphy used this to get what he wanted. In a precursor to his battles with Governor Sulzer,

Boss Murphy used his power and influence in the legislature to hold up the governor's appointments to essential executive positions until Governor Dix appointed Murphy's choices to important political posts.[20]

On example of how this worked occurred just after the protracted battle that ended with O'Gorman's appointment as senator. Governor Dix wanted his trusted confidant George C. Van Tuyl Jr. to be state superintendent of banks. The job was important to the state but also important to Dix because of the superintendent's power over the state's finances. Dix appointed his ally to the post but Van Tuyl needed to be confirmed by the state senate and specifically by the Senate Finance Committee. The committee staff prepared a report recommending Van Tuyl's confirmation, but the chairman of the Finance Committee was Senator James J. Frawley. Frawley was a staunch ally of Charlie Murphy's and such an important member of Tammany Hall that he served as a Tammany district leader (much more about Senator Frawley later in this book).[21] Week after week passed without the Finance Committee acting on Van Tuyl's nomination; all the while, this important post was vacant. It would continue to be vacant until Boss Murphy got what he wanted.

Murphy wanted to fill the vacancy on the Supreme Court left by O'Gorman's selection to the senate. The boss's candidate was an obscure lawyer named Daniel F. Cohalan. As a friend and advisor to Charlie Murphy, Cohalan's practice had quickly grown to large and lucrative proportions.[22] Until Murphy got what he wanted, his allies in the senate would make sure that Governor Dix would not get what he wanted. In the Albany slang, "Dix gets nothin' until the Gov comes across with Cohalan."[23]

Dix and Murphy—governor and boss—struck a deal. On May 18 Senator Frawley and the Finance Committee unanimously endorsed Van Tuyl to be superintendent of banks. Sixteen minutes later, a message from Governor Dix announced the appointment of Daniel Cohalan to the State Supreme Court.[24]

Under continuous pressure from Murphy, Dix appointed as public service commissioners the secretary of the Tammany committee (J.

Sergeant Cram), chairman of the Democratic State Committee (Huppuch), and his brother-in-law (Curtis N. Douglas).[25] The Public Service Commission was an important position of trust, and these appointments, as well as his appointments to the Civil Service Commission, caused the New York Times, which had been an ardent supporter of Dix's, to write, "It begins to look as if there was nobody in the State quite so careless about the success and the reputation of Governor Dix's administration as the Governor himself."[26] From the point of view of reformers, Dix did succeed at least in preventing a good deal of bad legislation. He vetoed over 100 bills, removed a corrupt borough president in Queens, and, after establishing a boxing commission that basically allowed unrestrained pugilism, he reversed himself and urged a safer, more responsible approach.* Still, this was much, much less than they had hoped for from the governor.

During Dix's tenure, there was also a marked change in Charlie Murphy. As district leader, he had his "hailing place" or unofficial office by a lamppost. By the end of Dix's term, Murphy held his meetings in a luxurious suite of rooms at Delmonico's, a fashionable restaurant at Fifth Avenue and Forty-fourth Street. This ostentatious show of wealth shocked many longtime political players who had mastered the art of simple appearances to hide their own illicit gains and used their practiced skill at the "common touch" to cover secret wealth. This practice did not help Murphy—or Tammany Hall—with the public, but Murphy, in the full flush of his newfound power, cared little for appearances. In time, both William Sulzer and Charlie Murphy would pay the price for Murphy not caring.[27]

---

* The removal of Queens borough president Lawrence Gresser, which was called for by Samuel Ordway, a special investigator appointed by Governor Hughes, might not have been so remarkable after all. It had the effect of strengthening the political faction in Queens led by Joseph Cassidy, a Murphy ally (Brown).

7

THE ELECTION OF 1912

THE YEAR 1912 WAS SHAPING UP to be an unusual one in politics. Although the deep fissures in the Democratic coalition were on public display during Governor Dix's tenure, they paled in comparison to what Republicans were facing. President William Howard Taft was running for reelection, but his predecessor in the White House, Theodore Roosevelt, had grown disillusioned with his former protégé's conservatism and was challenging him. Unable to wrest the GOP nomination away from Taft, Roosevelt bolted the party and formed the Progressive Party—or as it was more commonly called, the Bull Moose Party. Based as much on Roosevelt's personality as on common goals, the platform stressed cutting the power of Big Business through strict limits on campaign funding and lobbying; electoral reform, such as direct election of senators, women's suffrage, recall, and referendum; fiscal policy, including relief for farmers, a federal income tax, and inheritance tax; workers' policies, such as an eight-hour day, minimum wage laws, and workers' compensation; as well as other similar populist reforms.

The full break in the Republican Party, between conservative organization men and radical insurgents, played out across the country but nowhere more so than in New York. A New Yorker himself, Roosevelt was personally popular in the state, which was fertile ground for his progressive ideas. Moreover, New York was home to Wall Street and to many of the trusts that Roosevelt railed against with such eloquence and vigor. New York's senior U.S. senator, Elihu Root, was a leader of the reactionaries and a Taft man. (Root was the chair of the national convention and shepherded Taft's renomination through a fierce floor fight.)

For governor, the Republican old guard nominated Job E. Hedges, a prominent corporation lawyer (like Senator Root), while Roosevelt's Progressives nominated Oscar Straus, a former Roosevelt cabinet secretary and philanthropist. The question was whom the Democrats would nominate. The factional fights and Dix's ineffectiveness led Charlie Murphy to walk away from him.* Although Murphy was clearly in control of patronage and spoils, he feared that Dix would lose. The important thing to Murphy was winning.

An anecdote from William Riordan, the political reporter for *The Sun*, offers an interesting insight into Boss Murphy.

> On Independence Day in 1905, the Tammany faithful gathered, as usual, at the Wigwam, then located at Fourteenth Street near Irving Place—to hear patriotic speeches. On the stage sat the society's leadership, called the Council of Sachems, including the boss, Charles F. Murphy. All wore ceremonial sashes, medals, frock coats, stiff collars, and silk hats despite a room temperature of 105 degrees. After the ceremony and speeches, all rose to sing "The Star-Spangled Banner."

---

* As Dix's term came to an end, William Church Osborn (organizer of the Society to Prevent Corrupt Practices at Elections, New York State Democratic Chair, founder of the Citizens' Budget Commission, president of the Children's Aid Society and president of the Metropolitan Museum of Art) wrote a letter published in the *New York Times* under the headline, "Speaks Up For Gov. Dix." It contained this praise for the outgoing governor, "Let us admit at once that he is not dramatic; that he fails to realize the news value of situations and is not bursting with benevolent meddlesomeness" (*New York Times*, December 28, 1912).

Riordan was watching Boss Murphy closely. As the meeting broke, Riordan caught up with the Secretary of the Democratic County Committee.

"What's with Murphy?" Riordan asked. "He didn't sing the 'The Star-Spangled Banner.'"

"Perhaps he didn't want to commit himself," the Secretary replied.[1]

Charles Francis Murphy, Tammany's boss from 1902 to 1924, was shrouded in silence and mystery even while wielding enormous power.

It was said of him, "If silence can be flamboyant, then Murphy was an exhibitionist." Asked by a passerby for the time, he would gaze back benignly, pull out his pocket watch, and hold it up to the questioner's eyes, never opening his mouth.[2] He is said to have once offered this wisdom: "Never write when you can speak; never speak when you can nod; never nod when you can blink." And he lived by his own advice, leaving no records or writings, having given no formal speeches and granted no interviews of any consequence.[3]

His motivations were inexplicable to his closest friends, and one could only infer the obvious: politics was a road to success, honors, and wealth for an ambitious man who had been born poor.

Born in 1856 Charlie Murphy was the second of nine children. His father, Dennis, was an Irish immigrant, poor and illiterate, but he valued education and sent his children to public school until they were old enough to work. Charles became a manual laborer at the age of fourteen working in a shipyard as a caulker. It was rough work, and Murphy "not only knew how to use his fists, but he had no fear. In two years he was the acknowledged boss of the shipyard; he had literally fought his way into leadership."[4] In 1876 he organized a baseball team. He was a good catcher and received offers from professional clubs. Becoming a horsecar driver, he saved his money.

In 1880 Murphy used his life savings of $500 to open a bar, Charlie's Place, at Nineteenth Street and Avenue A. It was a rough, working-class neighborhood, and it served Murphy well. The saloon itself had one window and a narrow door, and everything inside was purchased secondhand. Beer and a cup of soup were sold for 5 cents, and Murphy frequently tended bar, always taking the time to listen to his customers.

One was a young man named James Hagan. Hagan wanted to run for the state assembly but neither Tammany Hall nor the anti-Tammany forces known as the County Democracy would endorse him. Hagan asked Murphy for advice. "Run independent," was all Murphy said. Managing Hagan's campaign, Murphy worked hard and used his influence at the shipyard and throughout the neighborhood to elect Hagan. Tammany's leaders took immediate notice of Murphy's skill and vote-wrangling abilities and in 1892 named him a district leader.[5]

Murphy always kept tabs on his voters, and if any Democrats in the district had not voted by 3 p.m., Murphy sent him a card by a messenger, respectfully inviting him to the polls. Murphy could be found standing under an old gas lamp every night outside his clubhouse, available to anyone who needed to see him. Hard work and accessibility piled up huge majorities for the Democratic ticket. By now, Murphy owned four taverns and his ever expanding clientele were the backbone of his political machine.

Conversations with Charles Francis Murphy were brief and one-sided. The petitioner spoke for a minute or two and then Murphy nodded yes or no. His promises were always considered carefully but once made they were binding, no matter how circumstances might change.

In 1897 Murphy was appointed a dock commissioner, and he thereafter preferred to be addressed as "Commissioner." The commission offered opportunities for what Riordan—in his classic satire of machine politics, *Plunkett of Tammany Hall*—called "honest graft": the then legal use of inside information and influence to make money. In one example, a brother of Murphy's organized the New York Contracting and Trucking

Corporation. The brother and two friends each owned five shares while the remaining eighty-five shares were owned by "an unnamed person who was never identified."

New York Contracting was soon granted inexpensive leases for city-owned docks, which were then sublet to international shipping companies at enormous profit. When the Pennsylvania Railroad began building Penn Station and its tunnels beneath the Hudson and the East Rivers, the Board of Aldermen stopped blocking the building permits only after the Pennsylvania Railroad awarded New York Contracting a huge construction contract—despite a bid 25 percent higher than the competition.

Richard Croker had been boss for almost two decades when Tammany lost the 1901 mayoral campaign. Having also failed to carry New York City in the 1900 presidential campaign, Croker had the sense to jump just before he was pushed. He resigned, sailing to Britain to live the life of an English country gentleman. Power fell to a triumvirate: Daniel F. McMahon, a district leader and contractor; Louis F. Haffen, the Bronx borough president; and Charles F. Murphy. Five months and five days later, Murphy put the others aside and became the chief. He would wield power for a generation.

Murphy's leadership style was to keep abreast of developments through the city, consult regularly with the lesser leaders, and test the views of others before advancing his own. His taciturnity led "the boys" to think that "he [always] had something in reserve...It was the cards he was holding back that gave him command of the situation." Many remarked at his ability to quickly grasp even the most complicated political or legal issue. Every week, he met with his district leaders: they would talk about their problems. He listened, said a few words, and then acted. Politics was his vocation and avocation. He worked at it furiously and exclusively, and he invariably enjoyed the effort.

Although he owned four saloons, Murphy rarely took a drink. He also did not smoke or swear and was known to keep his temper no matter the situation.

Murphy did not originate the political machine as an informal welfare

CHAPTER SEVEN

"Charles Francis Murphy"
Known as Silent Charlie for his reticence, Murphy was Boss of Tammany Hall from 1902 until his death in 1924. Under Murphy's leadership, Tammany Hall elected three governors, three mayors, and two United States Senators. No other Tammany leader ever had or would ever again enjoy such power.

system, but he expanded the district clambakes, support for widows, and food baskets for the poor. He had the vision to develop a stable of great candidates.

In this case, Murphy's political instincts told him it was time to dump Governor Dix, and he was not alone. Most of the Democratic leaders of the state went on record as opposing a second term for Dix.[6]

Enter Congressman William Sulzer, whose relationship with Tammany was complicated. Sulzer claimed that Tammany tried to ditch him twice while he served in Congress but he won anyway.[7] Yet he also called Tammany "the greatest vehicle" for accomplishment of good,[8] and in 1902 offered this powerful defense of the organization:

> The men who, in season and out of season, continually denounce Tammany and Democracy, who denounce its leaders, who revile it and prophecy all evil concerning it, know not of what they talk. Its organization is thoroughly, simply and absolutely Democratic.... Chronic faultfinding is unfair, sweeping denunciation is unwarranted.... Tammany is Democracy. Tammany needs no defense from any man. It needs no eulogy but its own history, its own record, and its own indefatigable efforts for its principles and the people. That record and that history speak in trumpet tones to the world more eloquently than words of mine. Read its history, read what it has done for the people in many a struggle, and for the Democratic party, ere you judge it and condemn.... Tammany will go on and on forever—to its truer and grander destiny.[9]

Sulzer was ambitious—he had sought the Democratic nomination for governor every year since 1896—but there were limits to Tammany's support of his efforts.[10] In fact Richard Croker, leader of the hall through 1901, openly ridiculed his ambition.[11] At the 1906 convention in Buffalo, Sulzer garnered serious support and even opened a campaign headquarters, but it was not to be.* After Dix was nominated in 1910 Sulzer reexamined his relationship with Tammany Hall, wondering if he could maintain even the appearance of friendly relations with the organization that was becoming increasingly hostile toward his ambition. After all, he was the only candidate who had refused to withdraw in Dix's favor.[12]

But 1912 was a strange year. Sulzer's district on the Upper East Side was heavily Jewish, and Sulzer's support and impressive victory margins there made him a good candidate to compete for the same voters as the Progressive candidate, Oscar Straus, the first Jewish member of the U.S. Cabinet. Sulzer's experience in foreign affairs, especially his leadership in abrogating the Russian treaty, added to his appeal with Jewish voters. Furthermore, Sulzer had an exemplary record on progressive issues like the amendment for popular election of senators, a federal income tax, and legislation to create the Department of Labor and reduce the tariff—a record that would help earn progressive votes for the Democratic ticket.

Sulzer was both attractive and still young at forty-nine and such a good speaker that he was known as a "spellbinder."[13] Still, it was not an easy decision for Charlie Murphy and Tammany Hall to nominate him. In his favor, Sulzer was tall and striking, very much resembling Henry Clay,[14] and he had also been a good soldier in the cause of Tammany Hall. As a congressman he had done good work to bring in the votes, and he had also been "one of the boys," obeying orders from Tammany bosses Richard Croker and Charlie Murphy.[15] Still, questions about his suitability remained.[16] He took his resemblance to Clay too far, making his imitations of that statesman's dress, speech, and mannerisms seem vain and self-important.[17] As one reporter who knew Sulzer said, "When it comes to preserving our liberties, William is a whole canning factory."[18] When "Big" Tim Sullivan, a Tammany leader, heard about the prospect of Sulzer's nomination, he

---

* In 1906, Sulzer's nominator denounced socialism and the Democratic "surrender" to Hearst. Sulzer came in second with 124 voters, while Hearst received 309 and future governor Dix got 17. Significantly, most of Sulzer's votes came from Kings County and not Murphy's New York County.

exclaimed, "You can't do that.... He doesn't amount to anything....We treat him down on the Bowery as a joke."[19] Later, Murphy would call his decision to nominate Sulzer "the greatest mistake of my life."[20]

The Democrats met in Syracuse on October 3, 1912. There were a number of candidates: Governor Dix, Supreme Court Justices Victor J. Dowling and James W. Gerard, and Martin Glynn, an Albany newspaperman and former state comptroller under Governor Hughes. The overwhelming majority of county chairs were for Sulzer, at least according to sources within the Sulzer camp, because of that ever important trait in politics, his apparent "electability." Martin Glynn, because of his record and an early speech to the delegates that was both strong and heavy on progressive ideas, was another favorite.[21]

In addition to nominating a gubernatorial candidate, there were several subplots unfolding at the Onondaga Hotel in downtown Syracuse. Would Sulzer be able to overcome the antipathy of Murphy and other Tammany leaders? In light of his disappointment (and disobedience) at the 1910 convention, would Sulzer even try to earn their support or simply try to overcome it? Could the Democrats heal the growing rift between the reform camp and the Tammany camp? All these questions were important and intertwined because of the very real danger that large numbers of reform Democrats could bolt the party—just as Roosevelt and his Progressives ditched Taft and the Republicans. In fact, that these disaffected Democrats could join with disaffected Republicans to elect Oscar Straus of the Progressive Party was quite a real possibility in 1912.

That Democratic presidential candidate Governor Woodrow Wilson of New Jersey weighed in on the convention, demanding a "free and unbossed" convention, and presumably an independent candidate, only heightened the stakes and served to put Tammany's Charlie Murphy further under the microscope.[22]

What would Charlie Murphy do? Could Murphy get the candidate he wanted without controlling the convention? If he controlled the convention, could his candidate win?

When balloting began, Murphy gave an indication that the convention would be "unbridled." On the first ballot, a roll call vote was requested. New York County, home to Tammany Hall, cast vote after vote to nominate Governor Dix for another term, as did many others from New York City. When the name of Charles F. Murphy was called, Tammany's boss arose and said, "I ask to be excused." One observer called Murphy's declination "the crown to the structure of freedom."[23] The first ballot results:

John A. Dix of Washington	147
William Sulzer of New York	126
Herman Metz of Kings	70
Martin Glynn of Albany	46
George Burd of Erie	38
Francis Harrison of New York	21

Various others received scattered votes. A total of 226 votes were necessary to be nominated.

Many Tammany men let it be known that their votes for Dix were more a sign of respect for a sitting governor than an earnest desire to have the governor run again. Nonetheless, on the second ballot, a roll call vote again being requested, New York County stuck with Dix, and again Murphy arose and said, "I ask to be excused." However, Sulzer picked up votes in several rural upstate areas. The second ballot results:

William Sulzer	141
John A. Dix	126
Herman Metz	68
Martin Glynn	48
George Burd	28
Francis Harrison	27

The move to Sulzer continued on the third ballot. Erie County's solid support for favorite son Senator George Burd dissolved with several voters moving to Sulzer while Onondaga County threw its entire nine votes to Sulzer. More significantly, Sulzer gained twenty votes from Charlie Murphy's New York County. The third ballot results:

William Sulzer	195
John A. Dix	87
Herman Metz	76
Martin Glynn	41
Francis Harrison	21
George Burd	9

The shift of so many Tammany delegates from Dix to Sulzer was significant, and Governor Dix removed his name.[24] Following the third ballot, Murphy held a conference with his advisors; the result was the very public release of his delegates to vote as they saw fit.

On the next ballot Sulzer had the momentum and soon had the votes. A Washington County delegate, who had placed Governor Dix's name into nomination at the start of balloting, arose and exclaimed, "I wish to withdraw the name of Governor Dix in favor of William Sulzer." Other candidates followed, and Sulzer was declared the winner on the fourth ballot. Martin Glynn, from Albany County, was nominated as lieutenant governor, and the convention, in an unprecedented and stunning break with tradition, appeared "unbridled and unbossed."[25]

However, Charlie Murphy worked even better in the shadows, and the appearance of independence was "only an illusion."[26] In fact, the convention was from the start manipulated by Murphy.[27] The whole time, it was, one delegate wrote, "absolutely in the hands of Murphy."[28] Newspaper reports said the whole thing was a charade, arranged beforehand by Murphy; Patrick E. "Packy" McCabe, the Democratic boss of Albany; and Norman E. Mack, Democratic National Committee member from New York.

Although the boss personally restrained from voting, Murphy told his delegates to watch how "Packy" McCabe voted and to follow his lead. McCabe voted for Sulzer.²⁹ Any doubts of Murphy's intentions were put to rest when Robert Wagner cast the solid vote of New York County for Sulzer.³⁰

As mentioned earlier, the questions as the delegates arrived in Syracuse were: What would Charlie Murphy do? Could Murphy get the candidate he wanted without controlling the convention? If he controlled the convention, could his candidate win?

The answers were clear, at least to those in the know: Murphy did control the convention and Tammany chose the candidate, but the power had been exerted behind closed doors, in the proverbial smoke-filled rooms, mostly in Suite 802 of the Onondaga Hotel—the room registered in the name of Charles F. Murphy. Sulzer was chosen, not because Murphy trusted him and not because the Tammanyites insisted on him, but because Sulzer was their best chance to win in November and by winning keeping the Democratic Party—and specifically the Tammany faithful—in power.

By hiding his own influence behind the scenes, Murphy allowed the convention—and the candidate—to appear unbossed. That made an election victory possible for Sulzer. It also set the stage for future conflict between the boss who wielded his power in secret and the candidate who publicly denied owing anything to that influence.

William Sulzer continued to set the stage for that conflict as he hit the hustings. After his nomination, Sulzer was asked why he wanted to be governor. He replied, "I hope to put the government back into the hands of the People" and added that he was "very confident" Murphy would help him get that done.³¹ Sulzer also declared, "William Sulzer never had a boss, and his only master is himself." Murphy, it is reported, heard the boast with a smile.³²

National Democrats were pleased with the convention and the candidate. The Democratic presidential candidate, Woodrow Wilson, called Sulzer "a man whose reputation for integrity and independence is unquestionable, a man of high principle, devoted to the public interest."³³ And three-time Democratic nominee William Jennings Bryan offered Sulzer his highest compliment, calling Sulzer "a man of the People."[34]

Reformers across the state accepted the "unbossed and unbridled" version of the convention and rushed to support Sulzer. The anti-Tammany reform group, Empire State Democracy, led by State Senator Franklin Roosevelt of the Hudson Valley and Thomas Mott Osborne of Syracuse, withdrew its slate in favor of Sulzer while the *New York Times* praised his nomination, saying Sulzer would govern "with ability, with independence, with good sense, and with good results to the State."[35]

The *New-York Tribune*, on the other hand, disagreed, calling Sulzer "a steadfast advocate of Tammany methods and Tammany theories of government"; the paper asked, "When had he ever shown independence?"[36] Progressive gubernatorial candidate Oscar Straus, equally skeptical of Sulzer's reform credentials, asked, "Will a man who has for thirty years been aligned with Tammany Hall and received all of his preferment at its hands be able to free himself from the clutch of the Tiger?"[37]

Although the convention had been well scripted, it merely offered Sulzer an opportunity to win. He still needed to run the right campaign, aided by party loyalists across the state. However, Sulzer's campaign lacked substance and many specifics for his program. Instead he offered platitudes about his experience, such as, "An ounce of performance is worth a ton of promise" and "The record of the past is the best guarantee for the future."[38] Most Sulzer rallies concluded with this promise:

> When I am elected Governor the latch-string of the door of the Executive office at Albany will always be on the outside, and it will not be so high but that the lowliest can reach it, and the humblest citizen of the State may come to Albany and see the Governor and be treated with as much consideration as the richest and most powerful.[39]

Sulzer's speech on accepting the nomination of the Democratic Party at the state convention in Syracuse offered this as his program:

> I will go into office without a promise except my promise to all the People to serve them faithfully and honestly and to the best of my ability. I am free, without entanglements, and shall remain free. If elected I shall follow the street called straight and the Executive office will be in the Capitol. When I take the oath as Governor I shall enforce the laws fearlessly and impartially, but with malice toward none. Those who know me best know that I stand firmly for certain fundamental principles—for liberty under law; for civil and religious freedom; for Constitutional government; for the old integrities and the new humanities; for equality before the law; for equal rights to all and special privileges for none; for the cause that lacks assistance; against the wrongs that needs resistance; for unshackled opportunity as the beacon-light of individual hope and the best guarantees for the perpetuity of our free institutions. No influence will control me but the influence of my conscience, and my determination to do my full duty to all the people, as God gives me the light.[40]

The lack of specifics in the Sulzer campaign made no difference. November 5, 1912, produced a Democratic victory across the board. Nationally, Woodrow Wilson became the first Democrat elected to the White House in thirty years. In New York, Democrats won a huge victory in statewide offices and took control of both houses of the legislature; in fact, the assembly basically flipped—its new makeup 103 Democrats, 43 Republicans, and 4 Progressives. The senate comprised 33 Democrats, 17 Republicans, and 1 Progressive. At the time, Sulzer's victory was the largest plurality in state history. Sulzer received 649,599 votes; Hedges, 444,105; and Straus, 393,183.

Sulzer's victory was all the more remarkable since Straus appealed to the same voters and offered a similar platform. Yet underneath, it was not as impressive as it first seemed.

The high number of blank or scattered votes (80,368) suggested unhappiness with any candidate for governor, while a majority of 268,097 votes actually were cast *against* Sulzer, although split among two other candidates. In fact Sulzer received the smallest vote of any Democratic candidate for governor in fourteen years: fewer votes than Dix had received in 1910 (649,599 for Sulzer to 689,700 for Dix), fewer votes than Woodrow Wilson had gotten in New York State, and even fewer votes than his running mate, Lieutenant Governor Martin Glynn.

PART TWO

8

GOVERNOR WILLIAM SULZER

WILLIAM SULZER WAS INAUGURATED as the thirty-ninth governor of the great state of New York on January 1, 1913. The weather in Albany was cold and brisk, and the day was threatened with snow throughout. It would make no difference: the campaign was over but, as always with Sulzer, the show would go on.

The governor of New York, ever since Colonial times, was escorted to his inauguration by a military procession. By 1913 that procession had grown grand enough that it could only be called a military parade. William Sulzer dispensed with the parade; the military majesty was not in keeping with his commitment to democratic ideals. Instead, "Plain Bill" walked alone from the Executive Mansion to the capitol, causing a sensation before he was even sworn into office.

The new governor sent the crowds into a frenzy. Shouts of "Hurrah!" echoed over and over as the excitement of the already boisterous crowd grew. The people regarded Sulzer's simple act as the greatest exhibition of simplicity its imagination could conjure. They flocked into the streets and took their place in the wake of the procession.[1]

"Newly Elected Governor William Sulzer and
Former Governor John Alden Dix"
*Sulzer pushed Dix out of office and was consistently critical of his predecessor.
Note the differences between Dix's immaculate dress in comparison with
Sulzer's disheveled and uncoordinated "Plain Bill" persona.*

Sulzer took to his Jeffersonian humility completely, wearing an old gray suit that, a contemporary chronicler noted, "had seen service in the last campaign, and possibly in other campaigns."[2] Sulzer's demeanor was friendly but not overly jovial, striking just the right balance between solemn respect for the office and genuine appreciation for the support shown by the crowd. This was all in stark contrast to Governor Dix, "who pays close attention to his clothes, [and] wore the attire demanded by the latest fashion."[3] In that same spirit, Sulzer first official act would rechristen the Executive Mansion as "the People's House."[4]

Whether this was the real Sulzer or simply the façade that the new governor had worked so long and hard to promulgate, the people loved it: "No high hat for Sulzer!" exclaimed one bystander. "He's just plain Bill."[5]

Charlie Murphy was noticeably absent for Sulzer's triumph.* Whether it was because Murphy was offended to be invited via a formal invite from the Inaugural Committee rather than a personal invite from the governor-elect or because Murphy wanted to spare Sulzer the inevitable questions about their relationship was never made clear.[6] The *Times*, under the subheadline, "Few Bosses Are Present," remarked that, "It is noticeable, though, that fewer politicians have come [to Sulzer's inauguration]. The number of bosses present could easily be tolled off on the fingers. A flock of job hunters are on hand, however."[7]

"The hour has struck, and the task of administrative reform is mine," said the new governor.[8]

---

* January 1, 1913, marked another triumph for Sulzer: the first day of operation of the Parcel Post Service provided by the U.S. Postal Service. He was long one of the loudest and most insistent advocates in the nation for the creation of a Parcel Post Service. The first package was sent by former postmaster general John Wanamaker in New York to then postmaster general Frank Hitchcock. The first package to be sent by a woman was mailed at Grand Central Station by Sophia Irene Loeb to Governor Sulzer. The establishment of the parcel post had a tremendously stimulating effect on the national economy, opening a world of opportunities for farmers and merchants. Rural Americans especially were able to purchase foodstuffs, medicines, dry goods, and other commodities not available to them previously (*New York Times*, January 1, 1913).

I grasp the opportunity the People now give me and am resolved to shirk no responsibility, to work for the welfare of the people, to correct every existing abuse, to abolish useless offices, and wherever possible consolidate bureaus and commissions to secure greater economy and more efficiency, to uproot official corruption and to raise higher the standard of official integrity, to simplify the methods of orderly administration, to advance the prosperity of all the People, to be ever dissatisfied with conditions that can be improved, to promote the common weal, to guard the honor and protect the rights of the Empire State, and last, but not least, to reduce Governmental expenditures to the minimum, and thus lessen as much as possible the heavy burdens of taxation.[9]

Sulzer made no mention of the outgoing governor in his address and instead offered mostly reruns of his campaign speeches.[10] After delivering his address to the full crowd in the assembly chamber Sulzer repeated it to an overflow crowd outside.[11] The public was crowded into "remote and inconvenient corners" and "somewhat roughly handled by Albany policemen," but that was because 18,000 invitations had been sent out and the chamber could hold a scant 1,500. The *Times* estimated the cost of printing, engraving, and postage (4 cents per invitation) at about $1,000 and noted, "It will be a case of first come first served and a terrible jam will probably be the result." They were right.[12]

New York's paper of record also noted another example of the Sulzer paradox. In jarring contrast to the Plain Bill Sulzer who walked through the streets of Albany, "The simplicity that marked the ceremony had been thrown to the wind in one regard. The decorations were as lavish as in other years. Exotic plants, palms, American flags and the State emblem entered into the scheme."[13]

The governor's address was packed full of progressive ideas, including

"SULZER ON THE CAPITOL STEPS"
Governor Sulzer on his way to address the state legislature. As a Congressman, his colleagues called him "Seltzer" because of the effervescence of his speech or the "the Siphon of Debate" for his long windedness.

direct election of senators, direct primaries, women's suffrage, protection of natural resources, an extension of the minimum wage, increased worker compensation, new restrictions on child labor, and an empowered Department of Labor with the power to investigate conditions and enforce violations.[14] With William Sulzer, there was never a shortage of promises... or pandering.

The same day, the governor sent his first message to the legislature. Traditionally the governor's message was similar to a state-of-the-state speech today. In it, Sulzer set out three main themes: his deep commitment to "the People," his hopes to pass progressive legislation, and his determination to elevate the economic condition of the state.

THE PEOPLE

Showing his confidence in "the People," Sulzer declared his support for the Seventeenth Amendment prescribing direct election of senators: "I favor this change in the Federal Constitution as I shall every other change that will restore the Government to the control of the People. I want the People, in fact as well as in theory, to rule this great Republic and the Government at all times to be responsive to their just demands." This was no academic argument. Reformers had agitated for direct election as early as 1828, and it was an important plank of the Progressive platform. *The Treason of the Senate*, a series of articles by the muckraking journalist David Graham Phillips, published in *Cosmopolitan* magazine in 1906, exposed corruption in the senate and accelerated this movement toward direct election. Protracted battles over appointments in state legislatures (such as the battle to replace Chauncey Depew in New York) did as well. However, important leaders in New York, notably Elihu Root, senior U.S. senator from New York, were opposed to the change. Root, who had won the Nobel Peace Prize in 1912 for his work to bring nations together, was a formidable opponent. He argued that state legislatures were more deliberative and less subject to the passing whims and fancies than the general electorate, as the founders had intended. The proof, Root argued, was in the fact that many distinguished senators had been appointed by legislatures and likely would never have been elected. Most importantly, Root made an argument based on federalism—that by having the entire state legislature choose senators, they were representative of the entire state and would zealously guard the important power and prerogatives of the states.*

Those sentiments held no weight for Sulzer. He was in favor of anything that put the people first. "The People can and ought to be trusted. They have demonstrated their ability for self-government. If the People cannot be trusted, then our Government is a failure and the free institutions of the

---

* The Seventeenth Amendment would be ratified in May 1913. Elihu Root took his opposition to the end, refusing to stand for reelection.

fathers are doomed. We must rely on the People, and we must legislate in the interests of all the People and not for the benefit of the few."[15]

He continued, "If Americans would excel other nations in commerce, in manufacture, in science, in intellectual growth, and in other humane attainments, we must first possess a people physically, mentally, and morally fit and sound."[16] He put a premium on smart, progressive business leaders: "We have had to change old customs and repeal antiquated laws. We must now convince employers that any industry that saps the vitality and destroys the initiative of the workers is detrimental to the best interests of the State and menaces the general welfare of the Government."[17]

Many of Sulzer's inaugural promises were as empty sounding as his campaign rhetoric:

> We must try to work out practical legislation that will apply our social ideals and views of industrial progress to secure for our men, women, and children the greatest possible reserve of physical and mental force. I hold it to be self-evident that no industry has the right to sacrifice human life for its profit, but that just as each industry must reckon in its cost of production the material waste, so it should also count as a part of the cost of production the human waste which it employs.[18]

The *New York Times* opined, "The message ... contained many recommendations for reform, but little in the way of helpful suggestions to the lawmakers along the lines of constructive legislation.[19]

But always, Sulzer put the people first:

> Let us then be just to the workers. No man can pay too high a tribute to "labor." It is the creative force of the world, the genius of accomplishment of the brain and the brawn of man, the spirit of all progress, and the milestones marking the advance of nations. Civilization owes everything to labor — to

the constructive toiler and the creative worker. Labor owes very little to civilization. Mother Earth is labor's best friend. From her forests and her fields, from her rocks and her rivers, the toiler has wrought all and brought forth the wonders of the world.[20]

PROGRESSIVE LEGISLATION

Sulzer's second main theme was progressive legislation—again, for the people and their wages: "Many of our States have enacted workmen's compensation or insurance laws. The production of our wealth in a large measure is a tribute to the ability and the efficiency of the workers. It is only just, then, that those who do the work should receive an equitable share of that which they have helped to produce. No compensation is fair which does not secure to each worker at least enough to permit him or her decent standards of life."[21] And to ensure living wages: "To secure for these less accustomed to the competitive struggle protection that other workers have won for themselves through organization, and we should carefully consider the establishment of wage boards, with authority to fix a living wage for conditions of work below which standards no industry should be allowed to continue its operations."[22]

Sulzer was against the exploitation of child labor:

> For the welfare of the State child life must be protected. Not only should the child be guaranteed the right to be born equal, but it must be given the chance to live, to grow, to learn, and to develop into useful and patriotic citizenship. The work period must not be permitted to infringe on the formative and the maturing period. Compulsory education laws and restrictions upon child labor properly enforced will secure to every child of the State its rightful heritage.[23]

On imposing state safety standards:

Another type of legislation beneficial to the State, that aims to conserve human life and health, is that which requires the use of safety appliances and establishes safety standards. Human life is infinitely more valuable than the profit of material things. The state, for its own preservation, has the right to demand the use of safer and more hygienic methods, even if at greater cost of production to the employer. Occupational diseases should be studied, and the results of careful investigation embodied in laws to safeguard the health and the lives of the workers.[24]

On a strong and active Department of Labor: "I recommend legislation to so reorganize the Department of Labor that it shall have greater powers and a more comprehensive scope with additional agencies sufficient to investigate conditions, enforce the laws, and accomplish the greatest good for the greatest number—along practical humanitarian lines."[25] The Department of Labor would go hand in hand with an energized Civil Service Commission:

As a consistent friend of the merit system in the civil service it is my purpose to co-operate with you in protecting its integrity and promoting its efficiency. Therefore I recommend: that the State Civil Service Commission initiate constructive work along the line of standardizing promotion examinations, by introducing and maintaining efficiency records of all competitive employees, and request the co-operation of the heads of department with the Civil Service Commission in enforcing the present rules or any supplementary ones which the State Commission may adopt to carry this plan into effect.[26]

This commission would recommend new civil services laws and rules: "The State Civil Service Commission, in my judgment, should continue its efforts to bring about a more systematic administration of civil service laws in the cities of the second and third classes by the adoption of a model set of rules, by uniform classification of position in the service of such cities, and by co-operation and assistance in conducting and rating municipal examinations."[27]

On revising the state criminal justice system: "The need of reform in civil and criminal law is urgent, and I recommend the enactment of such legislation as will relieve the present legal systems of the delays, the unnecessary expense, and the uncertainties incident to the present procedure."[28] And on protecting the state's farmers: "We must keep the needs of the farmer ever before us. What the farmer produces is real wealth. To-day, when consumption has caught up with production, it behooves us to give attention to the land and every kind of assistance to the tillers of the soil. Those of the cities who would return to farms must be encouraged, and those of the farms must be aided to great effort and larger profit. We are falling behind as an agricultural State."[29]

Besides these protections, Sulzer wanted to offer better incentives to promote farming:

> We should help our farmers to secure the advantages of long loans at reasonable interest rates.... I recommend that whatever is within the power of the Legislature to do to sustain, to promote, to upbuild the agricultural resources of the Empire State, should speedily be done. I will work heartily with you, as well as the rank and file of farmers, to make the next two years the most prosperous, in an agricultural way, that this State has ever known. When the farmer is prosperous the State will flourish.[30]

The whole program also called for infrastructure improvements: "The building and the maintenance of good roads, the continued conservation and development of our natural resources and the constant improvement of our waterways appeal to us now as they have in the past, and should have our earnest support and constant attention."[31]

THE ECONOMY

The governor spent the biggest part of the message showing concern—and setting out his program for—the economic situation of the state and its people. In 1913 the average yearly wage was $585 (roughly $13,000 in 2013 dollars) but then, as now, there was a large disparity between different professions, even among the working class. Those engaged in clothing manufacturing were paid only 25 cents an hour while cashiers and bookkeepers earned over $20 per week (though only $16.50 for women in the same jobs). Of course the cost of living was less as well. A loaf of bread cost just over 5 cents baked, or only 3 cents for a pound of flour. Potatoes were cheap and plentiful, costing barely over 1 cent per pound. Butter went for 40 cents a pound, cheese for 22 cents, steak for 24 cents, and milk for over 35 cents a gallon.

The year 1913 saw an increase in joblessness across the country and a corresponding rise in inflation, issues of great concern to Governor Sulzer. "For more than ten years the increasing cost of living mounting higher and higher each succeeding year has been the most immediate, the most pressing, and the most universally observed fact about economic conditions in this country." said Sulzer. "While wages have remained practically the same, the cost of the necessaries of life has grown more and more oppressive, until to-day the average man in our State, with a family to support, has about all he can do to make both ends meet."[32]

Sulzer continued, "I earnestly direct your careful consideration to this important matter concerning the People, and recommend that you take such action in the premises as you deem just and wise to reduce the high cost of the necessaries of life in order to make living less a struggle for physical existence."[33]

Sulzer concluded, "In view of the increasing expenditures in the administration of State affairs, mounting higher and higher each succeeding year, and necessarily imposing onerous burdens on our taxpayers, I recommend genuine retrenchment in every department of the State, to the end that expenditures be kept down to the minimum of taxation materially reduced."[34] He continued, "I am in sympathy with the oppressed taxpayers of our State and to the best of my ability will aid you in your efforts to lighten their burden.... The way to stop waste and extravagance is to retrench and economize. A cursory examination into State affairs convinces me that many expenditures can be stopped and efficiency prompted if every State officer will clean house, stop waste, and practice every economy consistent with good government and the orderly administration of public affairs."[35]

The Democratic legislature, having campaigned on the promise of a "short and businesslike session" did not adjourn for the usual week or ten days following the inauguration but instead set Monday, four days away, as the start of their legislative session.[36]

Never one to be outdone, Sulzer also got off to an active start, appointing a Committee on Inquiry, New York's first, to examine state spending, investigate the bureaucracy for efficiency, and root out waste, fraud, and abuse.

Sulzer immediately decreased appropriations in select departments and was unsparing in his criticism of Dix's stewardship of the state. The new governor had noticed, he said, "a lack of system and method in the administration of the business of the State, a wide departure from anything like uniformity and an unscientific and wasteful absence of appropriate provisions for the promotion of the economy."[37] Strong language indeed, especially for a predecessor from the same political party.

Governor Sulzer rapidly created a new Department of Efficiency and Economy, a State Board of Estimate, and a State Board of Contract and Supply, and gave the comptroller power to audit state departments. In his second week, the governor produced a commission on public health laws.

The governor was proud of his work and not shy about taking credit. At a dinner in the Lotos Club on February 18, Sulzer made this typically self-congratulatory statement: "As many of you know, from reading the newspapers, I have been a very busy man ever since I took the oath of office as the Governor of the State. To tell the truth," Sulzer continued, "I have been working on an average about eighteen hours out of the twenty-four, and this is the first public dinner, or reception, or entertainment, I have been able to attend since the first day of January. Being Governor of New York is no easy job—that is if you want to be The Governor."[38]

9

LEGISLATIVE PROGRAM

CONTROL OF BOTH the executive and legislative branches of government gave Democrats a unique opportunity to pass legislation. That opportunity was summed up by the Speaker of the assembly, Al Smith, who in taking up the gavel asserted that "the people in no uncertain terms gave our party the control of the affairs of this state.... It is our duty to show the keenest possible sense of that responsibility."[1] Instead of the fractured Democratic Party of 1910, Tammany was in full control as dawn rose on the legislative session. Murphy's handpicked choice for governor had won but equally important was that Murphy had bypassed the senior men[2] in both houses to install his own leaders in the assembly and senate.[3]

Murphy chose Al Smith to be Speaker of the assembly. Born on December 30, 1873, on Manhattan's Lower East Side, Alfred Emmanuel Smith quit parochial school after his father's death and went to work at the famous Fulton Fish Market at the age of fourteen. Smith's career in politics began in 1895. That year Smith was appointed as an investigator in the Office of the City Commissioner of Jurors, a position he owed entirely to Tammany Hall — a friend in the good graces of the organization had recommended

"Future Governor Al Smith and Mrs. Smith"
Smith would transform New York State as a four term governor but in 1913, he was chosen as Speaker of the State Assembly through the machinations of Tammany Boss Charles Murphy.

Smith for the job. Smith was known for his contagiously friendly demeanor and a photographic memory that allowed him to quickly memorize speeches and to speak on almost any topic for long periods of time. He put his natural attributes as an orator to work on behalf of Tammany candidates and causes and quickly advanced through the organization's ranks.

In 1903 Smith was elected to the state assembly. In Albany he proved himself a skilled politician and took a leading role advocating for progressive reforms. Smith would go on to serve as sheriff of New York County and president of the Board of Aldermen of Greater New York. Later, he was elected governor four times and was instrumental in passing significant parts of the progressive agenda into law. Smith's most lasting legacy may be his successful efforts to reorganize the state government, streamlining the budget process and introducing a consolidated and businesslike structure to the executive branch. Smith's last foray in politics was a losing race as the

Democratic Party's candidate for president in 1928 (and the first Catholic to lead a major party ticket). Toward the end of his life, Smith served as president of the corporation that built and operated the Empire State Building.

Smith's counterpart in the senate was Robert Wagner, Tammany's choice for president pro tempore. Born on June 8, 1877, in Germany, Wagner and his family immigrated to New York City in 1885. He was educated in New York and, as a lawyer, made his reputation fighting high-profile labor cases. Wagner left the state senate upon election to the New York State Supreme Court. From there he was elected to the U.S. Senate and was reelected for three terms. In Washington, Senator Wagner authored sweeping legislation that dramatically changed the American social and economic landscape. He served as chairman of the Senate Banking and Currency Committee during the New Deal era. Two of his most notable accomplishments were enacted into law in 1935: the Social Security Act, providing old-age pensions to Americans, and the Wagner Labor Act, guaranteeing labor's right to organize and to bargain collectively. "Whether you like his laws or deplore them," one journalist noted, "he has placed on the books legislation more important and far-reaching than any American in history since the days of the Founding Fathers."[4]

During their time leading New York's legislature, Smith and Wagner worked diligently to introduce basic labor standards along with enforcement measures, pass the Seventeenth Amendment for direct election of senators (sponsored by Wagner), and pass other important progressive legislation.

One of the defining events of this period was the Triangle Shirtwaist Factory fire. The fire killed 146 garment workers in New York City in one of the largest industrial disasters of its time. Inside the factory, the managers' efforts to maximize production and profits meant locking emergency exits to stop the workers sneaking outside for cigarette breaks. Making an already terrible situation worse, the fire department that responded was designed for an era before skyscrapers. Their ladders could not reach the ninth and tenth floors where many of the women were stranded. Over fifty of the victims—mostly young women and some mere girls—jumped to their deaths. The disaster touched the public consciousness, and people across the country demanded action.

In keeping with his promise to enact more effective worker safety legislation, Sulzer established a commission to investigate the fire itself and more broadly to examine the working conditions that led to the tragedy. He appointed Robert Wagner as commission chairman and Al Smith as the vice chairman. The Factory Investigation Commission held hearings across the state and hired field investigators to do unannounced, on-site factory investigations. Their investigation led to a series of groundbreaking reforms of labor laws and worker protections. Those that became law in 1913 alone included workplace sanitation rules, mandated better building access and egress, requirements for fireproofing and fire extinguishers, limits on work hours for women, requirements for fire alarms, insurance to protect workers, and widows' pensions. Sixty of the sixty-four recommendations of the commission were passed into law. Collectively, the fire—and the response—helped create a movement that is still felt today.

Together, Smith, Wagner, and Sulzer also advocated for women's suffrage, rules and regulations for the New York Stock Exchange, and the creation of a public utilities commission with the power to protect consumers. Frances Perkins, a leading advocate for much of this change (and an eyewitness to the Triangle fire), wrote of this time, "The extent to which this legislation in New York marked a change in American political attitudes and policies can scarcely be overrated. It was, I am convinced, a turning point."[5] Perkins went on to serve as U.S. commissioner of labor under President Franklin Roosevelt.

10

REFORMER

Although vitally important, passing progressive legislation was not in and of itself enough for Sulzer. He also wanted to clean up government. It is, of course, easy to be skeptical. Sulzer was a Tammany man through and through, but he was also ambitious. Was Sulzer a true reformer who desired the best for New York, or was he merely playing a political part for his own political gains? Most likely both answers were "yes"; the reality was complicated.

Sulzer's ambition, like most New York governors before and after him, was the presidency. There is no written record of these dreams but many contemporary chroniclers believed this motivated "Plain" Bill. It explains his later alliance with publishing magnate William Randolph Hearst and it sheds light on this newfound commitment to reform, an allegiance never before seen in Sulzer's work.

To see how a dedication to reform might further his ambition, Sulzer needed to look no farther than across the Hudson River. Woodrow Wilson had been elected governor of New Jersey in 1910. Just two years later, Wilson was elected president. The rapid rise from university president to U.S. president was due in great part to Wilson's status as a reformer, specifically

WILLIAM RANDOLPH HEARST

Hearst, owner and publisher of the nation's largest newspaper chain, was incredibly influential in shaping public opinion. Sulzer needed Hearst and his far reaching public relations machine to win that campaign. Furthermore, he was harboring dreams of running for president (has any New York Governor not had those dreams?) and Hearst's support could be just the vehicle to achieve that ambition. He was deeply bitter, having lost races for mayor and governor, he held Tammany Hall in general and Charles Murphy personally responsible for his defeats. Furthermore, Hearst remained ambitious and many suspected he had already cut a deal to run for United States Senate on a joint ticket with Sulzer in 1914. Together, they would run New York State and the state Democratic Party on their way to taking over the national party and the White House.

one who took on New Jersey's corrupt political machines. Wilson's most important reform was the introduction of primaries for statewide offices. Previously, statewide candidates—from governor on down—were chosen at state conventions that were controlled by and often dictated to by the party bosses. The ability to name the Democratic or Republican candidates (and, alternatively, to replace them) gave these machines much of their power because of the patronage in jobs and contracts that flowed from state government. Introducing a primary system—where voters could choose their preferred candidate—was a serious blow to the machine system. This made Wilson a big favorite among self-styled reformers. Significantly, the party machines retained this power in New York State.*

In 1913, politically speaking at least, being a reformer meant more than just passing progressive legislation. It required exerting power and showing independence of the dominant political machines... and the party bosses. Governor Sulzer wasted no time declaring his independent credentials. On the day after his inauguration, William Sulzer solemnly proclaimed to the press, "I am the Democratic leader of the State of New York."[1] Sulzer went even further to declare his political independence from Tammany Hall. He declared publicly that if Charlie Murphy wanted to see the governor, he would have to do it in the Executive Chamber and his advice would receive no greater consideration than that of any other New Yorker.[2]

Actually, the friction between the governor and Murphy started earlier, before Sulzer even took office. On December 21, 1912, a celebratory dinner

---

* Ironically, Wilson's own rise to power was helped in large part by Tammany Hall, albeit accidentally. At the 1912 Democratic National Convention, Tammany supported Champ Clark of Missouri for president. Clark, the Speaker of the House of Representatives, was seen as the front-runner at the time the convention opened in Baltimore. A Missourian, Clark had the support of a majority of the Democratic delegates during the early voting but could not reach the two-thirds vote necessary for nomination. When Tammany delegates declared for Clark, William Jennings Bryan turned to Wilson, who had been running second in the balloting. Bryan said he would support Wilson so long as Charlie Murphy and Tammany did not. On the forty-sixth ballot Indiana governor Thomas Marshall's delegates swung to Wilson, making him the Democratic nominee. Marshall was then nominated for vice president. Incidentally, Sulzer himself received 3 votes for vice president. Marshall received 389 (H. W. Brands, *Traitor to His Class* [New York: Random House, 2008], 66).

was held in honor of Governor-Elect Sulzer. It was planned to be a grand event attended by those who had taken part in the campaign and those who intended to play a role in government. Politicians from far and wide were there to fete Sulzer and his rising star... but Tammany Hall chieftain Charlie Murphy would not be there to celebrate the campaign in which he had played such an important role, beginning with selecting the candidate himself. According to contemporary observers, Murphy felt slighted because former congressman and three-time Democratic presidential nominee William Jennings Bryan was to be an honored guest at the dinner, personally invited by Sulzer. At the Democratic National Convention, Bryan had denounced New York City directly—and Tammany by implication (see footnote on page 87).[3] The *Times* described Bryan's conduct at the Baltimore convention as follows: "[He] laid his lash on Tammany."[4] In fact, Bryan "more than any one else was responsible for Murphy's failure to be a power of any sort in the great convention that nominated Woodrow Wilson."[5]

It may have been a good thing that Murphy stayed away. The hall was packed with an enthusiastic crowd, and the Great Commoner did not disappoint. The boss and Bryan would have been seated at the same table, and Bryan went out of his way to intensify his feud with Tammany. The three-time presidential candidate, nominated on the strength of his oratory, declared, "In New York, the People are at least learning that a boss is not essential to the prosperity of the State!"[6] Bryan brought the crowd to their feet when he pronounced the boss's control of national conventions over forever, replaced by direct primaries.

Former governor Dix was absent as well; Sulzer had recently been very critical of the Dix administration and what he called its "extravagance."[7] The whole affair amounted to a public slight of Charlie Murphy. Having helped Sulzer realize his ambition to be governor, the boss certainly expected more loyalty.

However, the trouble ran deeper than mere words. According to sources close to both Tammany Hall and the governor (many were a part of that axis), that same month Murphy had "rebuked [Sulzer] for 'butting in' with regard to some contracts to be let by a State department." To which Sulzer replied that he was going to be governor and Murphy retorted, "Like hell you are!"[8]

The situation escalated quite quickly as Sulzer railed in speeches against the "party lash" and began to cut off patronage appointments and freeze out Tammany contractors from lucrative projects.[9] With these speeches and actions, Sulzer was declaring his political independence from Tammany Hall and pursuing the Woodrow Wilson path that he believed would lead him to the White House.

Significantly, Sulzer began filling patronage positions across the state with men who would be loyal to him personally, not to Charlie Murphy or Tammany Hall. More than just trying to defang Tammany, the governor was building a Sulzer machine.[10] If his motivation for taming Tammany was altruistic, he would have hired the best and brightest—and simultaneously eliminated hundreds of patronage positions to protect the public treasury. Instead he was building his own power and burnishing his credentials with the public.

Murphy was equally petulant. According to the *Times*, "[Murphy] would not take the trouble to go to the capital for the inauguration of the new Democratic Governor-elect." It was quite a contrast from two years earlier when the boss was "conspicuously present at the Dix inauguration…and inconveniently domiciled at the capital for several weeks after, while State patronage was being parceled out."[11]

Sulzer faced one significant obstacle to his own political ambitions: Murphy still maintained his influence with the legislature. Assembly Speaker Al Smith and senate president pro tem Robert Wagner were "both faithful Tammany men."[12] Tammany also controlled the key committees in both houses, with one exception: the Judiciary Committee.* The

---

* The lieutenant governor, as head of the senate, had the power to make committee assignments in the senate. Glynn, an Independent Democrat, had refused Murphy's request to appoint Stephen Stilwell as chairman of the Senate Judiciary Committee. At the time, Senator Stilwell was facing bribery charges, and to Glynn, if not to Murphy, that disqualified him from running the committee tasked with enforcing

legislature—and Murphy—were therefore in a position to block, or at least seriously curtail, Sulzer's legislative plan.

Nonetheless, in one of the first major actions of 1913 the legislature passed Sulzer's Highway Department reorganization plan, placing the department under a single head. The significance was twofold. It presumably streamlined the department, promoting efficiency. An editorial in the *Times* called these changes "sound and wholesome."[13] Simultaneously it provided Governor Sulzer with much more direct control of the Highway Department. Giving away control of the department with the most patronage jobs was a significant concession from Murphy to Sulzer.[14] The legislature refrained from acting on Sulzer's request to rename the Department of Highways as the Department of Good Roads.

Still, Sulzer was facing the same trap that had ensnared Governor Dix before him: as much as Sulzer was defying and angering Tammany Hall, his reformer friends still expected more from him.

That was made clear on the night of March 18, 1913. It was the governor's fiftieth birthday, and his friends gave a celebratory dinner in his honor at the Café Boulevard, a popular restaurant located at Forty-First Street and Broadway in Manhattan.* A contemporary advertisement for the restaurant claimed it was "known to good livers for over 20 years." Attending to honor William Sulzer and likely also for the cuisine were representatives of the Wilson administration, the U.S. Congress, every branch of the state government, and many from the New York City administration.

---

state law. The senate examined the charges and voted not to expel Stilwell, but he was later convicted of criminal charges and imprisoned and, therefore, unable to attend the session (Brown, 297).

* Located in the Hotel Continental, the menu from a similar dinner held two months earlier at the Café Boulevard featured Appetizer Norwegian, Cream of Celery, celery, olives, salted almonds, paprika karpfen, new potatoes, Porkolt chicken, tarhonya, sorbet, roast young duck, compot, Salad Fantasie, apple strudel, and liptauer cheese and demitasse—along with clysmic, carmel wine misca, G. H. Mumms & Co. extra dry, milo cigarettes, and cigars.

"Representatives of Tammany, except Leader Charles F. Murphy, were conspicuous everywhere."[15]

The popular Sulzer drew a large crowd, even before the dinner was scheduled to begin. The governor was seated at a table of twenty-four, and the crowded restaurant erupted in cheers when he took his seat.

The financier Henry Morgenthau—chairman of the Finance Committee of the Democratic National Committee in 1912—was one of many speakers to challenge Sulzer, imploring him to stand up to Tammany Hall. Morgenthau gave an impassioned speech, imploring the governor to have his "wishbone converted into a backbone." He also laid down the gauntlet, telling Sulzer, "We look to you to be Governor of the Empire State and not to be the agent of undisclosed principals who hide themselves from public view."[16] These sentiments were echoed by others, including Manhattan district attorney (and future governor) Charles Seymour Whitman.

11

THE COMMISSION ON INQUIRY

In an era before the internet, before television—even before radio—newspapers were the most vital source of information. Indeed, everything the average citizen needed to know about the world could be found within the countless newspapers printed in a startling number of languages, catering to the ever growing New York population. The most compelling and essential news was printed on the front page, above the fold. It was here, in the January 28, 1913, issue of the *New York Times*, that Sulzer's intention to be the definitive reformer was categorically declared: "'If There is Anything Wrong I Want to Get at It,' says Governor."[1]

It had become the mantra of his administration. Only weeks before, in his January 1 annual message, Sulzer had announced he would create a Commission on Inquiry, whose goal was to "sift all the State departments with a view to checking useless expenditures, abolishing sinecures and promoting honesty and efficiency generally in the interests of the taxpayers."[2] The public was skeptical. Reformers wanted a serious investigation but did not expect one.[3] Tammany stalwarts wanted nothing more than a show but were worried by Sulzer's increasingly vehement rhetoric.[4]

The committee was intended to be a signature issue of the new administration. Aside from the obvious—saving money and improving efficiency—it was a textbook attempt at rewriting his public narrative—turning Sulzer from Tammany stalwart into a crusading reformer in the model of President Wilson. It foreshadowed the drama to come, and in another way, Sulzer's description of the elusiveness and confusing nature of government corruption also provided a glimpse of what was ahead. "As must be understood by every reasonable citizen," Sulzer told the *Times* in the January 28 article, "the Commission's task in this respect is most difficult, for corruption, graft, and dishonesty are cunningly contrived and skillfully concealed, and suggested avenues of investigation often lead into blind alleys without result, either because of the design of the corrupt or because of the indefiniteness, incompleteness, immaturity or rashness of the information offered for the commission's aid."[5]

In spite of his strongly worded attacks and pledge to reform the state, Sulzer's choices to serve as members of the Committee on Inquiry showed him to be taking the same middle ground already trod by Governor Dix—trying to please the reformers while also appeasing Tammany Hall.

John N. Carlisle, an independent and anti-Tammany Democrat from Watertown, was appointed as head of the committee. This pleased the reformers; the *Times* said Carlisle had been "active in almost all the movements ... to shake off the shackles of Tammany Hall."[6] Making up the rest of the committee was John H. Delaney of Brooklyn, the business manager of the *Morning Telegraph* newspaper, and H. Gordon Lynn of the Department of Commissioners of Accounts of New York City. Both were solid Tammany men.[7] Delaney had been an active participant in the reform fight against Kings County boss Patrick H. McCarren but had made peace with John H. McCooley, McCarren's successor.[8] The appointments aroused doubts in the minds of reformers as to whether the committee's work would be "on the level."[9] Legislation to pay for the committee's work passed the assembly unanimously, an indication that Tammany was pleased.[10]

Around this time, Murphy traveled to Albany for a few days. When asked about Sulzer, the Tammany boss replied, "I'm with Governor Sulzer to do anything to make his administration a success."[11] Was Sulzer back in the Tammany fold?

Some observers believed that Sulzer and Murphy had been in cahoots all along and that "the benevolent purpose of the Tammany chieftain in thus effacing himself... [was] for the good of the Sulzer administration."[12] Certainly, New York's top two Democrats went to lengths to put on a positive—or at least not a negative—face. The *New York Times* reported their exchange in the Executive Chamber as follows:

> Mr. Murphy—I wish you a happy New Year, Governor.
> Gov. Sulzer—I thank you, Mr. Murphy.

That ended the conversation between the two in the Executive Chamber. Nonetheless, "the visit of Mr. Murphy to Albany, following the installation of a new Democratic Governor," the *Times* noted, "was not so ceremonious as was his visit two years ago just after Gov. Dix had assumed office. At that time Mr. Murphy's suite at the Hotel Teneyck was the Mecca of all office seekers, as well as of those who were in quest of information as to what would happen next. Then Mr. Murphy was the center of things. His presence in the Capitol to-day was treated merely as an incident."[13] Further distinguishing this visit was the presence of Mrs. Murphy with her husband in Albany.

Whatever their motives, there were cloudy skies ahead for the relationship between the boss and the governor, and a new test would soon present itself. The term of William R. Wilcox (sometimes spelled Willcox), chair of the Public Service Commission for the First District, was expiring. The First District encompassed all of New York City. The Public Service Commission had broad powers, especially with regard to the New York City transit system. The failure of the transit system to keep pace with the rapid growth in both industry and population had become an increasingly important political issue. Now, after years of delay and studies and commissions, there was an agreement at hand for a "dual system" with both the Interborough and Brooklyn Rapid Transit Companies sharing control and responsibilities. The availability of cheap, reliable transportation across the booming metropolis was a top priority of the electorate.

Many in New York City supported Wilcox's reappointment, including Mayor William Gaynor and the majority of the Boards of Estimate and Apportionment. Concern for his reappointment was so widespread that a delegation of civic groups traveled to Albany to lobby for Wilcox's reappointment. The delegation was headed by former New York City mayor Seth Low.

Lined up against Wilcox was William Randolph Hearst and the Hearst media empire. The issue was very important to the publisher personally, and Hearst's papers had led a campaign for municipal ownership of rapid transit and against the Interborough and Brooklyn Rapid Transit deal. The governor had his own plan, wanting to appoint Henry Morgenthau. Morgenthau's extensive national fundraising network could be very helpful to Sulzer if—or when—the time came to finance a national campaign.[14]

Sulzer was in a bind. He needed Tammany and the New York City elected officials in order to be renominated for governor at the Democratic convention, but he needed Hearst and his far-reaching public relations machine to win that campaign. Furthermore, he was harboring dreams of running for president, and Hearst's support could be just the vehicle to achieve that ambition.

After a secret visit to New York City, Sulzer cut the baby in half. He nominated Edward E. McCall, a justice of the Supreme Court (he also nominated Devoe P. Hodson, a city court judge in Buffalo to fill a PSC seat in the Second District, a close confidant of William H. Fitzpatrick, Murphy's Western New York ally).[15] The confirmation was by a party vote in the state senate of 25-10.

Sulzer denied Tammany's will by not reappointing Wilcox but "the promptness with which the nomination was approved and the exceptionally laudatory comments about McCall made by the organization's spokesmen in the Senate ... strengthened the suspicion of Tammany influence."[16]

The independents and reformers were not pleased. Hearst's *New York World*, heretofore a strong supporter of Sulzer, editorialized, "At a time when he should have shown his strength and his leadership he has surrendered to Fourteenth Street [the headquarters of Tammany Hall] ... and shaken the fine promise of independence that he built up after his inauguration."[17] The *Times* was equally critical, saying the whole episode was "a spectacular, cynical, impudent display of Mr. Murphy's arbitrary power" and that Governor Sulzer's leadership had "vanished."[18]

Meanwhile, the Committee on Inquiry presented its report. It was damning and yet also quite limited in scope. The committee found problems throughout the state, the most serious being blatant abuses in the adjunct general's office, rampant graft and inefficiencies in the capitol restoration (following the fire of 1912), and questionable land purchases.*

In addition to exposing deficiencies, the report proposed changes in state operations. The boldest proposal provided for competitive bidding on future capitol repairs, long a demand of reformers.[19] Concurrently, Sulzer created the position of executive auditor, an effort to continue the work of the committee. For auditor, Sulzer choose John A. Hennessy, a New York newspaperman. Hennessy was given a broad profile, including the right of entry and examination into every department of the State government.[20] The executive auditor was also charged with stopping unwarranted expenditures.[21] This was a strong move by the governor as it gave him, through the executive auditor, the instrument to expose unsavory or villainous conduct, keeping those engaged in graft, including many from Tammany Hall, afraid of him.

However, as usual with Sulzer, nothing was cut-and-dried. Reformers were less pleased by Sulzer's handling of the State Architect's Office.

---

* One of the deals was land purchased by the state for an arsenal. Both the attorney general and the State Armory Commission had recommended against the purchase from First National Bank. Former governor Dix was a vice president of First National.

The state architect was responsible for overseeing the capitol restoration — and the project was coming in at twice the original estimated cost. The architect himself, Herman W. Hoefer, had been reappointed by Sulzer despite widespread accusations of incompetence, including a report by the American Institute of Architects detailing Hoefer's lack of skill and ability. The cost overruns detailed in the Committee on Inquiry report led to Hoefer's resignation, but by not bringing criminal charges or taking the inquiry to the next level to explain why the costs had doubled or who had profited, Sulzer and his committee had failed to meet the expectations of his reform-minded friends.[22] Sulzer would later argue that forcing Hoefer to resign caused "bitter hostility" from Tammany for Sulzer's "treason."[23]

This same month there was a more serious incident that deepened the divide between Tammany and the governor. The State Prison Department was headed by Colonel Joseph F. Scott, a well-regarded penologist during an age when prison experts were rare. Prisons employed large numbers of unskilled men for indeterminate periods of time, a godsend to any political boss who could provide paychecks for his troops, rewarding favored lieutenants with more pay and fewer hours. The best part? The monies were all provided by the state of New York. As such, Sulzer wanted to name a new warden at the Auburn Prison. His choice was Charles F. Rattigan, a Democratic state committeeman and lieutenant of Thomas Mott Osborne.* Osborne led a large Democratic faction in central New York and was a chief opponent and rival of Charlie Murphy and Tammany Hall. Along with State Senator Franklin Roosevelt, he had been behind the reform faction that blocked Governor Dix from appointing William Osborne, supporting Sulzer and Sulzer wanted to reward his organization.

---

* Osborne himself would go on to become warden of Sing Sing prison. He spent a week in Auburn and Sing Sing where he was treated like an inmate. His experiences led him to enact radical changes such as self-help programs for prisoners. He is regarded as a national leader in prison reform for his creation of Mutual Welfare Leagues. His *New York Times* obituary said, "Perhaps more than any other man, [he] has been credited with changing the viewpoint of modern society in the treatment of criminals in penal institutions."

Auburn Prison was the perfect plum since not only would Rattigan get a job with a good salary but Osborne's foot soldiers would, presumably, find work at the prison.[24] However, being a prison superintendent required senate confirmation and the majority of the senate, loyal to Tammany and Murphy, were not inclined to confirm Rattigan.[25]

Maybe the governor wanted to continue building his own organization outside of Murphy's reach (and adding Osborne's organization to his would help significantly) or maybe Sulzer had made a commitment to Osborne (or Rattigan) during the campaign, but nonetheless Sulzer was dead set on appointing Rattigan. To further this goal, Sulzer ordered an investigation into the Prison Department. The investigation reported ten charges of neglect in Auburn Prison alone, and the warden there was removed.

The prison superintendent, Colonel Scott, presumably responsible, insisted he would not resign; in fact he would fight the charges, but fearing a frame-up, he refused to appear for a hearing called by Sulzer's administration. On March 13 Sulzer removed Scott from office, calling him "inefficient, incompetent, derelict and neglectful of duty."[26] A number of senators objected, taking Colonel Scott's side. Senator John F. Murtaugh, an upstate Democrat not allied with Tammany, accused Sulzer of making the prisons "a football of politics."[27] Even the *Times* seemed disappointed when they wrote, "Col. Scott has not the slightest intention of appointing Mr. Rattigan to this post because he believes that it would be used by the latter in a local political fight. It was the refusal of Col. Scott to appoint Mr. Rattigan which first prompted Gov. Sulzer in his demand on the graft hunters that they get the Colonel's political scalp."[28] "Col. Scott's refusal to appoint Mr. Rattigan was a factor in bringing about the Superintendent's removal from office."[29]

Continuing his efforts to expand his own political machine, Sulzer appointed Judge John B. Riley to replace Scott as state prison superintendent. Riley was a lieutenant in Smith W. Weed's political machine, based in Clinton County, but also held sway in several of the northern counties of the state.

Allegations of fiscal irregularities, political misconduct, and other bad behavior soon surfaced about both nominees, and they were rejected by the senate with its majority of Tammany senators. In the sort of bizarre twist we expect as part of this story, Sulzer nominated George Weed as a replacement for Judge Riley. George Reed was Boss Smith Weed's son and Riley's law partner. He was also rejected. It would take some time to resolve these issues and fill these positions.[30]

In the meantime, a much larger fight was about to begin.

12

"GAFFNEY OR WAR!"

New York State has one of the oldest transportation networks in North America. The Boston Post Road, connecting Boston and the then small city of New York, was started in 1673. The road has expanded with the times and is now U.S. Route 1.

The growth of New York accelerated rapidly once the Erie Canal opened in 1825 and transportation followed that of technology. The canal gave way to the railroads and both would later be outpaced by the development of roads and highways, run in 1913 by the State Highway Department, a direct descendant of the Office of Surveyor General, created by the Colonial Dutch and reorganized in 1777 following New York State's first state constitution. Having undergone several name changes, the Highway Act of 1909 created the New York State Highway Department. Today, it is part of the New York State Department of Transportation.

The State Highway Department was also a major focus of the governor's Committee of Inquiry, which found a large number of irregularities there. The report charged corruption throughout, specifically implicating state superintendent of highways C. Gordon Reel and a number of Tammany-allied contractors. The governor put a stop to all construction until the inquiry was completed and then removed Reel from the Highway Department.[1] Tammany's friends claimed that the charges and Reel's removal were much ado about nothing, simply a "stage play" for the newspapers, but reports emerged that a number of threats were leveled at the governor.[2]

One threat, although repeatedly denied, was that Murphy wanted Sulzer to appoint his associate James Gaffney as the new head of the highway department. Gaffney was connected with New York Contracting and Trucking, owning five shares in the company. Eighty-five of the remaining ninety-five shares were owned by "an unnamed person who was never identified." Murphy himself was that silent partner in New York Contracting and Trucking.[3]

Allegedly, Murphy first asked Sulzer nicely to do his bidding, saying, "I want you to appoint Gaffney. It is an organization matter and I will appreciate it."[4] After no response from Sulzer, Murphy, who was not accustomed to asking twice, then sent the governor a message that said, "Gaffney or war!"[5]

Murphy denied the charge. "If I knew that Governor Sulzer had offered a place to Mr. Gaffney I would advise Mr. Gaffney to decline it." Murphy continued, "I am certain that if Governor Sulzer is questioned about this he will answer as I have answered."[6]

At stake was a sum of over $50 million, which had been approved as a bond issue by the voters for "good roads construction" by a vote of 657,548 for the measure and 281,265 against. That amount was a staggering sum in 1913 and enough to make the people who allocated those monies very rich, especially if such a person owned the controlling stake in a construction company.

Sulzer and Murphy's relationship continued to decline, deteriorating more rapidly from one day to the next.[7] Murphy believed Sulzer had leaked the whole Gaffney story to the press, and Murphy retaliated, reminding the public that Sulzer had his own relationship with Gaffney and had previously appointed Gaffney as the chairman of a group of nonpartisan experts to investigate road construction issues across the state.[8] Even more interesting, the day before the brouhaha, Sulzer had told the press that Gaffney would be a good man to head the Highway Department but was not a candidate.[9]

Refusing to allow Murphy the last word, the governor's team clandestinely released a story to the press asserting that Murphy *must* have known that other people were using Murphy's name to push Gaffney and to threaten the governor's legislative program if Gaffney was not appointed.[10]

Lieutenant Governor Martin Glynn, widely seen as an independent Democrat not beholden to Tammany, tried to defuse the situation. He told the press, "If the Governor is looking for a fight I am afraid he will have to manufacture it himself. I am going to tell the Governor that his constructive legislation is in no danger and this sort of talk will do neither him nor the party any good."[11]

It seemed like the conflict would be resolved when Gaffney himself went to see Sulzer in New York City, but the visit's only result was further division. To the newspapers, Gaffney claimed he told Governor Sulzer definitively and unequivocally that he was not interested in the highway position. Sulzer's people told the same reporters that Sulzer informed Gaffney, equally definitively and just as unequivocally, that he could not have the position, would not have the position, and that Sulzer would never support a person close to Murphy under any circumstances.[12] The same night, both Sulzer and Murphy appeared at the annual Friendly Sons of St. Patrick dinner in the Hotel Astor, and although they were seated near each other, the press was quick to note, they exchanged no greeting.[13]

The next day was Sulzer's birthday dinner at the Café Boulevard, and many politicos took note of the Tammany chief's absence.[14] In fact, the atmosphere was decidedly anti-Tammany, with Henry Morgenthau telling the governor that his only master should be "enlightened public opinion."[15] The result was that public opinion accepted Sulzer's position as being perfectly clear: He was aligned with the reformers.

Did Sulzer fear the power of Tammany Hall? Was the governor playing a dual role as a reformer in public and a loyal soldier in private? No matter his motivation, he was not ready to break with Boss Murphy.

The next day, Sulzer went to Murphy's rooms at Delmonico's Restaurant for a secret meeting with the Tammany chief. The two had a long talk, coming to an arrangement about distributing patronage.[16] The deal was simple: Tammany Hall would control patronage in New York County but have no say throughout the rest of the state, and Sulzer would have absolute independence to choose the more important state offices. It was an extension of Sulzer's belief, he said, in home rule, and they departed "the best of friends."[17]

In reality, nothing was clear. Both Murphy and Sulzer denied meeting or coming to any understanding, but they made conciliatory statements nonetheless. Sulzer said, "I'm at war with no man" when asked about Murphy and acknowledged that Tammany had a stake in patronage in New York City but that he would decide on patronage in other parts of the state.[18] Sulzer planned to work directly with the upstate Democratic leaders, creating his own followers and political operation.

The reformers continued to have doubts about Sulzer. The "hesitation of the reform element in rallying behind Sulzer arose not only on account of his long record of obedience to Tammany and his concealed vanity and ambition, but also on account of the distrust of his fundamental honesty, and uncertainty as to whether he possessed the mental grasp and moral equipment to take up the challenge."[19] An editorial in the *Nation* asked, "Is the Governor altogether sincere? Will he, when the time comes, back up his theatrical words by matter-of-fact deeds?"[20] To give the reformers more reason to question his motives, Sulzer continued to appoint Murphy loyalists to key positions, including to the important Public Service Commission.[21] The reformers also challenged Sulzer's tactic of fighting politics with more politics. Reformers felt that giving jobs to people recommended by the county chairmen was disingenuous since the county chairs would only offer people who were either acceptable to Murphy or people beholden to any number of smaller chieftains leading the smaller political machines throughout the state.[22]

The whole situation escalated with a visit from a contingent of Independent Democrats to the People's House (the Governor's Mansion). They forcefully urged Sulzer to make a full break with Murphy and his machine.[23]

Sulzer took it to heart and at the annual dinner of the Democratic Editorial Association of New York made a public proclamation of political emancipation. In his speech, Sulzer attacked the "invisible government" of the bosses and declared himself the leader of the Democratic Party. Reminding people (disingenuously) that he was chosen by a free and open convention, Sulzer said he had been elected without making any promises. The governor complained that once he took office, he found the whole government in shambles and rife with corruption, asserting, "I have never been an agent, and I never will be. No man, no party and no organization can make me a rubber stamp. I am the Governor. Let no man doubt that."[24]

Governor Sulzer wanted to get the people behind him, but he really had no issue on which to campaign since almost all of his bills had been passed by the legislature. As the governor's Committee of Inquiry finished its investigation, it made several recommendations: a State Board of Efficiency and Economy headed by a commissioner with powers to investigate; a State Board of Estimate with nine members, including independently elected officials and representatives from the legislature to improve budgeting; a State Board of Contract and Supply as a central purchasing agency; and legislation giving the state comptroller the power to audit state expenditures. These measures all passed the legislature without any real opposition.

The legislature also acted on the rest of Sulzer's program, including establishing a streamlined State Highway Department with one head, a reorganized State Health Department with real powers to regulate sanitation, and laws to improve factory conditions. The most significant legislation, owing much to the Triangle Committee's report, reorganized the State Labor Department, creating an industrial board with powers to investigate and regulate tenement labor, safeguard the employment of women and children, and protect workers from fire and industrial accidents all while creating new regulations and enforcement mechanisms to improve working conditions.

On January 27, Sulzer sent a special message to the legislature urging legislation to prohibit a series of alleged abuses on the stock exchange.

Stephen J. Stilwell, chairman of the Senate Codes Committee, and Aaron J. Levy, majority leader of the assembly, introduced the bills. The board of the stock exchange agreed on the need for protections but rejected any radical change. Nonetheless, six of the nine bills recommended by Sulzer were passed into law.

The Full Crew measure, an important railroad bill setting the minimum number of people required to work on certain trains, illustrates how Sulzer operated. The railroads were among the largest employers in the state, and as the richest businesses, they were significant political donors, usually to Republican or pro-business interests. These same railroad companies were quite strongly opposed to the bill, preferring that crew sizes continued to be set by the Public Service Commission.[25] The railroad bosses made a personal appeal to the governor, insisting that the Full Crew measure would cost them over $2 million per year, costs that would be passed on to the travelers themselves. Sulzer rejected their entreaties. Putting "man above the dollar," he set himself, as his office said, on the side of life rather than railroad dividends.[26] On the eve of signing the legislation into law, a "confidential letter" sent from John V. Fitzgerald, the legislative representative of the Brotherhood of Railroad Trainmen, was released. The letter, dated just before the 1912 election, was reprinted in the *New York Times* on April 5. In the letter, Sulzer promised to sign the Full Crew bill and said, "I would come out openly for the bill but if I did, the railroads would spend a barrel of money to defeat me." The letter showed Sulzer at his most duplicitous, playing both sides of the same issue and relying on subterfuge and mistruths to succeed. Nevertheless, Sulzer signed the bill into law.

Senator Elon R. Brown, the Republican leader in the senate, asked the Senate Judiciary Committee to investigate the letter. Such conduct, Brown said, rendered Sulzer ineligible for office.[27] At this time the state constitution required state elected officials to swear an oath before entering office declaring that they had not made any promises or offered any valuable consideration to influence voters. Sulzer's letter to Fitzgerald was sent *before* he was elected governor, promising to take a specific action *after* he was elected—seemingly a clear violation of Sulzer's constitutional pledge.

Calling him a "political fossil of the Paleozoic age," Sulzer accused William Barnes, New York State Republican chairman, of instigating the whole affair and tied Barnes to the "invisible government" that tries to run the state without any accountability to the people.[28] Beyond his usual attacks, Sulzer said that even if he had made such a commitment it would have been "all right." Senator Brown asked, rhetorically, if Sulzer's conduct was "treating public office as a public trust?"[29]

Sulzer would later cite this incident as one of the three factors leading to his impeachment.[30] Sulzer claimed that in retaliation for signing the bill, New York Central sent $300,000 to Albany booked as construction funds but really used to bribe legislators to impeach him. There is no independent corroboration of this, but it shows both Sulzer's mind-set and the importance of this legislation in 1913.

The attacks on Sulzer were also significant, in part, because of the attackers. State Republican chairman William Barnes and his lieutenant in the legislature, Senator Elon Brown, may not have been allied with Tammany Hall and Boss Charles Murphy, but they were defenders of the same political machine system. The Republican boss and the Democratic boss competed regularly for patronage plums from the Governor's Mansion on down to the various city halls throughout New York State. As beneficiaries of the same spoils system, they had an interest in perpetuating that system. Sulzer's challenge to that system—his disregard for the dictates of Boss Murphy—would be a precedent for future Republican governors to follow, and the attacks of Barnes and Brown show that the bosses would work together to protect the system that made them rich and promulgated their power.

Facing off against the bosses and without the strong support of the reformers and independent Democrats who doubted him, Sulzer was losing his grip on government. The consequences would be extraordinary.

13

JOBS, JOBS, AND MORE JOBS

SULZER ALSO FOUND HIMSELF with what could only be called a patronage problem. The governor had people he wanted to appoint to office but he needed the senate—controlled by Murphy loyalists—to confirm them. His reformer friends urged Sulzer to appoint great men with extraordinary qualifications, challenging the senate to confirm them (or daring them not to). Instead Sulzer chose another path, deciding to bargain and trade, appointing Tammany candidates to Supreme Court vacancies in New York City in exchange for confirmation of his candidates for other offices. The level of suspicion and distrust was so high that Sulzer had to send names to the senate one at a time, waiting for a confirmation to send the next one, saving the judges for last.[1] The senators soon decided enough was enough and refused to participate in this process. The result was vacancies in a number of key positions, including the commissioners of the newly empowered Labor and Health Departments, the new Commission of Efficiency, the Office of the State Architect, and several upstate Public Service Commission seats.

It was too much for Sulzer. He began to play down his feud with Murphy.

A source in the governor's office told the press, "If [Murphy] is willing to do the right thing by the Governor, the Governor is willing to do the right thing by him."[2] To facilitate this détente, Sulzer submitted a list of candidates on April 21 for public appointments. The list was a mix of Sulzer's own people, some Independent Democrats, and plenty of Murphy and Tammany people. All but two from the list were confirmed.

John Mitchell and John B. Riley were the only two who were rejected. Sulzer appointed Mitchell, the former head of the United Mine Workers and a national leader in the American labor community, as labor commissioner. The senate rejected Mitchell on the grounds that he had not lived in the state of New York for long enough (although the real problem seemed to be that he had not supported the Democratic ticket strongly enough to earn Tammany's support). Sulzer appointed John B. Riley, again, as state superintendent of prisons. As before, Riley was rejected by the senate as "unfit," although his alliance with Murphy's longtime foe Thomas Mott Osborne may have been part of the problem.[3] Finally, Sulzer settled on a compromise candidate, Herman Ridder, a German newspaper publisher, whom the senate confirmed easily. Whether by design or by coincidence, Ridder declined for "business reasons" after the legislature had recessed. This vacancy allowed the governor to make a recess appointment—an appointment that would not require senate confirmation—and Riley was appointed May 26. Riley immediately appointed Charles F. Rattigan as warden of Auburn Prison. Sulzer had gotten what he wanted; the appointment of Riley strengthened Sulzer's connection to the Weed political machine in the north country, and the appointment of Rattigan strengthened Sulzer's ties with Osborne's reform group and the central New York political machine based in Cayuga County.

Sulzer also tried to use his recess appointment power to appoint Mitchell, although the attorney general rejected the appointment since the vacancy in that office had occurred while the legislature was in session. Still, these actions further served to alienate legislators—Tammany and non-Tammany alike—who believed Sulzer had negotiated in bad faith and tried to hoodwink them.*

Regardless of the controversy, Sulzer continued his push to associate himself with good government, authorizing an investigation into the State Highway Construction Fund,[4] while a series of reports by George W. Blakey, a special commissioner of investigation in the prisons, revealed enormous amounts of "carelessness or graft" at Great Meadow, Sing Sing, Auburn, and others. At one prison, Blakey discovered misappropriation of $500,000 out of a budget of $1.1 million.[5] Overall, the report concluded that a "lack of system and waste of public money in experiments are the most conspicuous feature of the prison management."[6] As a result, the special commissioner of investigation recommended criminal charges against the superintendent of prisons.[7]

Sulzer's support of reform measures might earn him votes when running for reelection in 1914 or for higher office in the future. However, while garnering reform votes, Sulzer would be alienating Tammany Hall. And the 1913 Democratic State Convention—which would determine the Democratic gubernatorial nominee in 1914—would be dominated by Tammany Hall, just as in Rochester in 1912 and in so many conventions before.

That is, unless Sulzer could change the rules of the game.

---

* The Court of Appeals, in denying Sulzer's ability to appoint Mitchell, wrote that there is "no inherent power in the Governor that is superior to law," a stinging rebuke to Sulzer (*New York Times*, June 20, 1913).

14

DIRECT PRIMARIES

To many progressives, voter participation was the answer to all evils—the voice of the people, the *will* of the people, is what ultimately defined government. For that reason, direct primaries and direct election of senators had been a part of the Democratic Party platform for a number of years.

Still, the direct primary had been a problem for Governor Dix and a source of friction with Tammany Hall. Remember, under Dix, the legislative session had been held up by a fire and wrangling over a U.S. Senate appointment. When Dix finally sent a special message urging the passage of the Tammany-approved direct primary bill (called the Blauvelt Ferris bill) it was met with derision by reformers. Franklin D. Roosevelt and other insurgents called it "a fraud on the people" because it "intended to fasten the control of the bosses on the parties." The reformers also reminded Dix that he had formerly denounced the same legislation.

This bill provided for the direct nomination of congressmen, members of the legislature, and local officers, but the state convention would continue to nominate governors and other state officers. Just as important, the bill gave candidates designated by the party committees a preferential place on the primary ballot and the use of the party emblem (a significant help to gaining the votes of many illiterate immigrants who could recognize the symbol if not read the names), leaving candidates who were designated by petition at a disadvantage.¹ The legislation also allowed party committees to use party funds to support candidates in primaries.²

So far, the fights between Murphy and Sulzer had been behind the scenes; there had been no open break between the governor and Tammany Hall.³ The debate over direct primaries was about to change that. At issue were not actually direct primaries themselves but Sulzer's version of them and his tactics. From the beginning—his first message to the legislature—Sulzer called for the adoption of a direct primary bill.⁴ He urged this without asking for any specific provisions; instead, in classic Sulzer fashion the governor "favored the best that could be written."⁵

In 1913 the New York State Legislature was in session for approximately three months every year—January to March—making it one of the longest in the country at that point: government was—and is—serious business in New York. The statehouse, that towering mishmash of architectural styles ranging from Romanesque to Victorian, was at the time home to 150 assemblymen and 51 senators.

Although smack in the middle of the latest legislative session, to normal folks the evening of February 17, 1912, in Albany, New York, was an evening much like any other. Families gathered around the dinner table, shared stories of their day, washed up, and then retired to read the evening paper, whose headlines told the stories of the world beyond their front doorsteps, everything from the usual local mishaps to international politics.

Many of these readers would also learn that on this day their legislative leaders offered a bill that would become one of the most contentious of the session: a direct primary bill sponsored by Senator George A. Blauvelt. The bill attempted to reduce the expense of primary and general election campaigns, reduce signature requirements for independent nominations, and increase the number of offices to be voted on, but the legislation did not extend direct primaries to statewide officials.

The Blauvelt bill was debated in the legislature for almost two months without a word in favor or against it from Governor Sulzer. Then, toward the end of the regular session the governor sent a special message to the legislature outlining his plan for direct primaries and election reform. Quoting from the Democratic, Republican, and Progressive Party platforms of 1912, Sulzer declared that they were "irrevocably" bound to enact reform.[6] Sulzer emphasized that if the people were qualified to elect candidates, then the people were qualified to nominate their candidates—and if they were qualified to nominate some of the candidates, then the people were qualified to nominate *all* of their candidates.

Sulzer's plan eliminated the party emblem on the ballot, prohibited party funds from being used in primaries, created a process for candidates to develop party platforms, decreased the number of names required for nominating petitions, and required public disclosure of all expenses incurred in connection with campaigns.

Sulzer said, "The changes which I advocate in our primary laws are in harmony with the spirit of the times and of democratic institutions. They aim to restore to the people rights and privileges which have been usurped by the few, for the benefit of invisible interests which aim to control governmental officials, to pass laws, and to violate laws with impunity. To these invisible powers I am now, always have been, and always will be opposed."[7] The Progressives in the legislature immediately embraced the Sulzer plan. The Republicans in the legislature pointed out that they had introduced a very similar plan. The Democrats immediately expressed reservations.

Sulzer remained tenacious, insisting, "That message is my platform on this legislation." He demanded it be passed into law before the end of the year or he would "know the reason why." Sulzer also threatened to bring the legislature back with a special session until they got it done.[8] Sulzer called a conference in his office to rally support for the measure. Independent Democrats, independent Republicans, and some Progressives attended the conference. Sulzer told the group that he would fight Murphy to the finish on this issue and appointed a "war board" to lead the assault.[9]

For all his talk about restoring political rights to the people, there is no denying that the bill was advantageous to Sulzer's political aspirations. A direct primary would give him the opportunity to be renominated for governor in 1914, a privilege Tammany would certainly not extend at a state convention.[10] He had also watched Governor Woodrow Wilson, who had taken on the political bosses in New Jersey, advance from president of Princeton University to be the president of the United States in two short years.[11] One of Wilson's biggest successes in New Jersey was creating direct primary elections. Obviously, Sulzer was "aggrandizing himself at the risk of disrupting the party to which he owed every political preferment that had ever come to him."[12]

Although outside the statehouse, Albany was enjoying a mild late-winter day, with full sun and temperatures in the high forties, inside the chamber the atmosphere was charged with the smell of tobacco smoke, sweat, and more than a whiff of defiance. Clearly, Blauvelt's supporters were in the majority, including thirty-six-year-old rookie senator John Smith. Hailing from New York City's Third District, Smith was thin as a whippet and so fastidious in his dress that he was known to have two changes of clothing secreted away in his office in the statehouse. He ignored the darted looks shot his way by one of Sulzer's few supporters, longtime senator Harry Winston of Buffalo, whose face remained so red throughout the debate proceedings that even his opponents remained at the ready to administer smelling salts should he pass out from the stress.

Sure enough, the governor's wishes notwithstanding, the legislature passed the Blauvelt bill by overwhelming margins; 31-15 in the senate[13] and 104-21 in the assembly.[14] Livid, Sulzer vetoed the legislation, calling it "a fraud," "a miserable makeshift" effort, "a mere patchwork," "wholly fraudulent," and "a glaring breach of the pledged faith of every member of the Legislature."[15] Sulzer made clear he preferred his own version, which was, in the governor's analysis, "an honest, a sincere, a comprehensive, and a practical plan" for reform that empowered the people to destroy "the disgraceful secret alliances between the big business interests and crooked and corrupt politics."[16] He did not care much for the Democrats' objections to his bill, explaining, "No political party can make me a political hypocrite."[17]

Senator Robert Wagner, the Democratic majority leader in the senate, took great offense to the governor's rhetoric, noting that almost all of the governor's legislative priorities had passed both houses expeditiously. Now, because of minor differences between their election reform measures, the governor saw fit to accuse the legislature of dishonor? It caused, Wagner said, "pain and disappointment to us all."[18]

Republicans offered to support Sulzer's legislation, providing it was amended to continue the state conventions. Sulzer issued a formal statement, saying, "Neither the crossing of a 'T' or the dotting of an 'I' nor the changing of the simplest language in the bill will be tolerated." As if that was not clear enough, the governor reiterated, "My bill or nothing. That is the slogan."[19] The result was that organization Republicans in the legislature were in league with Tammany and the Organization Democrats. The end of party conventions would diminish Republican chairman Barnes's power just as much as it would to Democrats like Charles Murphy.

Sulzer was determined to win this battle. He solicited prominent Progressives and independent Republicans (or at least Republicans who wanted to depose William Barnes as state chairman) to write letters and send telegrams through the state supporting Sulzer's bill as the true path of reform.[20]

As for his own party, the governor summoned Democratic county chairmen from across the state to meet in his office.[21] On April 26, fifty-one out of the sixty-two chairmen came to Albany. Sulzer told them it was time to either be for the governor or they were most certainly against him. Sulzer threatened to expel anyone from the party who was opposed to him. "If any Democrat in this State is against the Democratic State platform," Sulzer declared, "that man is no true Democrat, and as the Democratic Governor of the State I shall do everything in my power to drive that recreant Democrat out of the Democratic party."

The governor continued, "If he is with me, I will be with him. If he is against me, mark well what I say, I shall be against him. He must either be a party to driving me out of public life, or I must be a party to driving him out of the Democratic party."[22] Sulzer ordered the Democratic chairmen to get the legislators from their counties to support him and to vote for the direct primary bill. Many of the leaders signed on to the Sulzer program, and several county committees even adopted resolutions endorsing the governor's bill. Only two said no outright, citing the impropriety of interfering with the legislative process.[23]

Of course, the legislators themselves were outraged. Assembly Speaker Al Smith said he depended on what his constituents wanted to make up his mind and that no one in his district was for the governor's legislation. Smith said that the existing primary law had not yet been given a "fair trial." Smith also took issue with Sulzer's reading of the state platform. Smith insisted that the statewide primary promise meant that there should be direct primaries in all parts of the state, not for statewide offices.[24]

John H. McCooley, the Democratic chairman in Kings County, maintained that upstate Democrats favored a convention because in a direct primary system New York City was too dominant. McCooley continued, "This talk that the Legislature is ruled by the bosses is all buncombe. It is no more controlled by the bosses than is the Executive of this State."[25] An unnamed legislator said, "No boss ever resorted to such unscrupulous methods to attain his purpose" as the governor has.[26] And the legislators sent that message very clearly: the governor's bill received just eight votes in the senate.[27]

In this debate, the merits of the governor's direct primary bill "were lost sight of as member after member stood up to censure the campaign of intimidation and cajolery carried on in the Executive Chamber."[28] Some of the most damning criticism came from John F. Murtaugh, a well-respected independent Democrat. Comparing Sulzer to Tamerlane, the fourteenth-century central Asiatic warlord immortalized by Christopher Marlow and Edgar Allan Poe and known for his cruelty, Murtaugh vividly described the governor erecting a pyramid with the heads of decapitated Democrats who happened to disagree with him.[29] Such strong criticism from someone not the least bit beholden to Boss Murphy shows just how strongly the legislature resented the governor's tactics. Sulzer was fighting Boss Murphy, but he had given up the high ground, was making enemies of anti-Tammany legislators, and only strengthening the resolve of the Tammany legislators themselves.

Majority Leader Wagner asked where Sulzer had been during the first four months of the year and of his term while the Blauvelt bill was being drafted and debated, and he criticized the governor's efforts at "self-advertisement" and publicity.[30] Wagner also read a letter purported to be from Chester C. Platt, secretary to Governor Sulzer, and sent to people who held jobs in state government. The letter said in part, "You are holding a lucrative office under the present administration. You are expected to be present and if possible speak for the bill."[31] Platt declared the letter "bogus" the next day, but the damage was done.[32]

Independent Democrats joined in the attacks on Sulzer, "enraged at being fought with the very weapons of the bosses in the name of emancipation from boss rule."[33] The legislature passed the Blauvelt bill again on May 3, only to have it vetoed by the governor.[34]

Legislators were so focused on the direct primary fight and meeting the governor's attacks that chaos reigned in Albany as the legislature ignored several emergency messages to focus their vitriol on Sulzer. The *World* reported, "The State Capitol to-day [May 2] resembled a Balkan war map."[35] As a few pro-Sulzer assembly members spoke in favor of his bill, the rest of the assembly broke out in an derisive chorus of "tra-la" and loud laughter while a large procession left the chamber and other speakers supporting the legislation spoke to empty benches.[36] The measure failed in the assembly by a vote of forty-seven in favor and ninety-three opposed. On the other side of the capitol, the governor's nominees for labor commissioner (Mitchell) and prison superintendent (Riley) "received short shrift." They were rejected without debate in the senate and without debate in the Democrats' conference earlier in the day.[37] Furthermore, Senator Elon Brown, Republican leader, announced his intention to bring libel charges against the governor.[38]

Sulzer, furious with the situation, exclaimed, "The battle for direct primaries has just begun. The fight will go on until the cause of the People triumphs."[39] He promised to bring back the legislature in an extra session and to stump the state, promising to visit the district of every legislator who did not support his bill. The governor announced that he would fight the bosses using patronage power and reprisals against his opponents, including firing workers and giving appointments *only* to Sulzer supporters.[40]

The conventional wisdom held that Sulzer had burned his bridges and staked his political future on fighting—and defeating—Tammany Hall.[41] It would be a fight to the death, but no legislator could be expected to change his vote; the governor would receive no help from the Republicans either.[42] The fight had been joined in 1909 and 1910 under Governor Hughes with help from Theodore Roosevelt—the two most popular Republicans in the state—and had failed, so there was no likelihood that the GOP would help a Democratic governor succeed.[43] At stake was not simply the primary bill but William Sulzer's hope to be renominated and reelected as governor and his goal of reaching national office.

Sulzer had another problem: Not all reformers were committed to the direct primary. Many "earnest and public-spirited reformers who approved of the principle of the direct primary deplored some of the changes Sulzer would make in the electoral machinery, particularly the abolition of the state convention."[44] The fact was that the state convention was a "time-honored institution valuable for the formulation of party principles and politics, and, if composed of delegates chosen by the enrolled voters, could become a thoroughly representative body." The alternative to the convention was that, to be elected, a candidate needed a powerful organization behind him to win statewide—or a great deal of money. And in an election with many contenders, a small minority of voters would choose the candidate. Furthermore, because of the difficulty of understanding judicial qualifications, the direct primary was not a positive development for an independent judiciary.[45] All these factors would allow the party machines to continue—or even expand—their determinative role in choosing candidates and winning elections.

Additionally, many reformers doubted that doing away with the state convention would get rid of the bosses or invite better candidates to participate in the process. In fact, many pointed out that state conventions had produced Governors Grover Cleveland and Charles Evans Hughes, reformers both and enemies of the bosses. The *Times* editorialized, "No inherent morality or immorality either in the caucus and convention, or in the committee designation and the direct primary, no evil that cannot be cast out if the people will take the trouble to do it."[46] Some observers even pointed out with a touch of irony that a convention had chosen Sulzer himself.

On May 8 the governor called a special session of the legislature for June 16 in order to resubmit his direct primary legislation. The next day, Sulzer held a rally in his office. It was attended by people who worked in the administration, anti-Tammany Democrats, some few independent Republicans, and a few members of the clergy rounded out with a few suffragettes.[47] Each of the state's sixty-two counties was represented when the governor reiterated that his legislation would become law.[48]

The group formed a campaign committee to fight for Sulzer's direct primary legislation. The committee was balanced with twenty-five anti-Tammany Democrats, twenty-five Republicans, twenty-five Progressives, and twenty-five unaffiliated voters. The committee was made up of luminaries including publishing magnate William Randolph Hearst; financier Herbert H. Lehman (future New York governor and U.S. senator); George Perkins, executive secretary of the Progressive Party and partner at J. P. Morgan; District Attorney Charles S. Whitman (future New York governor); president of the New York City Board of Aldermen John Purroy Mitchel (future mayor), influential publisher Ralph Pulitzer; and businessman and philanthropist William Vincent Astor.[49] Hearst was a strong advocate for Sulzer's bill. He put his newspapers behind the campaign, whose counsel and private secretary were also members of the direct primary campaign committee. Many observers believed Sulzer's interest in direct primaries stemmed entirely from an attempt to ingratiate himself with Hearst in an effort to have the support of the publisher's nationwide empire of newspapers and magazines in his future national campaign.

The campaign committee also appointed a Ways and Means subcommittee headed by Henry Morgenthau to raise money "for restoring to the people their rights."[50] Former president Theodore Roosevelt wrote an open letter on May 12 attacking the parties of "privilege" and "reaction," urging all progressives to support the governor in this fight. Roosevelt wrote, "The envenomed opposition of both the Murphy and Barnes machines to [the direct primary] is of itself sufficient proof that it is emphatically in the interest of the people as a whole."[51]

Words would not be enough to win this fight. On May 16 the governor began to act. His office announced that from that day forward Sulzer would recognize Daniel J. Dugan, a member of the direct primary committee, as the new Democratic leader of Albany County. Dugan would be replacing Patrick E. McCabe, the clerk of the state senate and a top Murphy lieutenant.[52] Throughout the administration, commissioners fired organization men from their jobs. Contractors were told by the governor himself to either fire McCabe's men or lose their contracts. No new men were to be hired unless William Sulzer personally approved them.[53] As a result, hundreds of men in the highway department were fired.[54]

Although not friends of Tammany Hall or the Albany County machine, reformers were not pleased. Sulzer was accused of trying to create his own personal machine under the guise of reform.[55] Others said the test of public service was being replaced by a test of personal loyalty to Governor Sulzer himself.[56] Many reformers and good-government groups were upset that civil service rules were frequently modified, changed, or simply ignored to get rid of Tammany's people and place Sulzer's in their stead.[57]

Sulzer's motivation was clear: Bind himself to Hearst and the Hearst publishing empire. The connection was Sulzer's best chance to realize his dream of being elected president. Hearst's reasons were equally personal. He was deeply bitter; having lost races for mayor and governor, he held Tammany Hall in general and Charles Murphy personally responsible for his defeats. Furthermore, Hearst remained ambitious, and many suspected he had already cut a deal to run for the U.S. Senate on a joint ticket with Sulzer in

1914. Together, they would run New York State and the state Democratic Party on their way to taking over the national party and the White House.

A Hearst loyalist pointedly said, "We have never felt sure whether the governor really is with us. His loyalty and sincerity from now on will be measured not by what he says in his speeches but by the number of heads of Murphy's henchmen which drop in the basket."[58] To many, this was further evidence that Sulzer's zeal for reform was less about a sincere commitment to change and more about a selfish attempt to ally himself with Hearst while simultaneously creating a political machine directly loyal to the governor.

Sulzer's efforts went far beyond patronage: the governor let loose with vetoes. He vetoed, again, the Blauvelt election reform bill. He vetoed a constitutional convention referendum (an effort by Tammany to change the fusion voting rules, helping the Democratic slate in the upcoming municipal election in New York City). He gutted $43 million in appropriation and supply bills. He cut hundreds of jobs in the state comptroller's office, the secretary of state's office, and various boards and agencies across the state. These jobs all had one thing in common: they were not under the personal control of the governor.

More significantly, Sulzer vetoed a workers' compensation bill sponsored by senate president pro tem Robert Wagner along with legislation to create a hydroelectric plant on the Mohawk River. The hydroelectric bill was a personal project of Lieutenant Governor Martin Glynn, and the governor had promised Glynn that he would sign the legislation. Glynn did not fight back, saying, "Governor Sulzer brags about being a friend of the people. When he vetoed this bill he was an enemy of the people and a friend of the corporations. Talk is cheap. Actions tell where a man stands."[59] Glynn pointed out that the 1912 Democratic platform included a pledge to support this hydroelectric plant that was just as important a promise to the people of New York as the commitment in the same platform for direct primaries. Glynn openly questioned Sulzer's motives, declaring, "Evidently only such provisions of the state platform are binding upon the Governor as suit his whims or the pocket-books of his corporation

"SULZER TAKES HIS CASE TO THE PEOPLE"

During Sulzer's statewide campaign swing, he took every opportunity to make his case directly to the electorate. This photo shows the Governor at the unveiling ceremonies for the memorial to the battleship Maine at Columbus Circle and 59th Street near Central Park in New York City. Sulzer had been a champion of raising the Maine as a member of Congress.

friends."[60] The governor took the opportunity to threaten legislators, telling them they were either with him or against him. Sulzer made clear there was no middle ground. The only test was to be the direct primary bill. Not only would Sulzer punish legislators who were against him but he would also remove any of their friends from office.[61]

On May 18 Governor Sulzer took his case directly to the people with what he called a "swing around the circle." He set out to tour the entire state with rallies in the district of each legislator who had voted against his direct primary bill. Accompanied by a full retinue, Sulzer expressed his full confidence that the people would "be aroused."[62] To coincide with the tour, Sulzer wrote a series of articles in the *World*, a Hearst paper, offering a direct challenge to the bosses, Democrat Charles Murphy and Republican William Barnes. It was war.

Back in New York City, Tammany and its allies refused to take things lying down. Senator Wagner, who had been chair of the Committee on Resolutions for the 1912 New York State Democratic Convention, went on the offensive. He declared that the platform had never been against state conventions (the major difference between the Blauvelt bill and Sulzer's bill). Rather, Wagner asserted that the goal had been uniform laws throughout the state providing for direct primaries. Contemporary sources back up Wagner's assertions. Just after the state convention in 1912 the *New York World* denounced the Democratic platform on direct primaries as "fraudulent" because it "left the state nominating convention untouched."[63] Wagner also pointed out that Sulzer's veto of the state convention referendum, the hydroelectric project, and the workers' compensation bill were in clear violation of the Democratic platform. Wagner struck a conciliatory note, too, pointing out that the legislature and governor had passed more progressive and more beneficial legislation than in any previous legislative session.[64]

Throughout the tour, Sulzer traveled by car, often an open car so that the people could see him, and with a full entourage, including stenographers, secretaries, newspapermen, and members of his entire campaign committee. In most cities, the governor filled his day meeting in his hotel suite with political allies—most usually those out of power who were willing to take a stand against the local organization—between addressing a local businessman's committee for lunch and maybe a meeting with the local naval or militia commanders. At night, Sulzer spoke in two or three locations per city, usually at convention halls, theaters, or the halls in various ethnic communities. The crowds were always large, representing Sulzer's personal popularity, varying from 1,000 to as many as 8,000 or 9,000 in some places. Usually about 25 percent of the crowd was made up of women and children who had come to see Sulzer rather than hear him or rally to the cause of a direct primary election. (Women would not be granted suffrage until 1917 in New York and 1920 nationally.)

Sulzer would invariably open his speech by calling upon the audience, asking if they were in favor of direct nominations. The crowd would answer with a resounding "Aye!" The governor would continue with some small variation on the theme of trusting the people to choose their candidates. For instance, "It is self-evident to me that if the people are competent to directly elect their public officials they are also competent to directly nominate these officials. If it is important for minor officers to be nominated by the people, it is still more important that the people be given the power to nominate candidates for United States Senator and for Governor."[65] Sulzer would then launch into a long attack on the bosses. This part of his speech garnered the most applause and enthusiasm. The conclusion was a long discussion about the merits of direct primaries over conventions and a detailed discussion of the advantages of Sulzer's bill over anything and everything else. By the end, close to half of the audience was likely to have left, having shown much less fervor for the details of direct primaries.

Sulzer's tour began in Buffalo. He spoke at rallies organized by the Progressive Party and the William "Fingy" Connors faction of the local Democratic Party.* In what would become an oft-repeated speech, Sulzer framed the issue as the people versus the bosses and declared the convention system as inadequate to convey the wishes of the people. Sulzer said, "Political conventions must go. Disgraceful secret alliances between special privilege and crooked politics must cease." He continued, "The spirit of true democracy is summed up in the slogan: *let the people rule.* They cannot rule until they obtain a successful method of nominating the candidate of all political parties."[66]

Sulzer pulled no punches: "I am convinced that every member of the Legislature is solemnly bound in honor, and by the highest moral and

---

* Fingy Connors himself was locked in a battle for control of the Erie County Democratic Party against William H. Fitzpatrick, a Murphy loyalist. Connors had been a vocal opponent of direct primaries when former governor Hughes had pushed them, lending credence to the widely held belief that this was a fight of power and control and not of principle or for democracy (*New York Times*, May 20, 1913).

political obligations, to vote for its enactment; and those who fail to do so will be forced to yield to public opinion."[67] He drew a line in the sand, declaring, "Let us keep the faith. That is where I stand, and I will stand there to the end. If any Democrat is against me in my determination to keep Democratic faith, I must of necessity be against him…and as the Democratic Governor of the State I shall do everything in my power to drive that recreant Democrat out of the councils of the Democratic party."[68]

He also played the patronage card. "Not another job will go to Erie County from the Executive Chamber," said Sulzer, "until the legislators see fit to vote for my direct primary bill."[69] Erie County's two senators and eight assemblymen had opposed the Sulzer bill and seemed unmoved. An unnamed legislator told the press that they were ignoring "Sulzer's ravings."[70] County Democratic chairman Fitzpatrick declared that Sulzer's rallies had not changed a single vote.[71]

From Buffalo, the governor's tour went to Elmira, Corning, and Schenectady. Sulzer's biggest response came when he would ask his audience if they wanted to nominate their leaders or leave it to three men, "one in New York, one in Buffalo and one in Albany," a clear reference to Democratic bosses Murphy, Fitzpatrick, and McCabe.[72]

In Elmira, in the middle of the rally, Sulzer turned to Senator Murtaugh and asked him to join the governor's fight, saying with his support, "The backbone of the oppositions would be broken." Murtaugh, when called upon to speak, instead spoke slowly and rationally, questioning the merits of Sulzer's proposal and denying vehemently that a vote against Sulzer's particular brand of direct primary legislation said anything about his honor or reform credentials.[73] Before the governor left Elmira he had threatened to drive Murtaugh out of public life.[74]

The same scene played out in Schenectady where Sulzer accused Senator Loren H. White of disloyalty and "virtually read him out of the party."[75] The governor did not miss an opportunity to ratchet up the rhetoric, saying, "I think I know the Tiger's place. It should be in a cage and that's where we will put it before we get through."[76] Sulzer renamed the direct primary bill the

"the People's bill" because "the People are for it." The only ones opposed, at least according to Sulzer's rhetoric, were political bosses and newspapers beholden to the special interests. Taking it even further, Sulzer declared, "Who dares to challenge my bill? Any one who does it is an enemy of the State, an enemy of the People, and enemy of the hope of every one."[77]

Returning to Albany, Sulzer was confident of victory.[78] Many on the tour disagreed privately with that assertion. The governor was clearly personally popular, but he had not swayed a single vote.

Meanwhile, the Organization Democrats and Tammany Hall were not leaving the governor's attacks unanswered. Senator Wagner, speaking to the Richmond County Democrats, said the state convention was indispensible to the development of party opinion. Beyond answering Sulzer's attacks, Wagner went on the offensive, lauding the important progressive legislation passed by the senate and assembly and detailing the positive benefits to the people of New York. Taking the fight directly to Sulzer, Wagner professed that no political boss would have ever threatened Senator Murtaugh as brazenly as Sulzer had threatened him. Wagner concluded, "If we in the Legislature, standing courageously by our convictions, undeterred by threats or promises, and responsive to what we believe to be the will of the People, are enemies of the People, the People may well beware of its self-designated *friends*."[79]

Senator Blauvelt, the author of primary reform bill that the legislature had twice passed, said, "The Sulzer bill is simply the bill of William Randolph Hearst."[80] Senator Griffin wrote an open letter accusing Sulzer of being a tyrant and asking, "Are you the high priest of direct nominations with a mission from Heaven to put on the rack all who do not worship at your shrine?" Griffin's letter concluded with this warning, "No man in civil life, no matter what his talents for depravity may be, could be half so dangerous a party boss as the Chief Executive of the State."[81]

On May 28 the governor took his direct primary tour to New York City, making no secret that he hoped to use the issue to build his own party apparatus there.[82] He held more than a dozen meetings, featuring supporters including District Attorney Charles Whitman, New York City comptroller William Prendergrast, Manhattan borough president George McAneny, president of the Board of Aldermen John Purroy Mitchel, and the leader of the Progressive Party, Bainbridge Colby. The rallies were crowded and featured Sulzer's standard denunciations of Charles Murphy in his biting rhetoric: "I warn anybody who attacks me that I will strip him of his hide, and tack the hide on the ceiling of the Capitol at Albany."[83] The crowds liked the attacks on Tammany but showed little or no enthusiasm for the direct primary or the governor's legislation.

A telling moment in the campaign came when Sulzer did not show up at a huge rally organized by the Direct Primary League, a nonpartisan organization founded to support this fight. Sulzer had been scheduled to speak on his cause de célèbre: the direct primary bill. But the league declined to allow William Randolph Hearst to speak, and as a result, Sulzer skipped the event. It caused Charles H. Duell, the chair of the league, to remark that the whole thing was politics pure and simple, and its "purpose was a new alignment of the Democratic forces of the state under the dual leadership of Sulzer and Hearst."[84] Perhaps this alliance had been longer in the making than it seemed, Sulzer traveled to his inauguration with Hearst, a fact much remarked upon at the time.[85]

The governor was, again, pleased with his direct appeal to the voters, but most observers remained convinced that he had made no real progress.[86] To further illustrate that, the Democratic senators and assemblymen from the Bronx and New York County met at the Hotel Knickerbocker on June 4 and agreed the governor's tour had no effect on public sentiment in their districts and that they would hold fast to their positions. The legislators also condemned the governor's methods.[87]

Senator Wagner emerged as a leader of the Tammany forces. Born in Prussia in 1877 Robert Ferdinand Wagner immigrated with his parents to the United States in 1885, settling in a tenement neighborhood on New York City's Lower East Side. Robert attended public schools and graduated from City College and New York Law School, being admitted to the bar in 1900.

CHAPTER FOURTEEN

"SENATOR ROBERT F. WAGNER"
Senator Wagner was the public face of Tammany forces fighting against Sulzer's public campaign to discredit Murphy's machine ... and replace it with his own. This photo is from 1937 when the Supreme Court upheld the validity of the Wagner Labor Relations Act.

He quickly abandoned the law for Democratic Party politics. He gave speeches and worked to turn out his mostly immigrant neighborhood for Tammany candidates. His successes earned him a nomination for the New York State assembly in 1904. Four years later he was elected to the state senate. His work on social legislation — especially trying to protect the immigrants in his district who were constantly exploited — and chairman of the State Factory Investigating Committee earned him plaudits as a progressive leader in the Democratic Party.

Having served as both majority leader and minority leader in the state senate, Wagner was elected a justice of the New York Supreme Court in 1919, where he served until his election to the U.S. Senate. He would serve three terms, resigning in 1949 because of ill health.

In Congress, Wagner was instrumental in writing the Social Security Act, and he originally introduced it in the Senate. He also helped draft the National Industrial Recovery Act (1933), the Federal Emergency Relief Administration Bill (1933), the law establishing the Civilian Conservation Corps (1933), and the Wagner-Steagall Housing Act of 1937, among many others.

His son, Robert Wagner Jr., would serve as mayor of New York City from 1954 through 1965.

Senator Wagner was a staunch Tammanyite, in large part because, in his point of view, only Tammany folks cared about the people in his neighborhood: the poor, the immigrants, the people in the same vulnerable position his family had been when they came to America. Wagner had a sterling reputation as honest and above board, but he was not afraid to fight.

Wagner accused Sulzer of trying to "disrupt the Democratic party and make himself leader, using as a cloak a direct nominations bill which, it should be apparent by this time, the voters of this State do not want." Wagner also called the governor's bluff, telling him to make good on his accusations that legislators were involved in graft or to retract his threats.[88] Wagner also gave it back, accusing Sulzer of the "vicious and vindictive use of veto" and promising to investigate any legislator who changed his vote on the legislation seeking evidence of intimidation or bribery. Senator

Wagner accused the governor of trading appropriations for votes, threatening legislators, and being in the pocket of the state's power interests as evidenced by his veto of the Mohawk hydropower bill.[89] Wagner issued a final challenge to Sulzer: "It was time the mask was torn from the hypocritical face and after this direct primaries campaign is over we will show who is boss and who is making corrupt bargains to veto and sign legislation."[90]

Senator Wagner was not alone in fighting back against Sulzer. Democratic National Committeeman Norman E. Mack and some former state officeholders published a sixteen-page booklet titled, "The Truth About Direct Primaries." The pamphlet took a mostly rational approach to the issue, coming out strongly against direct primaries. In detail, it noted that state conventions had, in recent history, nominated Samuel Tilden and Grover Cleveland for governor, both reformers and neither friends of the bosses. Heck, the authors noted, a convention had even nominated William Sulzer for governor. More scientifically, the booklet noted that less than 25 percent of the general election voters had voted in primaries in 1911 and 1912, most of those votes coming from New York City. Furthermore, the authors noted that Sulzer's bill could hamper voting and abolish safeguards against fictitious independent nominations, while the provision abolishing party emblems was of doubtful constitutionality.[91]

Sulzer had his own allies, and he received some help from former president Theodore Roosevelt, who toured Buffalo, Rochester, and other upstate cities in support of Sulzer's direct primary bill. Roosevelt echoed Sulzer's attacks, calling state conventions "mere devices for registering the decrees of the big and the little bosses."[92] The former president also got the same results: large crowds, thundering applause for TR's attacks on the bosses, little to no enthusiasm for the direct primary campaign, and a complete failure to change the vote of a single member of the legislature.

Sulzer continued his tour, winding again through upstate and ending in New York City. Like the earlier version, this tour was a whirlwind. Scheduled to end just before the special legislative session, Sulzer turned up the rhetoric, comparing his enemies to Boss Tweed and declaring that they would meet a similar fate. (Boss Tweed died in jail.) The final meeting of the direct primary campaign was held June 14 at Cooper Union. Sulzer headlined it, and prominent Progressives—including Sulzer's gubernatorial opponent Oscar Straus and Progressive Party chairman Bainbridge Colby—joined him. The tour also, for the first time, included William Randolph Hearst. Hearst was in fine form, calling out "Hon. Charles 'Finance' Murphy" and Senator "Elihu 'I.O.U.' Root."[93] In what perhaps was the most fearsome threat to Murphy, Hearst threatened to bolt the party for the New York City municipal campaign if the direct primary bill did not pass.[94] Sulzer, in his confident way, claimed to have made a long line of converts to his cause.[95]

Charles Murphy took Sulzer's attacks to heart and realized their break was irrevocable. Since Sulzer was clearly not going to be doing Tammany Hall any favors, the boss told legislators they should defeat his proposal even if it took all summer.[96]

The public may have supported Sulzer (and Hearst) on the direct primary bill, but no one, not even Sulzer's closest allies, supported the legislation with much enthusiasm. The public just did not trust the messenger. A contemporary analyst wrote, "Sulzer was simply incapable of inspiring a popular uprising because the People had no great confidence in his fundamental sincerity, even when he was apparently striving for reforms in the public interest."[97] The *New York Evening Post* agreed, editorializing, "The People did not rally to the Governor because he did not talk or act like a governor." He lacked "dignity or self-respect," the *Post* continued; Sulzer's "constant violence of speech and tumultuousness of action had no success against a vicious and perverse legislature."[98] The people liked William Sulzer. They came out in droves to see him, but they simply did not trust him. The people wanted someone to challenge Tammany Hall and the countless other political machines but did not trust William Sulzer to do the job. Furthermore, the people objected to the graft and corruption that sustained the political machines, not state conventions, and therefore they had no enthusiasm for the direct primary fight.

Maybe they were right. Disturbing allegations indicated that perhaps Sulzer was playing both sides of the issue. Lieutenant Governor Glynn would later claim that, during this time, Sulzer asked him to serve as a messenger to Murphy. The message? Tell the boss to ignore the governor's rhetoric and that soon they would "fix up matters to their mutual satisfaction." Glynn refused to make the entreaties.[99]

On the eve of the special session to consider Sulzer's direct primary legislation, Patrick E. McCabe, the clerk of the senate and Tammany leader of Albany County, issued an authorized statement. In it, he said that Sulzer had sought—and received—secret conferences with Murphy at the Tammany leader's home in New York City.

McCabe offered four specific times and places: February 2, March 2, March 17, and April 13. The later two occurred *after* the public break between Sulzer and Murphy. In his statement McCabe wrote, "On the evening of March 17, Governor Sulzer attended the dinner of the Friendly Sons of St. Patrick at the Hotel Astor, made a noise in which he railed against the thing he calls 'invisible government' and sneaked around to see Mr. Murphy the next day and spent several hours with him."[100] Although reports of the meeting appeared in the press and Tammany Hall secretary Thomas F. Smith corroborated it, Sulzer vehemently denied it ever occurred.

Even more damaging, McCabe said that on April 13, after dinner at the National Democratic Club, Sulzer roused the Murphy household at 1:00 a.m. begging for an audience and, once admitted, stayed three hours. According to McCabe, Sulzer said he had come from a meeting with William Randolph Hearst and that Hearst had abused the governor for not pushing direct primaries. The result, McCabe said, was that Sulzer urged Murphy to "deceive Hearst" but that Murphy declined, even though Sulzer offered a patronage package including two public service commissioners, the commissioner of labor, state superintendent of prisons, and anything else the boss wanted. McCabe continued, "When this was refused he begged with tears in his eyes but Murphy was obdurate."[101]

A frequent target of Sulzer's attacks himself, McCabe was unsparing in his denunciation of the governor, calling him "an over-heated Executive with an insane political ambition." He was particularly harsh on Sulzer's hypocrisy for pretending to care about working men while vetoing the Mohawk hydropower project at the request of the power trust. Even so, McCabe's strongest attack on the governor was for his veto of a constitutional convention. McCabe called that "the most criminal political act ever perpetrated on the party by a Democrat of any type."[102]

Sulzer's immediate response was, "I do not care to answer this until I learn who has written it. Most of it is absolutely false."[103] At a direct primary rally in Albany Sulzer called McCabe "a little Boss Tweed," "a cats-paw," and "a squealer." He said the report was "deliberately planned and executed by crafty enemies of direct primaries" to stop the direct primary campaign.[104]

The plot thickened when, despite Sulzer's denials, Hearst conceded that he and Sulzer did meet—and disagree—on the night of April 13.[105]

Two days later, McCabe made a second statement to the press: "I charge Governor Sulzer with publicly denouncing Mr. Murphy and surreptitiously calling upon him and assuring him of his everlasting loyalty and friendship, and I challenge Governor Sulzer to answer that he did or did not call upon Mr. Murphy at the times mentioned."[106]

Sulzer responded with a prepared statement but did not specifically address the charges: "For the present I shall treat that vile and villainous matter with the contempt it deserves.... Suffice it to say that I have taken my stand for good government and political righteousness, and all the mud and all the slime and all the filth they now hurl against me will not deter me in the performance of my duty as I see the right and God gives me the light. I cannot be intimidated, and I have no fear of political or personal consequences."[107]

The special session that started on June 16 opened with more attacks on the governor. Legislators accused him of trading appropriation and supply moneys in exchange for votes. Even the Republicans had had enough. Republican assemblyman Hinman said,

> Governor Sulzer's vision of the truth is somewhat clouded by vivid dreams of his further political preferment. He needs a censor. Ambitious men seem to find it difficult to be honest. The attitude of the present overlord of all New York impels the deduction that it is ambition, not patriotism, which is leading him headlong on in his career. In his eye constantly is his own name written on the future pages of history. The public are entitled to the truth about the Governor's attitude on the subject of direct nominations. He is waging his war upon a false presentation of facts.[108]

Under the New York State Constitution, the executive has the power to call special sessions of the legislature and the exclusive power to determine the agenda of those sessions. This special session agenda had only one item: direct primaries. The governor continued to insist that public opinion compelled him to force the issue. Direct democracy, Sulzer said, is essential to the freedom of the American people: "Every other government is a mere form of despotism." The legislation was basically the same bill and the message the same rhetoric. Again, Sulzer cited the platforms of the various political parties to insist that every legislator from every party was bound to support the bill.[109]

Nevertheless, not a single legislator stood up or spoke up for the governor.

Senator Wagner offered a direct answer to Sulzer: "The time has come when the Senate will look more deeply into accusations that have been made against Senators and more deeply into what has been done since the Regular Session. The truth will come to light. Let us have patience and the People will know when it has been done what promises and corrupt bargains have been made to get votes for a bill the Governor is so anxious to pass."[110] Legislator after legislator took to the floor to reject the governor's demands, insisting that no one in their districts cared about direct primaries.[111]

Not one to be deterred, the governor continued to hold rallies, including one in the Executive Chamber attended by about 500 people. One of the speakers, a minister, said Governor Sulzer was "sent by God to lead us to victory."[112] The rest of the speakers were virulently anti-Tammany and seemed to treat direct primaries as a "panacea to eradicate all political evils."[113]

The legislators continued to reject Sulzer's plan decisively. The assembly vote was ninety-two against to fifty-four in favor, a gain of seven votes from the first time it was considered, but three of those new "yes" votes came from members absent earlier in the year. Sulzer claimed it as a victory since assembly Democrats from outside of the cities of New York and Buffalo all supported it, suggesting, at least to Sulzer himself, that he was in charge of the state party (or at least the party outside of Buffalo and New York City).[114]

In the senate, the direct primary bill was debated for over seven hours. An unnamed senator told the press that Sulzer was "the Judas of the Democratic Party. The Governor has fed at the public crib for 25 years. What right has he to complain?"[115] That was illustrative of Sulzer's support in the senate. The final vote was ten in favor and thirty-eight opposed.

To add insult to injury, both houses repassed the Blauvelt bill by wide margins, a 77-59 party-line vote in the assembly and a 32-16 vote in the senate.

Just prior to the end of the special session, the legislature passed a concurrent resolution, proposed by Senator George Thompson, authorizing an investigation into Governor Sulzer's alleged use of patronage and his veto powers to inappropriately influence legislators as well as Sulzer's campaign fund financing his direct primary fight.

The governor, as usual, continued to send conflicting signals. On June 25 he told the press the fight had "just begun."[116] The next day, June 26, the governor welcomed any "honorable" compromise.[117] That day, Edward McCall, a Tammany man appointed to the Public Service Commission by Sulzer, came to Albany and met with Sulzer, giving rise to speculation that McCall had come as an emissary of Murphy to negotiate peace.[118]

Meanwhile, state government was in chaos. State comptroller William Sohmer, since 1910 the treasurer of Tammany Hall, stopped the work of the Highway Department (since purged of Tammany workers and Tammany contractors by Sulzer's fiat) by refusing to approve payrolls and delaying contracts while also rejecting payroll requests from the Department of Prisons.[119] Meanwhile, a fight between Sulzer and Tammany members of the public trustees held up contracting. The vacancies on the Public Service Commission held up all business in front of that commission while the Department of Efficiency and Economy came to a standstill because no money had been appropriated by the legislature for its operations.[120]

The crisis to come would make the conflict of these few weeks seem like child's play.

15

THE SCANDALS

THE WAR IN THE PRESS CONTINUED. McCabe unleashed another broadside aimed at the governor, accusing him of unprofessional conduct in a lawsuit where Sulzer was a counsel in Vermont in 1890. The accusation was that Sulzer deserved to be prosecuted for perjury.[1] Eventually, the judge from the case exonerated Sulzer but not until after the allegations had a thorough airing in the press.[2]

The governor accused Tammany Hall of hiring detectives to follow him and investigate his background, and he challenged his enemies to produce "all the other libelous stuff" they have on him.[3] He wanted, Sulzer insisted, "to treat Mr. Murphy right," but the demands were too high. The governor continue to broadcast his refusal to be "part of a criminal conspiracy to loot the state."[4]

After a week of unanswered questions about Packy McCabe's disclosure, Sulzer finally responded, making a brief statement to the newspapermen crowded outside his office in the capitol. Sulzer acknowledged meeting Murphy three times since he was elected governor. The first time, when Murphy was in Albany as a presidential elector, Sulzer said he only saw Murphy publicly and insisted he refused to meet Murphy privately. The second meeting was in New York City. Asked about their discussion, Sulzer would only reveal that Murphy "said things which hurt" the governor's feelings. The final meeting between the boss and the governor, according to Sulzer's disclosure, was on April 13 and was a failed attempt to patch up their differences. Reflecting on the that meeting, Sulzer said he was so sick of the fight that he wrote out a resignation letter, deciding, only at the last moment, to stick to his guns.[5]

Boss Murphy replied, issuing a rare statement, "Gov. Sulzer is absolutely in error when he accuses me of being a party to any so-called conspiracy to discredit him." Murphy denied hiring any detectives or releasing the files from Sulzer's case in Vermont or pushing Gaffney (or anyone else) as highway chief. In fact, Murphy asserted his own serious doubts about the governor's truthfulness, revealing that he always insisted on a third person being present when he met with Sulzer, because "the Governor would not hesitate to swear my life away if he found it to his political advantage to do so." Current events, Murphy noted, proved his point.[6]

Things got even stranger when a Miss Mignon Hopkins sued William Sulzer for breach of a marriage contract. Hopkins, a cloak model in a Philadelphia department store, said she and Sulzer became engaged in 1903, keeping it a secret so as not to interfere with his political career. They lived together at different times over the years, said Hopkins, and he introduced her to people as his wife. Hopkins said Sulzer's marriage to another in 1908 had destroyed her life, and she sued for commensurate damages.[7]

Not surprisingly, the governor denounced the allegations at "stale and fishy," declaring the matter a "frame up" and a blatant attempt to blackmail him. Sulzer said that Hopkins' charges were "part of the plot of Boss Murphy and his political conspirators to discredit me because they cannot use me for the nefarious schemes to crook the state of New York." Again, nothing involving Sulzer was cut-and-dried, and the governor admitted that he knew Hopkins. "Suffice it to say that I knew this Hopkins woman years ago. I was a friend of her family in their distress but I deny emphatically that I ever agreed to marry her; that I ever wronged her; that I ever lived with her, or that I ever held her out to be my wife."[8] Yet he admitted that she had sued him before, a case settled out of court by cash considerations.[9] In an excuse Sulzer would use again and again in the months to come, the settlement "was on account of the precarious condition of Mrs. Sulzer."[10]

The next allegation involved a mining scheme that bilked investors out of huge sums. Sulzer conceded that he had been involved with the Alaska Industrial Company, but he called it an entirely legitimate business endeavor and denied the allegations of cheating the shareholders, saying unequivocally, "It's a pure fake."

A similar claim had surfaced earlier. The *New York Evening Post* had published a story on October 22, 1912, about Sulzer being sued by a missionary in Alaska, a suit that was settled for $100,000. Sulzer denied it, claimed it was being pushed by his opponents, and said he was in no way connected with the charges.[11] In October, Sulzer admitted he had owned a few shares of the company but claimed to have gotten rid of them a long time before the allegations surfaced — and besides, he said, it was an honorable company. Incidentally, the officers of the company were Samuel I. Frankenstein, Sulzer's law partner; Louis A. Sarecky, later secretary to Governor Sulzer; and the governor's brother Charles A. Sulzer.[12]

The regular disparagement was clearly taking its toll on the governor. Sulzer was so incensed that he asked New York County district attorney Charles S. Whitman, a regular ally, to initiate a John Doe inquiry in order to find the person or persons responsible for leaking the Vermont information, the breach-of-promise suit, and a "new conspiracy" that Sulzer believed was being plotted.[13] He claimed he was being followed by "thugs"[14] and threatened by the "Tammany crew."[15] Still, the attacks kept coming and kept getting worse for the governor. A lawyer named Joseph F. Darling accused Sulzer of using his position in Congress as chairman of the Foreign Relations Committee to help a group called the Spriggs-Clark syndicate obtain a valuable concession for minerals in Guatemala from that country's despotic ruler Manuel Estrada Cabrera. The kicker was that Sulzer had a personal financial interest in the syndicate.[16] Sulzer responded with his usual attacks, saying of Darling that he is "a man with criminal instincts and a menace to the community" and denying any connection.[17] The *New York Times* published a series of letters written by Sulzer that seemed to prove his involvement in the scheme.[18] The circumstantial evidence was also striking. Sulzer's law office was located next the office to syndicate head A. E. Spriggs, the former governor of Montana, with whom Sulzer admitted he was "intimate, both as a friend and attorney." Sulzer also conceded he was familiar with the terms of the Spriggs concession and that he traveled to Guatemala to meet with President Cabrera immediately prior to the agreement being signed. Sulzer also became a strong public proponent of Cabrera after it was signed, in striking contrast to the opinion of almost every other American observer who visited Guatemala.

This was not the only allegation that Sulzer used his congressional office to enrich himself. During the same time period, Sulzer was accused of serving as a confidential advisor to a Cuban contracting firm seeking help from the U.S. State Department in collecting a claim of $500,000 for a waterworks project in Cuba. Letters and telegrams, including notes on House of Representatives stationery, showed that Sulzer was paid from the money collected. Sulzer's response, once again: "There is nothing to it. It is a pure fake."[19]

Sulzer's defense of Guatemala's despotic president Cabrera continued to be helpful to his friends. In 1909 Sulzer helped another company led by former governor Spriggs obtain a valuable mining concession in Guatemala. Some connected the mining concession with Chairman Sulzer's zealous advocacy to move coffee from the tariff-restricted list and onto the free-trade list, a boon to that country's economy. The companies that benefited from Sulzer's advocacy in Guatemala had another element in common: Louis A. Sarecky, who would become secretary to Governor Sulzer, was the secretary of both companies.

Some of the charges were not new, having surfaced during the gubernatorial election but the drip, drip, drip of scandalous revelations continued to damage the governor's public standing, while his habit of seeming to give different answers to similar questions continued to erode New Yorkers' confidence in Sulzer's veracity. However, these scandals were only vetted in the press. Soon, Sulzer would face a more difficult examination of his conduct.

PART THREE

16

THE FRAWLEY COMMITTEE

O N MAY 2, 1912, THE PENULTIMATE DAY of the regular legislative session, the assembly and senate passed a joint resolution appointing a committee "to investigate into the conduct of the various State departments." The broad scope of the investigation included almost all the official acts of the governor and his men. The committee was given subpoena power and the ability to take testimony under oath, as well as to compel witnesses to appear in court and to mandate the production of relevant records.

The resolution passed the senate unanimously and the assembly by a vote of 137-8. James J. Frawley (D-New York County), the head of the Senate Finance Committee and the author of the joint resolution, was appointed as chairman. The other members of the committee were Senators Felix J. Sanner (D-Brooklyn), Samuel J. Rampsberger (D-Erie County), Elon R. Brown (R-Jefferson), and Assemblymen Myron Smith (R-Dutchess), Wilson R. Yard (D-Westchester), and LaVerne P. Butts (D-Otsego). As counsel, the legislature named Eugene Lamb Richards, and as secretary of the committee, Matthew T. Horgan, deputy commissioner of efficiency and economy. Horgan was also a close longtime associate of Governor Sulzer.

The governor was, as usual, dismissive. He said they were looking to "show [him] up" and that the committee was made up of his enemies. According to a source friendly to Sulzer, Senator Frawley had said, at a conference of Tammany men on May 20 at Delmonico's, "It is either Sulzer's life or ours!"[1] Senator Sanner was close to Chairman McCooley, the Democratic leader in Brooklyn, and Senator Rampsberger was close to Chairman Fitzpatrick, the Democratic leader in Buffalo. Even Brown and Smith, the Republican members, were not friendly to Sulzer. Brown, the minority leader in the senate, had called for the governor's impeachment following the revelations that Sulzer had promised to pass the Full Crew Railroad legislation before his election. Horgan, who had been with Sulzer during his congressional days in D.C. and was his constant companion on the campaign trail, was later called "a Tammany spy" and "traitor."[2]

During the special legislative session, on June 25, George F. Thompson, a Republican senator, offered a concurrent resolution to expand the Frawley Committee, as the investigation became known, to probe the governor's use of patronage and veto threats to pass his direct primaries legislation as well as to inquire into Sulzer's fundraising to pay for both his gubernatorial campaign and the campaign to pass his primaries bill.

Senator Thompson insisted his resolution was unplanned and uncoordinated, but the fact that it passed unanimously and without debate suggests that his fellow legislators knew it was coming.

The legislators, even before the investigation began, announced that it was not a "fishing expedition" and that they already had enough information to "show the Governor in his true light to the voters."[3] There were hints that William Randolph Hearst had financed Sulzer's campaign secretly and in violation of election law and, in another campaign law violation, was promised favors in exchange for these donations. The story continued that Sulzer's fight against Tammany Hall was in order to help the publishing magnate Hearst with his goal of being elected as a U.S. senator. Hearst's ambition had too often been thwarted by Charles Murphy and other Tammany stalwarts.

Leaks to newspapers suggested that the governor had threatened state legislators, that he had approved money and appropriations in the millions of dollars as rewards to legislators for their votes, and that he allowed important state positions to go vacant with the sole aim of furthering his battle with Tammany Hall—vacancies that resulted in serious harm and damage to the state.[4] Reports attributed to Tammany men said that Sulzer would be "thrown out of office before October first."[5]

The Frawley Committee commenced with private hearings in advance of the public hearings scheduled to begin on July 3. The first target was George W. Black, the governor's special examiner of the prisons. The committee raised questions about his expenses: he had been announced with great fanfare as serving without compensation but was in fact receiving $25 per day. Under a barrage of questions, Black admitted to changing witnesses' testimony and withholding favorable testimony.[6]

Frawley also asserted that most of Blake's prison abuse allegations were based on nothing more than hearsay and assumptions.[7] The committee exposed the authorities on whom Black relied to be incompetent and unreliable. To wit, although one so-called expert had ten years of experience in the New York City restaurant industry, he more recently had worked as a "manager of fake circuses and exhibitor of chariot races at county fairs."[8] Another "expert" spent only one and a half days conducting his interviews, doing his research, and writing his report. A third supposed construction expert actually had no knowledge of, or experience in, brick or concrete work.[9] An "expert" on building costs was really only the treasurer of an accident insurance company. Another admitted his testimony was not "conclusive" and was really nothing more than "an off-handed opinion."[10]

The investigation did more than just undermine the investigation of the prisons; it cast doubt on all of the investigations, crusading, and reforms that Governor Sulzer had undertaken—and announced—with great fanfare. Senator Frawley summed up this phase of the investigation well, stating that Blake and the others were "a pack of scoundrels of the worst type, going about the State telling falsehoods about honest and competent public officials."[11] Perhaps the investigated state workers were not all "honest and competent," but there was no reason to believe anything that Blake and his team had said.

In its follow-up, the Frawley Committee issued a subpoena to the governor's secretary, Chester C. Platt, asking for the originals of the prison reports and the transcripts of interviews with witnesses. The suspicion was that these transcripts had been tampered with before the final report. Platt claimed executive privilege, insisting that the committee had no right to *any* of the chief executive's papers.[12] Frawley objected strongly to this claim. The governor, who was absent from the capitol during Platt's initial testimony, tried to diffuse the situation upon his return, promising to provide all relevant papers to the committee.[13] However, after further reflection, Sulzer modified his answer, agreeing only to provide papers "within the sphere of [the Frawley Committee's] legitimate powers" that were also "not incompatible with the public interests."[14] The final result was that the governor only provided the letter from himself to the state comptroller officially appointing Blake as the special investigator and withheld all of the reports and testimony from the Frawley Committee.

Sensing, perhaps, that the investigation was not going well for him or his administration, the governor did what all good politicians do. He changed the subject—or at least tried to blur the situation. The governor initiated a grand jury investigation of road contracts in every region where the contractors had ties to Tammany politicians. Sulzer convened a special grand jury in Rockland County and ordered the Supreme Courts to meet in extraordinary session in Suffolk, Putnam, Washington, and Dutchess Counties to immediately try charges stemming from Blake's original report.[15] Sulzer also appointed Hennessy as a special commissioner to investigate basically anything. All throughout, the governor and his people were continuing to fire any workers loyal to Tammany Hall.[16]

Sulzer also continued to use his official powers to strengthen his political hand—cutting appropriations in departments and commissions unfriendly to him, throwing his enemies out of office, or cutting the pay of anyone he could not fire. The governor also aided his supporters and potential allies by boosting the pay of faithful commissioners and of people helpful in building the independent Sulzer political machine. The raises were as much as 66 percent in some cases. These partisans also had their staffs increased and found new offices created to reward their loyalty.[17] To illustrate his independence Sulzer appointed Dr. Eugene H. Porter as health commissioner and Martin Decker as chair of the Public Service Commission, Second Department. Both were Republicans. He also appointed James M. Clancy, an enemy of Charlie Murphy, as warden of Sing Sing, and John H. Hanify, the manager of his direct primary tour, as state hospital commissioner.[18]

In the meantime, the Frawley Committee continued its investigations. Phase II concerned the use — or abuse — of the governor's patronage and veto power. A number of assemblymen and senators were interviewed under oath by the committee. These legislators testified that the governor had vetoed legislation important to them *only* because they would not support Sulzer's direct primary legislation. None offered any specific proof, but taken together the testimony painted a picture of a man dead set on a direct primary — and willing to trade anything to have his bill approved — no matter the important and beneficial legislation that might suffer or the consequences to the state.

On July 23 the Frawley Committee offered a preliminary report to the legislature asking for more time to continue its investigation because of the "many important matters" that still required the committee's attention. Rather than adjourning, which would have ended the legislative year, the legislature kept itself alive by recessing its extraordinary session, thus ensuring that the members would be available to take official actions on the matter as needed.[19] Of course, and this was perhaps equally important, this action blocked the governor from making any recess appointments or filling many of the positions from which he had fired Tammany loyalists.[20]

The governor was not amused. Valentine Taylor, Sulzer's top legal advisor, issued a statement, "regarding the power of the Frawley Committee to annoy and harass the Governor and other citizens of the State." Taylor said the committee had no right to do many of the things it wanted to do, and it especially had no right to question Sulzer's campaign fund because such an investigation violated the separation of powers. Moreover, the state constitution limited the legislature's business while in special session to subjects specifically brought up by the governor.[21]

Through Taylor, Sulzer asked Attorney General Thomas Carmody for an opinion on the power and jurisdiction of the Frawley Committee. Senator Frawley was outraged, saying, "The pitiful thing is that the Governor should try to stand on technicalities to avoid inquiry into his conduct."[22] The attorney general agreed. Carmody shot down the governor and his legal team on every point and explicitly declared that the Frawley Committee had the power to investigate Sulzer's campaign fund.

His campaign fund would prove to be worth investigating.

17

THE SULZER CAMPAIGN FUND

ON JULY 30, 1913, THE FRAWLEY COMMITTEE began public hearings. The immediate focus was Sulzer's 1912 campaign committee. New York State election law, under a provision commonly known as the Corrupt Practices Act, provided that all candidates for statewide offices had to sign a sworn statement detailing their campaign contributions and campaign spending. William Sulzer had signed a statement to conform with this act on November 13, 1912, in which he claimed that from September 23, 1912, through November 4, 1912, he raised $5,460.00 from sixty-eight contributors and spent $7,724.09.

The first piece of evidence examined by the Frawley Committee, a check for $2,500 from prominent banker Jacob H. Schiff, raised serious questions about Sulzer's sworn statement. Dated October 14, 1912, the check had written on its face: "Mr. Schiff's contribution towards William Sulzer's campaign expenses." It had been deposited into Sulzer's campaign account but was not listed on Sulzer's detailed report to the secretary of state.

Next, the committee called its first witness, Louis Sarecky, who had long been in the employ of William Sulzer as an assistant and secretary.

Sarecky refused to answer any question put to him about Sulzer's accounts and campaign funds. Instead, he continually requested an appearance by his counsel in order to "bring out the whole story and not one side of it."[1] Sarecky also repeatedly challenged the legitimacy of the Frawley Committee on technical grounds relating to the timing of its creation and the timing of the legislature's adjournment.

The Frawley Committee was outraged by Sarecky's refusal to answer questions and in retaliation asked the committee's counsel to prepare an arrest warrant for Sarecky for being in "contempt" of the legislature. Almost immediately, the committee also produced a $500 check from Abraham I. Elkus (counsel to the Triangle Fire Committee) that was not listed on Sulzer's sworn statement. Implicating him further, the committee produced an October 5, 1912, letter signed by Sulzer acknowledging Elkus's contribution and produced evidence proving that the check was deposited into William Sulzer's personal bank account.[2]

Clearly, appearances were against the governor. As he had so many times before when things were not going well, Sulzer went on the attack, issuing a lengthy statement accusing Charlie Murphy of perpetrating a "gigantic fraud" in order to "shield the thieves." The whole thing, Sulzer claimed, had been made up by Murphy to shift the blame to the governor and away from himself because it was Murphy himself who personally gained from campaign monies.[3]

Throughout this whole affair—as he had during the course of his career—Murphy laid low, out of the public eye, preferring to send messages through subordinates and refusing to speak to the press. Sulzer's latest attack was too much even for the taciturn Murphy. The Tammany leader sent an open letter to the Frawley Committee. In part, the letter read, "If Governor Sulzer has any information as to misconduct on my part relating to campaign contributions I request him to furnish it to your committee, and I will appear for examination at any time."[4] Offering to take the witness stand—offering sworn testimony—was unprecedented for the boss.

Sulzer ignored Murphy's challenge to produce evidence, preferring to continue his attacks on the boss. Everywhere he went, the governor declared that he would have no trouble with the legislature if not for Murphy's "outside influences and...dictations."[5] Sulzer also kept up the rhetoric of a man martyred for his cause: "The proposition is a simple one. I am trying to put the great issue to the front—graft and crooks—my enemies are constantly trying to put me to the front. My personality is nothing compared to the issue at stake."[6] Sulzer also suddenly remembered Murphy's threats to have him impeached if he would not go along with Tammany's plans, accusing Murphy of threatening him at their April 13 meeting (a meeting that Sulzer first denied ever took place), saying, "In six weeks I will have you out of office!"[7]

Continuing to characterize himself as the victim, the governor said he knew how to have avoided this fight. "All I had to do," said Sulzer, "was to sit tight, do what the boss told me like a nice, good little Governor, and be given the nomination for Governor next year, and the nomination for the Presidency of the United States thereafter."[8]

Sulzer's rhetoric was working...to some extent. Many of the governor's friends supported him in spite of the revelations surrounding his campaign fund and the discrepancies in his sworn statement, but that support came with the caveat that they urged him to come clean about any irregularities during his campaign. A friendly editor in the *New York World* wrote, "In a matter of this kind the issue cannot be shifted. The Governor cannot vindicate himself by refusing to testify or by accepting a Scotch [not proven] verdict. Such charges against a Governor are charges that have to be disproved. They are not charges that can rest unproved."[9]

The governor's first effort to come clean failed. Sulzer said he had been away on the campaign trail when the Schiff and Elkus checks were deposited. His office, Sulzer insisted, had handled the transactions and his office staff had simply made a mistake. On October 8, 1912, however—a date after the checks were deposited—he had declared in his voluble campaign style that "William Sulzer was a man of the People" and as such he had no collector of campaign contributions.[10] Much more damaging than the obvious doublespeak was this fact: Sulzer did not leave for his campaign swing until October 18, several days after the checks were deposited.[11]

The evidence against Governor Sulzer, both in front of the Frawley Committee and in the court of public opinion, was already quite damaging and one has to wonder why—or even how—Sulzer could insist so resolutely on his innocence. Was he delusional, truly believing he had done nothing wrong? Or was he, like so many politicians from Julius Caesar to the present day, a man capable of embodying the qualities of both saint and sinner, with no moral qualms whatsoever? Or perhaps William Sulzer had simply danced out of so many scrapes over so many years that he trusted his supporters to believe in his charm more than the Frawley Committee's facts and voters to hate the graft and corruption of the Tammany organization enough to obscure his own crimes and erase any memory that he owed his political career—and even the governor's chair—to that same political machine.

Certainly, the Frawley Committee was not impressed by Sulzer's charms nor would they be deterred his obfuscation, misdirection, or allegations. They were on a roll and moved their hearings to New York City, specifically the city council chambers. The move was intended to bring the committee closer to witnesses and, significantly, closer to several banks.[12] These hearings picked up where the Albany hearings had left off, producing more damaging evidence against Governor Sulzer.

Most notably, the committee heard testimony and examined evidence of additional unreported contributions and reports that Sulzer spent extraordinary large sums on stocks, all purchased on margin. The unreported checks were from prominent donors including William F. McCombs, chair of the Democratic National Committee ($500); Henry Morgenthau, chair of the Democratic National Committee's Finance Committee ($1,000); and John Lynn, financier ($500).

Evidence presented to the committee showed that there were ninety-four checks and significant cash deposits made into the Sulzer campaign account between October 1, 1912, and November 12, 1912, the date when Sulzer signed the statement—all in all, a total of $12,405.93.[13] Sulzer's secretary, Louis Sarecky, had made most of the deposits personally. Sulzer had even sent a letter to his bank on October 12, 1912, giving Sarecky the power to endorse checks in his (Sulzer's) name.

In addition to the campaign deposits, evidence presented to the committee showed sizable deposits into Sulzer's personal bank accounts roughly corresponding to the period when Sulzer became a candidate (September 1, 1912) through the end of the year (December 31, 1912). The deposits — mostly cash — totaled $24,395.31, for a balance at the end of the year of $22,527.47.[14] That amount of $24,395 would be equivalent to $532,178 today.[15]

In addition to the deposits into his personal account, the Frawley Committee heard evidence that Sulzer avidly speculated in stocks during his campaign for governor. Stocks and brokerage firms had played a prominent role in earlier New York State scandals and were a favorite means of corrupting, or at least influencing, state legislators. In 1910 state superintendent of insurance William Horace Hotchkiss undertook a special investigation into corruption in the capitol at the request of Governor Charles Evans Hughes.

Hotchkiss's report showed that in a single month in the summer of 1903, an agent of the New York City railway interests sent the sum of $40,000 to the firm of Ellingwood & Cunningham. The money was sent without vouchers or receipts. Hotchkiss established that this brokerage house was the firm that served as a "clearing-house" for the money supplied to members of the legislature by a lobbyist for the railway interests.

Furthermore, the report showed that Senator Louis F. Goodsell and Assemblyman Louis Bedell, prominent Republican leaders, had received large amounts from the Metropolitan Railway Company, as much as $24,800 for Goodsell and $21,750 for Bedell. Goodsell admitted that he had "bought" stock without putting up any margin.

In fact, it appeared that at least ten prominent Republican legislators who had ruled important senate and assembly committees for years had speculative accounts with Ellingwood & Cunningham. At the same hearings, H. H. Vreeland, president of the Metropolitan Street Railway Company, testified about paying out fully $250,000 in "taking up" stocks that legislators and other politicians had been carrying with brokerage houses and which they desired converted into cash.[16] Now Governor Sulzer was accused of having similar brokerage accounts and making large purchases of stock on margin without collateral.

Testimony in front of the Frawley Committee established that Sulzer had a brokerage account at the firm of Fuller and Gray, and during the campaign he purchased 200 shares of Cleveland, Chicago, Cincinnati, and St. Louis stock, colloquially known as "Big Four" stock. A congressman from Manhattan purchasing stock was not, in and of itself, a problem. The problem was that Sulzer had always carefully cultivated an image as a man of the people and was generally thought to be poor or, at the very least, far from wealthy. The problem, as the Frawley Committee saw it, was that the account at Fuller and Gray was quite suspicious and other, more independent observers agreed.

First, the stock account was not recorded, as was tradition at Fuller and Gray, under Sulzer's name or address but instead was mysteriously listed as "Account Number 500." Second, the "Big Four" stock was purchased with $11,800 in cash ($257,476 in today's money). Third, Sulzer had not paid for the stock himself, but a man named Frederick L. Colwell had delivered the cash to purchase the stock. Finally, testimony in front of the Frawley Committee established that Sulzer's identity as owner of the account was generally known among the firm although Colwell himself had refused to answer the committee's subpoena and had instead gone into hiding (earning him a charge of contempt similar to that levied against Sarecky).

More testimony produced evidence of a second secret account, this one at the firm of Harris and Fuller. Mr. Fuller, following in Sarecky's and Colwell's footsteps, initially refused to testify or answer any questions from the committee before returning a day later under threat of contempt charges. At that point he offered to answer all questions that the committee might be pleased to ask.

Under questioning, Fuller admitted his firm kept an account for Sulzer and that in an effort to keep Sulzer's identity a secret, the account was listed only as number Sixty-Three. Fuller testified that Sulzer had bought 500 shares of Big Four as well as 100 shares of stock in both American Smelters and Southern Pacific Rail Road. The total value of the stock was $48,599.39. Using the Department of Labor numbers, that would be worth over $1 million today. The stock had been all purchased on margin. As stock market conditions worsened, Harris and Fuller asked Sulzer again and again to pay his debt but were ignored. Harris and Fuller took matters into their own hands, selling some of the stock but a debt for the enormous sum of $26,739.21 remained due for some time. After the Frawley Committee was convened, on July 15 Lieutenant Commander Louis M. Josephthal—a member of the governor's military staff—paid the remaining balance and closed account Sixty-Three.

Every day of testimony in front of the Frawley Committee seemed to produce more and more donations to the Sulzer campaign that were not accounted for in Sulzer's sworn statement. Many were endorsed by Sulzer himself, and a few of them were traced by the committee to a third brokerage firm, Boyer, Griswald and Company. The committee heard evidence that the aforementioned Frederick Colwell had purchased an additional 200 shares of "Big Four" stock at Boyer, Griswald and Company. These shares were paid for in part with a personal check from William Sulzer for $900. The balance was paid with $7,125 in cash and certified checks for $4,000. The certified checks were made out to Sulzer's campaign and signed over to the brokerage firm.

Senator Frawley summed up the findings of his investigation this way: "When our committee began work we had a hunch that the full account of the Governor's campaign expenditures had not been published as the law requires, but it was a surprise to all of us to find that he had used some of the money constituted for his political expenses to try a flyer in Wall Street."[17]

On August 8, 1913, Senator Frawley offered the opinion of the committee that William Sulzer knowingly violated the Corrupt Practices Act and there was no point in the committee continuing its investigation further. Instead of the committee continuing its work, Frawley declared, it was time for action.

18

IMPEACHMENT

There was no doubt that the Frawley Committee had uncovered inflammatory and damning information on Governor Sulzer, but there were differing opinions among Tammany's leaders on how to proceed. Some feared a backlash from hounding Sulzer too aggressively, and they suggested turning the committee's evidence over to a special prosecutor or district attorney to prosecute.[1] But leaving Sulzer to the courts could take months and would almost certainly extend things past November, and the entire legislature was up for reelection in November.

Meanwhile, Sulzer's support was dropping precipitously. "Sulzer's failure to utter a single word during the hearings regarding the serious disclosures made and his apparent determination to suppress vital testimony was constituted by many, even those who were kindly disposed towards him, as a confession of guilt."[2] A New York City reformer went on the record, "There were signs on all sides that he was losing the support of persons of independent political tendencies, who had applauded the fight he had been making ... against Boss Murphy."[3]

The normally loquacious Sulzer—answering every charge and allegation with fierce denials and truculent counterattacks—had turned silent.

The governor went into seclusion, avoiding his office where the press corps was lying in wait, and refusing to speak to reporters who had the pluck to try to call on him at the People's House. His credibility shattered along with his political future, the ever expansive Sulzer perhaps had a crisis of confidence or may just have been plotting his next move. Whatever the cause, he would not utter a single word in his defense until the end of the committee hearings when he would, somewhat anticlimactically, read and review the record.[4]

Belated attempts by the governor's allies to respond to the growing list of charges not only rang hollow but also fell far short of what was needed. On August 7 the governor's secretary, Chester Platt, issued a statement that said, "Some of these charges are false, some are distorted truths, easily explained, and some of these charges are insinuations about which, at present, the Governor is wholly ignorant."[5]

The majority of the press, up until now supportive of Sulzer—or at least supportive of his fight against Tammany Hall—found it difficult to defend him.

In a stinging editorial, the *New York Times* wrote,

> The people of New York do not want to believe these shocking things of the Governor of the State but if the charges are untrue, why does not Mr. Sulzer deny them at once? If he has any explanation, why does he not make it? To make countercharges against Mr. Murphy and to seek to ferret out wrongful practices, chargeable to the Murphy influence, in the State departments is no answer to the evidence affecting Mr. Sulzer's reputation and honor. Can he be so blind as not to see that his silence be construed as confession, that any attempt on his part to baffle the committee in its work or to evade a full investigation will also be construed as confession.[6]

The *New York World* was equally unsparing: "It was not Murphy who signed William Sulzer's name to a false statement of campaign contributions and expenditures" or diverted campaign funds. The editors urged Sulzer to "spare the State of New York further shame and humiliation" by resigning.[7] Sulzer's argument (that these forces were only allied against him because he was succeeding in his fight against corruption) was also falling apart with this loss of support from newspapers and independent reformers.

The *New-York Tribune* had also had enough:

> The prostitution of all the agencies of government to the purposes of a factional fight between the Governor and Murphy has been a sickening fight for all right-minded citizens. It is not half as sickening as to see a Governor who went into office with bright prospects and who had the People's confidence and support while they believed he was honestly fighting corruption, remain silent under disgraceful charges affecting his personal integrity and his political honor.[8]

The *New York Evening Post*, an independent voice, regarded as neither a Tammany nor a Sulzer paper, wrote, "The man who has dragged the good name of New York in the dirt should take himself out of its sight." We prefer, they wrote, "a plain, unadulterated Tammany rascal, who stands for what he is, to a single political sinner turned saint for a moment and calling for aid to overthrow his quondam pals and bosses in the name of that political justice, decency, and honestly he so long helped to violate."[9]

Even William Randolph Hearst's *American* wrote, "The undeniable fact that the offenses charged are at variance with Governor Sulzer's entire career and known character before his nomination does not change the pitiless fact that Governor Sulzer cannot escape impeachment and removal from office, and possible conviction of crime, unless he can answer them."[10]

Apparently the criticism was hitting home with Sulzer. After meeting with his top advisors, the governor issued the following written statement at 1:00 a.m. on August 11, 1912, refuting the allegations:

> I deny that I used any campaign contributions for personal use. I deny that I speculated in Wall Street or used money contributed for campaign purposes to buy stocks either in my own name or otherwise. I never had an account with Fuller and Gray or Boyer and Griswold. I never heard of these firms; do not know the members and knew nothing about the transactions which these firms testified to before the Frawley Committee until recently threatened with exposure and the alleged transactions were brought to my attention by the Farley Committee. The stock matter with Harris and Fuller was not a speculative account or matter, but a loan made upon stocks as collateral, which stocks had been acquired and paid for years before my nomination for the office of Governor and from other sources than Harris and Fuller. Certain checks given to me for campaign purposes were deposited to my personal account, and thereafter I paid the amount of said checks to my Campaign Committee. In filing my statement of receipts and disbursements with the Secretary of State I relied on information furnished me by the persons in immediate charge of my campaign, and in whom I had, and have, the most implicit confidence, and I believe the statement furnished by them to be accurate and true.[11]

The response, such as it was, was full of holes and inaccuracies and failed to address the most serious charges. But if the governor's statement went out with a whimper, the battle in the legislature was set to be a true bang.

On August 11 the assembly was scheduled to receive the report of the Frawley Committee, and legislative leaders spent a great deal of the day in conference, trying to get their story—and their plans—straight. When the assembly gaveled into session, slightly after 10:00 p.m., the atmosphere was electric. The immense assembly chamber is the largest room in the New York State capitol, and it was filled as a record crowd of curious spectators crammed the galleries. Fewer than 100 of the 150 members of the lower house were in attendance. Many members were in an angry mood; some showed fight. The spirit of belligerency transcended party lines. The Moorish Gothic–designed interior appeared spooky as the shadows flickered through stained-glass windows.* The August heat, a high of seventy-eight on this day, was as stifling in the sandstone room.[12]

As for the governor, Sulzer's usual habit when the legislature was in session at night was to visit the capitol himself. Not this night.[13] The session began with a number of parliamentary maneuvers by the pro-Sulzer forces—procedural attempts to put a stop to the proceedings. Assemblyman Hinman, the Republican leader in the assembly, urged the reconsideration of the vote to approve the Assembly Journal of July 23. Included in that journal was the vote to recess, a vote that Sulzer and his partisans would afterward claim lacked a quorum. A vote to reject the Assembly Journal would have rendered these whole proceedings technically moot and put the legislature into adjournment.[14] In what was a harbinger of things to come, the motion failed by a vote of 30-66.

Nonetheless, Hinman's vocal support of Governor Sulzer came as a surprise to Democratic leaders. State Republican chairman Barnes saw the whole Sulzer/Murphy feud as an interparty squabble and was intent to "leave them to it," and Democrats expected Hinman to follow Barnes's lead.[15]

Senator Frawley presented his report: "We submit to the Senate and Assembly that the facts stated are sufficiently serious in character and are so volatile of the laws of this State and the rules of fitness for, and conduct in, high office, that the public interests demand some action in reference thereto whether through the exercise of the powers of the Legislature, or by referring the facts and evidence to other duly constituted officers charged with duties in respect thereof." Frawley continued, "The questions here involved are vital to clean government. They are above party or

---

* Today's assembly chamber, while impressive, bears little resemblance to the original 1879 chamber. As the foundation in the capitol began to settle, the stone ceiling cracked and broke. A new ceiling obscures the beautiful murals but protects the assembly members.

partisanship. They are vital to the citizens of the state and call for prompt and well-considered action. They call for an answer from Governor Sulzer because both his obstructive tactics and his silence warrant the conclusion that the charges can neither be answered nor explained." Senator Frawley also recommended the punishment of Sarecky and Colwell for being in contempt of the legislature.[16]

Frawley conceded that although his committee had not prepared a full report, there was enough evidence to proceed. He declared that it was time, not for further reports, but to act. Assemblyman Hinman forcefully disagreed. The Republican leader wanted to remain aloof from the "disgraceful" quarrel within the Democratic Party, but, he insisted, a response was still necessary to preserve the good name of the state of New York.[17] Hinman argued, "While Sulzer may not have been a good official, he is entitled to fair treatment. We are not concerned with Sulzer the man, but Sulzer the governor. We have our own dignity to maintain."[18] Assemblyman Michael J. Schaap, leader of the Progressive Party in the legislature, joined Hinman in Sulzer's defense. "I ask you," said Schaap, "to look well into your consciousness before you adopt without reading recommendations based on this testimony.[19] The House voted 65-35 to adopt the Frawley report.

In the senate, the debate went the same way. Senator Duhamel, a Hearst man through and through, elected with the support of both the Democratic Party and Independence League, said that the Frawley Committee had set out deliberately to crucify the governor. Frawley immediately denied it, claiming to be a friend of the governor and saddened by this tragic chain of events but "was drown[ed] out by the loud laughter of the spectators."[20] Having received the report, Aaron J. Levy, the Democratic majority leader, introduced a resolution that restated the many charges against Sulzer and called for the governor's impeachment "for willful and corrupt conduct in office, and high crimes and misdemeanors."[21] The resolution was set down for consideration the next day. Some objected to the rush. Assemblyman Gibbs, for instance, said, "If William Sulzer were the greatest wretch that ever crawled this earth, you are not giving him a square deal. I blush for my

"IMPEACHMENT"

Assembly Majority Leader Aaron J. Levy (at bottom left) reads the charges and called for the Governor's impeachment "for willful and corrupt conduct in office, and high crimes and misdemeanors." Meanwhile, the crowd in the Assembly Chamber was eight deep. The Albany police were called in to reinforce the Capitol orderlies, hoping to keep the peace.

party and its leadership to have to say so."[22] Nonetheless, Hinman's resolution to wait a week for consideration and further review was defeated by the same 64-30 vote.

On the next day, August 12, 1912, the assembly convened at 11:00 a.m. and immediately adjourned until 8:30 that evening. In the meantime, deputy sergeants at arms scattered throughout town compelling members to take their seats. A crowd "larger than any that ever stormed the Capitol in the memory of the oldest attendant poured through the doorways hours before the time set."[23] The crowd was eight deep, and the Albany police were called in to reinforce the capitol orderlies, hoping to keep the peace.

Rumors were rampant. One had Sulzer's supporters rushing the Speaker's room and adjourning the session sine die. Another had the governor, as commander in chief of the state, calling out the militia and refusing to allow the legislature to sit.[24] Neither likely had any basis in fact, but access to the floor of the legislature was nevertheless limited to those carrying a card signed by the assembly Speaker and countersigned by a second member of the assembly.[25]

Hour after hour, the debate continued with various moves by the major players. Sulzer summoned Tammany legislators to the Executive Mansion. One of the few who answered the call, James C. Campbell of New York County, reported the governor to have implored, "I have tried to do what is right. If you have a heart, if you have red blood in your veins, you ought to stand by me."[26] Senator Frawley reported his exchange with the governor thus: "Jim, this has gone too far. I didn't expect anything like this and I know you didn't." When Frawley rejected the governor's pleas, Sulzer responded, "Let me tell you that if I am impeached there will be a revolution in New York within twenty-four hours. The people elected me and they won't stand for me being removed this way."[27]

The governor was also frantically working the phones and telegraph. Most of the telegrams followed the same pattern as this one to an ally in Buffalo:

> Will you telephone or telegraph Assemblyman Geoghan [a Buffalo member] immediately? He voted for Frawley report yesterday, but I think if you can reach him you can prevent him from voting for the impeachment. Answer. Can you help with other Assemblymen? You ought to be in Albany.[28]

When the telegraph bill of the Executive Mansion was reviewed later, there was evidence to suggest that Sulzer had been communicating with Franklin D. Roosevelt, assistant secretary of the navy, and John Purroy Mitchel, collector of the Port of New York, in an attempt to get President Wilson to intervene on his behalf.[29] Throughout it all, Charlie Murphy was at home in New York City, monitoring events by phone.[30]

While the members were being rounded up throughout Albany,[31] the assemblymen "smoked, chatted, read the papers, giving no sign in their demeanor that anything serious was at hand."[32] A few minutes after 10:00 p.m., Speaker Al Smith announced, "The gentlemen in the gallery will kindly stop smoking," and the body was called to order.[33]

The floor of the legislature was a battleground. The charges of the pro-Sulzer faction were exemplified in the words of Assemblyman Gibbs: "Everybody knows that the reason why Sulzer is being demanded as a victim is that he had the manhood to refuse to be tied to the wheels of a certain political chariot."[34] The governor's supporters argued also that the legislature was in special session and therefore lacked the power to impeach.* The leaders denied both charges. Impeachment, they maintained, was appropriate—and in fact necessary—whenever there was malfeasance. The assembly leadership (all Tammany men) insisted Sulzer was being impeached because he was unfit to hold his office, not because of who his friends were. Protecting the people knew no limits.[35]

A shockwave hit the legislative chambers around 2:00 a.m. with the revelation that Mrs. Sulzer had confessed to everything. The surprise was audible as word of her confession reached the galleries.

The former Miss Clara Rodelheim of Philadelphia had been, to this point in her husband's career, "noted chiefly for her attention to the duties of her household." A nurse educated in the Graduate Nurses' College at Columbia, she was the archetype of a dutiful political wife. Her public persona was typified by interviews such as this: "I love to read, and to sew, and to cook, and to make cake, and to attempt new dishes. I like visiting my friends, and I do like above all other things to have a new friend to lunch and to cook every particle of food myself. It is genuine liberty to sit down and serve yourself without a black-browed servitor standing by idly, scowling at you if you linger."

---

* According to the New York State Constitution, the legislature, while in special session, could only consider matters brought to its attention by the governor. Sulzer had clearly not asked the legislature to consider his impeachment.

CHAPTER EIGHTEEN

"Mrs. Clara Sulzer"

The Sulzer forces continued after the vote to insist that Mrs. Sulzer would testify at his trial, telling the truth and ending the inquiry. Her husband's handlers later put out word that she had a nervous breakdown and was unable or unfit to testify when the time came. More likely the whole episode was a sham.

Mrs. Sulzer, according to a "source close to the family," had told the governor and Louis Marshall, one of his lawyers, that she had signed her husband's names to checks received as campaign contributions. The declaration, and the realization of its impact on her husband and his political career, had left her "prostrated" and in the midst of a nervous breakdown so severe that Sulzer "telegraphed to New York for Dr. Abrams, a nerve specialist."[36]

Her claim was that she had, without Sulzer's knowledge, put campaign checks into the stock market to revive the family's finances. The governor, she said, had "gallantly refused to allow her to be drawn" into the fray, which is why she had remained quiet until the last minute.[37] Assemblyman Hinman and the governor's other friends seized on this as the perfect justification to delay the vote. Levy and the Democratic leadership labeled this as just another attempt at delay, noting that Sulzer's stock speculation had started *before* his marriage and that the correspondence from Harris and Fuller had been addressed to *William* Sulzer.*

The debate concluded with an almost two-hour speech by Majority Leader Levy just after 3:00 a.m. At that point, one observer remarked, "Those not assuredly asleep were not discernibly awake, save for the party leaders and their active lieutenants."[38]

The impeachment resolution was passed after the assembly had been in session for over seven hours of long speeches, debate, and delay. Tammany Hall had not achieved so much electoral success without having mastered the essential political skill of vote counting, and the organization's floor managers knew they lacked the necessary votes to pass the impeachment resolutions.

Instead, they resorted to another timeworn political technique; they stalled until key Tammany votes, summoned during the early hours from New York City, arrived in the assembly chambers. Assured of victory, the floor leaders gave the necessary signal and the long debate was suddenly

---

* The Sulzer forces continued after the vote to insist that Mrs. Sulzer would testify at his trial, telling the truth and ending the inquiry. Her husband's handlers later put out word that she had a nervous breakdown and was unable or unfit to testify when the time came. More likely the whole episode was a sham.

called to a halt, replaced with a rapid fire of legislation resulting in the adoption of the impeachment resolutions.

The vote was seventy-nine in favor—three more than necessary for impeachment—with seven GOP members voting with seventy-two Democrats to impeach Sulzer. Voting against the measure were twenty-six Democrats, sixteen Republicans, and three Progressives.

The result was unprecedented in the history of U.S. politics: William Sulzer, forty-second governor of the state of New York, elected in November 1912 with 649,559 votes, had been impeached for "willful and corrupt conduct in office, and high crimes and misdemeanors."

In fact, many members had been slumbering in their seats during the tedious hours of the prolonged debate while others leaned back in their chairs and closed their eyes. There were audible sounds of deep and labored breathing from some of the members. Speaker Smith had enough of the rows of men with their heads thrust down on their chests and their eyes closed.

"A number of the members, I take it, are asleep in their chairs," Smith thundered, bring his gavel down with a resounding thump on his desk. More whacks of the gavel on the Speaker's desk, reinforced by thumping by newly awakened members on their desks, aroused the sleepers, and the rest of the assembly's business was concluded quite quickly. The assembly's final act, repassing the Blauvelt elections bill by a vote of 108-5, added a final insult to the injury.[39]

The assembly adjourned at 7:30 a.m. Two hundred spectators were all that remained of the crowd that had filled the capitol earlier in the day to witness this historic event. What the *New York Times* called "the heaviest guard of uniformed police ever sent into the Capitol, each armed with nightstick and revolver," joined those departing the galleries and the elected officials as they exited the assembly chamber, leaving behind the stale odor of half-smoked cigars, hundreds of torn papers littering the floor, and lights slowly being put out.

The official action of the assembly had also appointed two committees, one to officially inform the senate of Governor William Sulzer's impeach-

"Stand Firm! The People Believe in You."

The furtive, hurried manner in which Sulzer's impeachment was conducted changed the tide of public opinion. A formerly castigating press and general public now voiced their outrage at the process and the outcome, preferring to ignore Sulzer's sins and focus on those of Tammany Hall. The sign behind Sulzer, the gift of loyal constituents, reads: "Our Governor: **Stand Firm!** *The People believe in you. The attempt to overturn the Head of Government is TREASON."*

ment and another to draft the formal articles of impeachment. After a recess of only an hour, the official articles of impeachment were presented to the senate by the committee led by Majority Leader Aaron J. Levy.

The eight articles of impeachment were expansive. The first charged Sulzer with making and filing a false statement on his campaign accounts with the secretary of state. The second charged perjury in verifying this statement. The third, bribing witnesses before the Frawley Committee. Fourth, suppressing evidence by threats. Fifth, preventing a witness from testifying. Sixth, larceny in using campaign contributions for personal use. Seventh, threatening to use the power and influence of his office to influence the action of other public officials and threatening to veto bills unless assemblymen interested in them supported his legislation. Eighth, corruptly using his influence to affect current prices of securities by urging legislation relating to the New York Stock Exchange and then attempting to withdraw the subject from the consideration of the legislature, which concealed his interests in exchange transactions.

The assembly had also appointed nine members to serve as impeachment managers or prosecutors to present the case in favor of impeachment to the Court of Impeachment. The managers were:

- Aaron Levy, Democrat of New York County and majority leader of the assembly
- Patrick Joseph McMahon, Democrat of Bronx County
- Abraham Greenberg, Democrat of New York County
- William J. Gillen, Democrat of Kings County and chair, Assembly Committee on Electricity, Gas and Water Supply
- Theodore Hackett Ward, Democrat of New York
- Joseph Vincent Fitzgerald, Democrat of Erie County
- Tracey P. Madden, Democrat of Westchester County and chair, Assembly Committee of Penal Institutions
- Thomas K. Smith, Republican of Onondaga County
- Herman Ferdinand Schnirel, Republican of Ontario County

On August 13, at 11:00 a.m., the senate officially received Sulzer's impeachment. Senate president pro tem Robert Wagner set the Court of Impeachment for October 18 at noon.* The senate also passed, by a unanimous vote, the Blauvelt elections bill before recessing through October 19.

---

* The constitution provided that a month must pass between an impeachment and the convening of the Court of Impeachment.

19

THE FALLOUT

It was dawn when word of the final vote on the impeachment resolutions reached William Sulzer. He was sitting on the porch of the Executive Mansion with John Hennessy, his trusted political advisor. His faithful friend Samuel Bell Thomas was staying at the mansion and throughout the hours of debate had been running messages back and forth to the assembly chamber, in an effort to stave off the inevitable defeat.

Barely four hours later, the now impeached governor reached the capitol, walking with his friend Samuel Bell Thomas. Whether he had endless depths of optimism or was merely putting on a good show, it had an impact, even on the hardboiled reporters, who reported he looked "refreshed." Sulzer paused on the steps of the capitol to accommodate the photographers, but "It's a fine breeze" was all he would say in response to persistent requests for a statement about his future plans.

Although Sulzer did not appear at his desk, he spent hours closeted with supporters, including the editor in chief of the *Knickerbocker Press*, a fervent anti-impeachment paper, and his legal counselors. As he left the building just before six in the evening, Sulzer barely missed Patrick McCabe, the clerk of the senate and political boss of Albany County with whom he had feuded so publicly. McCabe was headed to the Executive Chambers to serve the governor with the complaint and summons as well as an official copy of the Articles of Impeachment.

Leaving the capitol, Sulzer would only tell the reporters that on the advice of counsel, neither he nor his wife would have any public statement until the impeachment trial convened.

Silence may have been more than a legal strategy. It was a very good public relations strategy as well.

The furtive, hurried manner in which the impeachment was conducted changed the tide of public opinion. A formerly castigating press and general public now voiced their outrage at the process and the outcome. The *Philadelphia Record* stated the change succinctly, that it is impossible "to believe that a man who had the moral courage to defy the powerful boss, with foreknowledge of the consequences, could have been guilty of such mean and dishonorable conduct in the administration of his campaign funds."[1]

The labor leader Samuel Gompers was disgusted "to see that some of the men with whom I had the honor of being associated in the [Triangle Shirtwaist Factory Fire Investigation] Commission... have been worked up, or are working themselves up, in a frenzied effort to 'get' the governor." As a result, Gompers cut off all contact with Senator Robert Wagner.[2]

The reversal of fortune continued. Jacob Alexis Friedman, author of one of the few objective histories on the impeachment, wrote, "Assuming even that [Sulzer] had been guilty of indiscretions and improprieties before coming into the governorship, many argued, he was deserving of a full pardon for the courage he revealed when he deliberately chose the road to possible ruin instead of the path to security and higher honors."[3] The Albany *Knickerbocker Press*, in an editorial on August 12, said that Sulzer had been impeached for seeking to deliver the state "from the clutches of professional spenders of the public treasury and the rule of the political

"A NUMBER OF THE MEMBERS, I TAKE IT, ARE ASLEEP IN THEIR CHAIRS"
The scene in the Assembly Chamber shortly before members voted to impeach Governor William Sulzer. Al Smith, sitting in the Speaker's chair (far left), needed to whack his gavel to wake up slumbering members. The vote was 79 to 45 in favor of impeachment.

bosses."[4] There was a widespread belief that the "prosecution was begun for purely political reasons, and that whatever truth there might be in the charges, they would never have been brought to light had he been a complaisant servant of Tammany Hall."[5] Others said, "It was not for his faults but for his virtues that he was being crucified."[6] "His crime, in Tammany eyes, was not that he made false returns of campaign contributions," said still others, "but that he tried to snatch the leadership of the Democratic party from Murphy's grip."[7] One of the more colorful analogies was that the Tammany boss ordered the governor's impeachment "as he would order a beefsteak at Delmonico's and a servile assembly voted the impeachment with more obsequiousness than a self-respecting French waiter would show to a grand duke."[8]

Even former president Theodore Roosevelt weighed in on the matter. In a letter to Sulzer he wrote, "I have yet to meet a single person who believes, or even pretends to believe, that a single honest motive has animated the proceedings of your antagonists.... We have never seen a more startling example of the power of the invisible government under the present system."[9]

Some publications acknowledged that Sulzer may, in fact, be guilty of certain indiscretions but that the alternatives were far worse. *The Nation*, for instance, stated, "It is not that Sulzer is admired or trusted but that Murphy is detested and feared. In the face of the grave charges against Governor Sulzer which are so strongly evidenced and which he has not met in a way at all satisfactory, he could hardly have a friend—or, at any rate, a defender—in the state, were it not for one circumstance. That circumstance is named Murphy. Hatred of him almost takes on the guise of love of Sulzer."[10]

The *Syracuse Journal* blatantly asked, "Which do you prefer—Sulzer, who grievously sinned before he became Governor, but who has been assailing vice in Tammany's citadel ever since that time, or Murphy in absolute control of the government?"[11]

The *World's Work* even asserted that the governor's guilt did not "particularly matter." It had been clear for some time, it said, that Sulzer had been unfit, and his unfitness was not the reason for his removal; he was impeached because of "his refusal to hand over the powers of his office to Tammany."[12] Some of the harshest words came from the *Knickerbocker Press* in Albany, which devoted countless pages to the hitherto "untold story" of "the most brazen attempt in the history of the world to overthrow constitutional government without resort to bloodshed."[13]

The criticism was universal throughout the country, from Democratic and Republican papers alike. Representative were the Louisville *Courier-Journal*, which held up Sulzer's impeachment as proof that the people of New York were "incapable of self-government,"[14] and the Baltimore *Sun* which advised its readers to "see in [the impeachment] what it is—the organized effort of an unscrupulous political making, which has always stood, and still stands, for all that is worse in politics and business, to maintain its supremacy and to keep the people out of their rights." Also the *Atlantic Journal*, "though Sulzer be guilty, the really dangerous criminal is not he, but his hypocritical accuser."[15]

Still, there were a few voices of dissent. Friedman points out, "The sole fight was for good government and clean politics; that the real enemy was political corruption which, at the time, was personified by Sulzer."[16] The *New York Times* asked, "Is there no way to combat Tammany save that of condoning all of Sulzer's faults and marching to the fray behind that inspiring leader, brandishing in one hand his Wall Street margin accounts and in the other his incomplete affidavit of campaign receipts and expenditures? Because Murphy is known to be a sinner, must the Sulzer transgressions one and all be overlooked?"[17]

Harper's Weekly joined in, condemning the "incomparable hypocrisy" of Tammany attacking Sulzer—its own selection—for his crimes, but noted, "Governor Sulzer cannot excuse himself by showing how bad is Tammany Hall. He must stand or fall by his own performances."[18] Theodore Roosevelt, never shy, advised the governor to give a "full and straightforward explanation and answer" to the charges at the "earliest opportunity." The former president said Sulzer owed it to himself—and to his supporters—to come clean.[19]

The *World*, historically a pro-Sulzer and anti-Tammany paper, called the impeachment "the most startling revelation of the degradation of government that New York had ever known." But the *World* gave Sulzer his share of the blame as well:

> A Governor is supposed to keep his skirts clear and his hands clean. He is supposed to respect the dignity of his great office and keep himself out of the clutches of political blackmailers. If he violated the law, if he plays fast and loose with his own integrity, if he deceives his supporters and betrays the principles which he pretends to represent, he must take the

consequences. He has betrayed the confidence and trust that honest men imposed in him, and that in itself was a form of moral treason.[20]

The *Springfield Republican* published this statement:

The country has been shown no such blatant hypocrisy in a public man in many a year. While gambling in stocks with recklessness that financially embarrassed him during his campaign for Governor, he was particularly vociferous about walking "in the street called straight" and after his election, this gubernatorial margin speculator became a zealous reformer of stock-exchange practice through legislation. That his fall may be traced to Wall Street gambling seems clear; but the man's brazen deception of the people in his public life makes that ordinary stock market trader seem a saint by comparison.[21]

On September 4 the Frawley Committee held its final meeting. They established that Sulzer's direct primary committee had raised $17,243.54 from donors with names like Morgenthau, Pulitzer, Astor, and Hearst. The final revelation (of sorts) was that the governor exceeded the state appropriation of $7,000 for his printing and publicity. The spending, according to the committee's counsel, violated the state constitution "by incurring expenditures in excess of the sum explicitly allowed for that purpose."[22] Nonetheless, the committee basically went dark.

Just as the Frawley Committee faded from the scene, the Assembly Impeachment Committee began holding hearings in its headquarters at 39 Wall Street. Their evidence conflicted with Mrs. Sulzer's "confession," from the checks being endorsed by Sulzer himself to the testimony of one of the stockbrokers—Melville Fuller—that he had never met or corresponded with Mrs. Sulzer. More damning was Fuller's production of a letter from the governor on July 14. The letter showed that "before his stock speculation with campaign funds had been exposed, Sulzer was already preparing to throw the entire blame on his wife."[23]

The hearings held by the assembly impeachment managers also found more unreported checks, including a number from brewery interests and "direct testimony that he made promises of favor and reward."[24] Other evidence showed that Sulzer was in debt $26,500 to Hugh J. Reilly (who had previously contracted with Sulzer to help with his claims against the Cuban government) from a loan without security or collateral.[25] The money from Reilly looked a great deal like a contribution. On the basis of the testimony, the managers considered "submitting supplementary impeachment articles to Assembly for adoption."[26]

The pro-Sulzer forces were not resting. A fund of $100,000 was raised to campaign against impeachment.[27] The crusade was led by the Albany's *Knickerbocker Press*, edited by former judge Lynn J. Arnold. The paper also printed weekly articles to expose Murphy's "dastardly attempt to seize the government of the State." The *Times* speculated that Arnold "was as interested in keeping Glynn out as Governor as keeping Sulzer in as Governor." Lieutenant Governor Glynn was also the publisher of the *Times Union*, a competing Albany Democratic paper. Arnold was a member of Sulzer's "war board" and, according to an advertisement in the *World*, promised his expose would prove that compared to Boss Murphy, "Aaron Burr was a novice and Tweed a piker" when it came to corruption.[28] Arnold also promised to expose bribery, perjury, and corruption, enough to indict Speaker Smith and both Senators Frawley and Wagner.

Meanwhile, Special Investigator Hennessy (who, as the governor's closest advisor, had sat with Sulzer through the impeachment vote) "speeded up his investigation of all Tammany-controlled state departments, despite the fact that the Comptroller's office had cut off his funds."[29] It was understood that private individuals provided means for the investigation to continue.[30] "Fraud," said Hennessy in a letter to Sulzer, "stands out as clearly as a mountain peak from a valley. All we need is the men and the time to get the legal evidence." He claimed to have a $5 million "trail of graft" leading to government officials and prominent Murphy lieutenants in upstate.[31]

But Sulzer's impeachment broke the force of Hennessy's investigation. Horgan, Delaney, and other important witnesses summoned by Hennessy refused to appear, maintaining that the impeachment had removed Sulzer, and with it, Hennessy had lost all power as his "personal representative."[32]

Sulzer, in a message to supporters, said,

> I am having a terrific struggle to resist the seizure of the State by those who have looted it, and would prostitute its government for private gain. When Mr. Murphy and his allies found out that they could not make a tool of me they attempted to block me every step. They could not, however, stop the machinery of justice, which I had set in motion against the criminals throughout the State, who have robbed taxpayers of millions of dollars. There was only one way for my enemies to prevent me from sending these thieves to the penitentiary, and that way was to impeach me and get me out of office.[33]

There were reports in the press that Sulzer's "war board" would ask for the indictment of Al Smith, Aaron Levy, and other assembly leaders for conspiring to coerce certain members to vote for the impeachment resolution, in obedience to Murphy's orders. The whole impeachment, Sulzer's war board alleged, was "part of a criminal plot of the Tammany Boss and his Board of Strategy to seize control of the government of the state for Tammany Hall."[34] Like the rest of the attacks on Tammany Hall and Boss Murphy, these allegations would never be more than mere rhetoric.

In an interesting aside, James C. Garrison, a newspaperman and publicity agent for Sulzer, made a speech where he "declare[d] now and positively that Tammany paid cash for the four votes it needed to pass the impeachment resolution."[35] Garrison was called before the assembly Judiciary Committee, where he refused to answer any questions, instead telling the committee to "call Murphy" and get "some real information."[36] The assembly found Garrison guilty of contempt for offending the body's "dignity" and "the honor and integrity of its members."[37] He was arrested in the assembly chamber on September 18 and kept in a penitentiary until after the impeachment trial, when he was released on a writ of habeas corpus.[38]

Throughout this time, the legislature was meeting at irregular intervals to pass appropriation and deficiency bills, including an appropriation of $75,000 to cover the expense of the impeachment trial (plus a supplemental bill to pay $121,000 to cover additional expenses and counsel for the board of managers and $40,000 to pay Sulzer's lawyers).[39] The legislature also passed concurrent resolutions declaring Colwell and Sarecky in contempt of the legislature. Levy, chair of the managers, outright accused Sulzer of hiding Colwell to prevent him from testifying.[40]

On the eve of the trial, both sides were optimistic. "I expect a fair trial," said Sulzer, "and I know that I shall be acquitted."[41] Assemblyman Levy, on the other hand, said the trial would offer evidence so "horrifying and repulsive that the court could not help but convict."[42]

Senator Wagner, a little less confident, said the decision of the court would be "in accordance with the evidence." Wagner was also pushing back on the Sulzer-as-victim narrative: "I am getting tired of all this talk that William Sulzer is being persecuted by Tammany Hall. Neither Tammany Hall nor any other political organization will sway the result of the impeachment trial. The verdict will be influenced neither by the sentiment of the Senators nor by public opinion. Every Senator will feel as fully the responsibility resting upon him as if he were a Judge of the Court of Appeals."[43]

The Court of Impeachment would determine who was right, but not before a constitutional power struggle of astonishing proportions.

20

GOVERNOR GLYNN?

THE IMPEACHMENT OF GOVERNOR SULZER raised a vitally important question: Who was in charge of New York State? Lieutenant Governor Martin Glynn had gone to great lengths to avoid the spotlight during the impeachment fight. Glynn was an independent Democrat, not allied with Tammany Hall. In fact, he had a great deal of support from reformers at the 1912 Democratic State Convention that ended with William Sulzer's nomination for governor. Having served in Congress and as New York State comptroller, Glynn was the editor, publisher, and owner of the *Albany Times Union* when he was nominated for lieutenant governor.

For the first six months of the Sulzer administration, the lieutenant governor and governor had a strong working relationship: Sulzer conferred with Glynn regularly, and the latter felt his advice was at least valued, if not always taken. That was until Governor Sulzer vetoed legislation to create the Mohawk River Hydro Power Project. Cheap and plentiful power was a legislative goal of Martin Glynn's, and the Mohawk River Hydro Plant had been a particular priority of the lieutenant governor, who had lobbied fiercely, personally twisting arms and cajoling legislators to pass the measure. In fact, at the insistence of Glynn and his allies, the 1912

Democratic State Convention platform had committed the Democratic Party to increased hydropower production and specifically to this project, just as it had called for the passage of a direct primary law. That Sulzer would fight so very hard for the primary legislation and not only not fight for the hydropower bill—but to actively use his veto power to kill the hydropower legislation—was a serious blow to Glynn and effectively ended his working relationship with the governor.

Although he took no active part in impeaching Sulzer—or in whipping votes to pass the impeachment—the lieutenant governor could not have been disappointed with the final vote. The next day, August 13, Martin Glynn announced to the legislature, "I regard myself as acting Governor of New York State and I believe there should be a test as soon as possible to determine this definitely."[1]

Sulzer, however, disputed the legitimacy of the assembly impeachment proceedings at an extraordinary or special session of the legislature (the terms are interchangeable), and he refused to surrender the executive authority to Glynn.[2] Sulzer even continued to issue orders as governor from the executive chamber, while in the lieutenant governor's rooms, Glynn performed executive acts. "I shall continue to exercise and discharge the constitutional duties of the Governor of the State of New York," Sulzer said, "first, among other things, because I am advised that the Assembly at its present Extraordinary Session possessed and possesses no power or authority to proffer article of impeachment, and, secondly, because the Lieutenant Governor of the State is not authorized to act as Governor in case of the impeachment of the Governor, unless such impeachment is sustained."[3]

Sulzer suggested finding a test case, but Glynn, ever mindful of the law, rejected this, issuing a strong statement: "It is beyond any power to barter away any of the functions attaching to the office in which I am placed by your impeachment. Any attempt on my part to do so or to stipulate a method by which it might be done, would properly place me in the position you now occupy—that of being impeached for malfeasance in office. I cannot and I will not attempt to do it."[4]

But Sulzer would not move, firmly declaring, "I am the Governor no matter where I may be transacting business."[5]

Rather than get drawn between the conflicting camps, Attorney General Thomas Carmody decided on a middle ground. He issued a ruling that the seal of the lieutenant governor, under existing conditions, carried with it the same authority as that of the governor's seal.[6] Lieutenant Governor Glynn (or was he Acting Governor Glynn?) also tried to defuse the situation. "I do not intend to enter into any physical contest with Mr. Sulzer over the office of Governor. As far as I am concerned, there will be no circus or military maneuvers about occupying the Executive Chamber. The law is supreme."[7] The governor's counsel did the same, saying Sulzer "will meet the charges made against him in an orderly and dignified way and will do nothing unbecoming the dignity of the State and will engage in no physical scramble to assert his rights to discharge the functions pertaining to the office of Governor."[8]

That said, Sulzer was taking no chances on losing control: he put the records of the Executive Department under lock and key while securing the great seal with a steel chain and the governor's private office with a new lock.[9] To further protect the accoutrements of his office, Plain Old Bill Sulzer ordered a squad of armed guards to patrol the corridor outside his office every night.[10]

Nonetheless, the situation — two men claiming to exercise the power of the governor's office — constituted a constitutional crisis. No one could say for sure who was in power. To solve the problem of extraditing a fugitive, for instance, one West Virginia sheriff solicited the signatures of both "governors" just to be safe.[11] Back in New York, the issue quickly reached the courts. Joseph G. Robin, a banker imprisoned for financial irregularities, asked to be released because of a pardon signed "William Sulzer, Governor of the state of New York." Justice Hasbrouck, sitting in Supreme Court special term in Kingston, ruled the pardon void since the governor had been lawfully impeached.[12]

Obviously, the challenge of running state government without a clear leader was not conducive to efficient government. Unsure of who they answered to, many government officials simply lined up with their favorites. According to the *Times*, "Officials of anti-Tammany departments and those personally associated with Sulzer continued to look to him for orders, while the Legislature and those whom the Legislature controlled transferred their allegiance to Glynn."[13]

The situation was untenable. On August 18, at the request of Secretary of State Mitchell May, Attorney General Carmody declared Glynn in charge pending the impeachment trial. Sulzer responded to the attorney general's opinion by changing the combination of safes in the executive offices and blatantly ignoring the directive.[14]

Glynn, after meeting with department heads, made clear he had no intention of offering new policies or changes. "Under me as acting Governor," Glynn said, "there will be no political earthquakes and no factional reprisals."[15] Glynn slowly took control of the reins of government, and on August 27 the legislature recognized him, the Assembly Speaker declaring from the chair, "The Lieutenant-Governor is now acting governor."[16]

Sulzer's last-gasp effort was an application to Supreme Court judge Alden Chester to restrain the Court of Impeachment. Chester denied the application, finding that the Supreme Court was powerless to interfere with the prerogatives of a court of higher jurisdiction and that the Court of Impeachment alone could decide if the impeachment was valid.[17]

On the day after the impeachment began, Chester Platt, secretary to the governor, transmitted certain papers necessary for keeping the state running to Martin Glynn, who was now recognized throughout government and the state as acting governor. William Sulzer retired to the People's House, where no attempt was made to disturb him.[18]

Part Four

21

COURT OF IMPEACHMENT

THE HIGH COURT OF IMPEACHMENT gathered at noon in the senate chamber on September 18, 1913. While not as grand as the assembly, the senate chamber is more detailed and intricate. First occupied in 1881, it is acclaimed as one of Henry Hobson Richardson's finest designs. The chamber's central feature is an acoustically perfect debate area created by the deep-paneled recesses carved into the rich oak ceiling. The walls are covered with beautiful, shimmering twenty-three-carat gold leaf and include marble from Italy for the large arches, red granite from Scotland for the pillars, and Mexican onyx panel on the walls to the north and south.

The court itself consisted of all nine justices of the New York Court of Appeals (the highest court in the state) and forty-eight senators.* Of the latter, thirty-one senators were Democrats and seventeen Republicans. The legal teams comprised a "strong array of counsel" on both sides.[1]

---

* Franklin D. Roosevelt had resigned to become assistant secretary of the navy, and Stephen Stilwell was in jail for attempted extortion, leaving two vacancies in the senate. Senator John C. Fitzgerald was ill and would be absent for the trial, and Judge John Clinton Gray was abroad in Europe.

CHAPTER TWENTY-ONE

COUNSEL

The impeachment managers appointed by the assembly had the right to appoint special counsel to act on their behalf. They chose a very imposing group of legal talent:

- ALTON BROOKS PARKER. At sixty-one, Parker had already had an amazing career as chief judge of the Court of Appeals and Democratic candidate for president (1904). A native of Upstate New York, at the age of twelve or thirteen, Parker watched his father serve as a juror and was so fascinated by the proceedings that he resolved to become a lawyer. Parker practiced law in Kingston, where he became active with the Democratic Party and was an early supporter of Grover Cleveland. During this time, Parker also became a protégé of David B. Hill, managing Hill's 1884 gubernatorial campaign; Hill won in a landslide.

After his election, Hill appointed Parker to fill an 1885 vacancy on the State Supreme Court. The next year, he was elected to his own fourteen-year term in the seat. Three years later, Parker became a trial judge when Hill appointed him to the newly formed Second Division of the Court of Appeals. In November 1897 Parker successfully ran for the post of chief judge of the Court of Appeals.

As a judge, Parker was notable for independently researching each case that he heard. He was generally considered to be pro-labor and was an active supporter of social reform legislation. Parker upheld the death sentence given to convicted murderer Martha Place, who became the first woman to be killed by the electric chair.

In 1904 he resigned to run for president, defeating publisher William Randolph Hearst for the nomination. After a disorganized and ineffective campaign, Parker was defeated by 336 electoral votes to 140, carrying only the traditionally Democratic solid South. He then returned to practicing law, serving as the president of the American Bar Association from 1906 to 1907.

Reentering politics, Parker managed John A. Dix's successful 1910 campaign for governor of New York and delivered the keynote address of the 1912 Democratic National Convention, nominating Woodrow Wilson for president.

In fact, Sulzer had reappointed Parker's brother, Fred H. Parker of Kingston, as a member of the State Hospital Commission.[2]

- JOHN B. STANCHFIELD. As a lawyer in Elmira, John Barry Stanchfield was a prominent litigator and the law partner of Governor David B. Hill. Elected as district attorney of Chemung County, mayor of Elmira, and a member of the New York State Assembly, Stanchfield was less successful as a statewide candidate, losing races as the Democratic candidate for governor to Benjamin B. Odell Jr. in 1900 and as the Democratic candidate for U.S. Senate in 1903 to incumbent Thomas C. Platt. He was fifty-eight when the Court of Impeachment convened.

In addition to the Sulzer impeachment, Stanfield would play a leading role in another important New York State Legislature conflict: the expulsion trial of five socialist members of the assembly elected in 1919 and expelled on the first day of the legislative session—a vivid example of the Red Scare. All five were elected again in special elections held in September of 1920. Stanchfield would again appear for the state of New York, acting on behalf of then Speaker Thaddeus C. Sweet.[*]

- EDGAR T. BRACKETT. Born in 1853 in Emerson's Corners in Wilton,

---

[*] On January 7, 1920, at the first session of the assembly, Speaker Thaddeus C. Sweet attacked the assembly's five socialist members, declaring they had been "elected on a platform that is absolutely inimical to the best interests of the state of New York and the United States." The Socialist Party, Sweet declared, was "not truly a political party" but was rather "a membership organization admitting within its ranks aliens, enemy aliens, and minors." The evidence? The Socialist Party had supported the revolutionaries in Germany, Austria, and Hungary. The assembly suspended the five by a vote of 140-6, with just one Democrat supporting the socialists. A trial in the assembly, lasting from January 20 to March 11, resulted in a recommendation that the five be expelled. They were expelled on April 1, 1920.

Opposition to the assembly's actions was swift, widespread, and nonpartisan. From the start of the process, former Republican governor, Supreme Court Justice, and presidential candidate Charles Evans Hughes defended the socialist members and Democratic governor Al Smith, now on the opposite side as Stanchfield, denounced the expulsions: "To discard the method of representative government leads to the misdeeds of the very extremists we denounce and serves to increase the number of enemies of orderly free government."

New York in Saratoga County, Edgar Truman Brackett was a prominent lawyer who represented the counties of Saratoga, Schenectady, and Washington in the state senate, serving from 1896 until 1906 and from 1909 to 1912. A prominent Republican who served as party leader in the senate, Brackett added a bipartisan appeal to the prosecution.

- EUGENE L. RICHARDS JR. A graduate of Yale University, Eugene Lamb Richards had a distinguished family tree. His great-grandfather was wounded at the siege of Quebec and was present with General George Washington when Lord Cornwallis surrendered. Washington appointed General Lamb as the first collector of customs for the Port of New York. Richard's grandfather was New York secretary of state under Governor Tompkins and was national president of the Order of the Cincinnati.

The fifty-year-old Richards, a native of Staten Island, was the counsel for the State Conservation Commission before taking the same post for the Frawley Committee. He would go on to serve as the New York State superintendent of banking.

- ISIDOR J. KRESEL. A former assistant district attorney, New York County; former assistant counsel to the Legislative Investigative Committee (Edwin Merritt, chairman), and future counsel for the Bank of the United States.

- HIRAM C. TODD. Prominent Albany attorney and future U.S. attorney for the Northern District of New York under President Warren G. Harding.

Governor William Sulzer's defense team included the following:

- D-CADY HERRICK. Born in Schoharie County in 1846 Herrick was a classmate of future president William McKinley at Albany Law School.*

---

* Herrick was baptized Cady Herrick. According to the *New York Times* (September 23, 1904),

> That pleased his mother. It did not please his father. The latter thought that Cady might be softened by fools into Katie—and the child was a big, bouncing boy. When that boy attained a few years Jonathan Herrick told his son to write his name D-Cady Herrick. He said to him: "The D will only signify the letter of the alphabet for which it stands. If people choose to think that it stands for a name instead of a letter, they may. But as for you, write your name D-Cady Herrick, D to please me and Cady to please your mother. Then we'll both be represented." This explanation, so true and so simple as to be difficult of adoption, is absolutely correct. Judge

Having lost in his first attempt, he was elected and then reelected at Albany County district attorney. He was a protégé of Albany Democratic boss Daniel Manning. After Manning was named U.S. secretary of the treasury, D-Cady Herrick took his place and would continue as Democratic leader, even on the bench. Resigning as district attorney, Herrick served as corporation counsel of the city of Albany until his election to the New York State Supreme Court and was later elevated to the appellate division. In 1904 he was nominated for governor of New York, resigning from the bench and as party leader. He was nonetheless defeated by Frank W. Higgins.

- IRVING G. VANN. Born in Tompkins County, Irving Goodwin Vann was mayor of Syracuse and later elected as justice of the New York State Supreme Court. On December 31, 1895, Vann was appointed by Governor Levi P. Morton to the Court of Appeals, replacing Rufus Peckham Jr., who had been appointed to the U.S. Supreme Court. Elected to a full term on the Court of Appeals, he served until 1912, when he reached the constitutional age limit of seventy years. At seventy-one, he was the oldest of Sulzer's lawyers and the only one who received any monetary compensation from the state.

- HARVEY D. HINMAN. Only forty-eight when the Court of Impeachment met, Harvey DeForest Hinman was the youngest of Sulzer's representatives. A state senator from 1905 until 1912, Hinman was a key strategist and advisor to Governor Charles Evans Hughes. In 1914, at the urging of Theodore Roosevelt, he was a candidate for the Republican nomination for governor, losing to future governor Charles Whitman.

Hinman continued working as a lawyer and as a Republican Party activist. He was instrumental in the establishment of Harpur College, the forerunner of Binghamton University, where Hinman College is named in his honor.

- LOUIS MARSHALL. Born in 1856 in Syracuse, Marshall was respected as a constitutional lawyer and civil rights activist. Among the founders of the

---

Herrick is so stalwart in person and in character that the imputation of "parting his name in the middle" has never hurt him. He has none of the qualities that sometimes go with men who "part their names in the middle."

American Jewish Community and a director of the National Association for the Advancement of Colored People, by the end of his legal career he had argued more cases before the U.S. Supreme Court than any other private lawyer of his generation.

• AUSTEN G. FOX. A former special district attorney in New York County and member of New York City Committee of Fifteen, a New York City citizens' group active in the fight against prostitution and gambling. This committee hired investigators who witnessed vice and reported on it.

PRELIMINARY MOTIONS

The avowed strategy of the defense was to obfuscate, delay, and obstruct.[3] That approach began with an effort to deny several senators their seats on the Court. As members of the Frawley Committee—which had recommended impeachment to the legislature—the defense argued that Senators Frawley, Rampsberger, and Sanner had already decided that Sulzer was guilty and, thus, denied Sulzer his right to an "impartial jury." Sulzer's team also argued that in the case of the governor's removal from office, the president of the senate—Robert Wagner—would become acting lieutenant governor and thus had a personal stake in the outcome (the lieutenant governor was paid almost twice what legislators earned) and could not be objective. D-Cady Herrick, for Sulzer, argued that the Court of Impeachment, like any other American court, must be impartial. Alton Parker, in a forceful argument that included a detailed look at President Johnson's impeachment, argued that the Court had no power to exclude any qualified members. The Court agreed with Parker without dissent (the four senators themselves declined to vote).

The next line of defense was a motion to dismiss, challenging the validity of the impeachment itself. It was, they argued, "without jurisdiction and null, void and of no effect.[4] Why? The impeachment had been brought in an extraordinary session, and Sulzer's team argued that impeachment proceedings had historically only been initiated at regular legislative sessions. In fact, the New York State Constitution stated explicitly that during an extraordinary session the legislature could only act on matters specifically raised by the governor. Allowing otherwise, Louis Marshall argued, would create "a vicious precedent." In a long, well-reasoned, and detailed address Marshall outlined the history of impeachment up through the present day and asserted that any deviation from that path threatened to open the door to serious abuse of the impeachment power.[5] The crux of the argument was that even when acting as an accusing body, the assembly had to adhere to the limitations and restraints of the constitution. To do otherwise, said Marshall, would seriously weaken the checks and balances that kept our nation strong.[6]

As he would for much of the trial, Judge Alton Parker took the lead for the impeachment managers and refuted these arguments, asserting that impeachment power is "absolute and complete" and can be used at any time.[7] Matching Marshall in scope and detail, Parker offered an exhaustive analysis of the state constitution and the use of impeachment in New York State. At an extraordinary or special session, Parker said, the Legislature is restrained by recommendations of the governor only on exercising their *legislative* powers. Impeachment, he argued, is not a legislative act. Rather, impeachment is an exercise of *judicial* power and not to be restrained, certainly not by the executive. Edgar Brackett, supporting Parker, took the argument further. Brackett argued that the public interest demanded the impeachment power to be unrestrained as to time or place. Public officials, Brackett said, need to always be subject to the constraint or threat of impeachment in order to protect the public. He also made very clear what he, and many others, thought of the Sulzer strategy of pursuing technicalities, delay, and obfuscation, quoting Congressman Charles Sumner during President Andrew Johnson's great impeachment trial: "Great God, is there any question possible except is this man guilty?"[8]

Louis Marshall, responding for the defense, rejected those arguments. Marshall contended that the state constitution was clear on what was germane during extraordinary sessions. As for the argument that public interest urgently demanded the impeachment of a corrupt or criminal officer, Marshall offered the penal code as a more appropriate remedy. He also took a shot back at the legislature, continuing his argument that the legislature could not meet anywhere at any time no matter how pressing impeachment or other actions might be. Marshall said, "Of course articles of impeachment could not be presented to the President of the Senate on 14th Street in the city of New York or at the Throne Room at Delmonico's in that city and make of that an impeachment."[9] Fourteenth Street, as we know, was home to Tammany Hall's offices, or its "wigwam," and Delmonico's was a favorite haunt of Boss Murphy's and his primary place of business.

The Court went into executive session to address the question, and by a vote of 51-1 denied the motion to dismiss. Chief Judge Edgar Cullen, clearly and succinctly, offered the opinion that while the assembly did not have the ability to impeach at any time, it did possess the power to impeach during an extraordinary session.

The final defense motion was to dismiss some of the more serious counts (the First, Second, and Sixth Articles of Impeachment) because the alleged acts occurred prior to Sulzer entering the office of governor. Employing extensive arguments from Thomas Jefferson, Alexander Hamilton, and many others, Herrick made the case that impeachment was only a remedy to corrupt acts taken by a public official in his public capacity *in office*. These charges—making a false statement of campaign contributions and swearing to it—were *outside* of the scope of his office and, furthermore, outside of his term of office. This distinction, Herrick argued, was essential to blunting the sharp edge of the sword of impeachment in order to prevent partisan abuses. Herrick offered this forceful point:

> If the Assembly can impeach for any cause that it sees fit, for acts done by an official during his term of office, as well as for acts done by him when a private citizen before he had become a public official, thereby suspending him indefinitely from discharging the duties of his office, then the door is opened wide to an unscrupulous majority to impeach an official whose conduct in office has been upright and honest, who has stood

in the way of graft and corruption, but who, perchance, before coming into office has been guilty of some indiscretion, or worse. To impeach, in fact, not for official misconduct, but because of his refusal to abuse the powers of his office.[10]

Herrick also offered more technicalities. The defense asserted that, under the Penal Code and the Corrupt Practices Act, a candidate was required to file a statement of contributions made *by* the candidate rather than contributions made *to* the candidate. Furthermore, they contended the law did not actually require an oath. As a result, even if the sworn affidavit was incorrect it was not perjury since it was never required by law. Austen Fox took this point further for the defense. According to Fox, the silence or "terseness" of the constitution was not the same as a grant of unlimited power. Reciting a litany of judicial precedents, Fox offered that never in the history of New York or anywhere else in the United States had an officer been removed by judicial process for acts committed while not in office. (Judge George G. Barnard of the New York State Supreme Court had been impeached for acts during a prior term of office.) Fox contended that it was the assembly that had broken the law by usurping power for political gain. "This action of the Assembly," said Fox, "is nothing more or less than an attempt to induce the State of New York to trample under foot its own fundamental law, in order that a present advantage may be gained in the restriction and repression of an individual unpopular with certain factions in the State."[11]

Fox also argued that no one had ever been impeached for acts committed while not in office (again noting that Judge Barnard had been impeached for actions committed during a prior term of office). Unsurprisingly, the counsel for the impeachment managers disagreed. They argued that the impeachment power exists specifically for *any* type of crime that may demonstrate unfitness for office.

For his part, Judge Parker examined each of the state constitutions, from 1777 through the present, showing that each new constitution broadened the definition of impeachment. The 1777 constitution allowed the assembly to impeach "for mal and corrupt conduct in their respective offices." In 1821 the new constitution added additional grounds for impeachment "for high crimes and misdemeanors," while the constitution of 1846 removed all limitations: "The Assembly shall have the power of impeachment by vote of a majority of all members elected." The 1846 language was repeated in every constitution up through Sulzer's time in office.[12]

Edgar Brackett took another tack to refute Herrick's claim. Brackett maintained that in fact Sulzer's actions were unquestionably and inseparably tied to the office of governor. To make the connection, Brackett quoted former governor Samuel Tilden, who along with former governor Charles Evans Hughes remained the gold standard of gubernatorial ethics and integrity: "Misconduct wholly outside the function of an office may be of such a nature as to exercise a reflected influence upon those functions and to disqualify and incapacitate officers from usefully performing those functions."[13]

Under the Corrupt Practices Act, Brackett argued, the campaign finance laws and reporting requirements served as "an official vestibule" to office. Misconduct on the campaign trail, he insisted, follows a candidate into public office. "Wickedness in a candidate," the lawyer argued, "is as surely inherited by the official as any hereditary taint by the child from the parent."[14]

Isidor Kresel, closing for the prosecution, took aim at the defense team's refuge in—and readings of—the technicalities of election law. Kresel reviewed the history and purpose of election law regarding campaign contributions and expenditures. The purpose of these laws, Kresel maintained, was to give the broadest possible publicity to political contributions and therefore included contributions made *by* him but most certainly also those made *to* him or his agents.

Following the arguments, Chief Judge Cullen suggested deferring a decision on this issue until after the testimony had been heard. It was, Cullen offered, essentially a question as to what constituted an impeachable offense. Deferring a decision would allow the introduction of evidence bearing upon the question of Sulzer's guilt or innocence. By a vote of 49-7, with each of the Court of Appeals judges in the majority, the Court of Impeachment backed Cullen's recommendation to postpone a decision.

THE CASE FOR THE PROSECUTION

On September 24 the Court came to consider the merits and evidence of the impeachment itself. It began with the clerk reading the formal answering of the charges by Sulzer's legal team. The defense denied all the allegations, adding that in reply to the charges on the making and filing of the statement, Sulzer had believed that the statement he filed was both true and accurate.

Eugene Richards opened the case for the managers, offering facts based mostly on the work of the Frawley Committee, of which he had been counsel. "We shall show," Richards promised, "that [Sulzer] was busier in getting money and in trying to get it than he was in getting votes. He went at his campaign for money with system, with cool deliberation and cunning schemes to conceal what he got."[15] Most of the evidence would focus on Articles One, Two, and Six of the impeachment: the false statement, perjury, and stock market charges.

A stream of witnesses followed, many of whom had already appeared in front of the Frawley Committee. Their testimony revealed many more checks to the campaign that had not been included in Sulzer's sworn statement. The unreported contributions came from bankers, liquor dealers, lawyers, brewers, and politicians. There were political reasons for Sulzer, the "man of the people," to conceal these contributions. Of the thirty-nine donors who testified, only four had appeared on Sulzer's report.[16] For the most part, "The witnesses were manifestly reluctant to testify and acted as if they would have preferred to avoid any public discussion of their contribution to Sulzer's campaign."[17]

Even this evidence caused a fight. Sulzer's lawyers argued that any contributions—whether they had been reported or not—could only be considered by the court if they were included in the Articles of Impeachment. The managers rejected any limits on the evidence they could introduce. The additional campaign contributions, they argued, showed that Sulzer had received and failed to report other items, all as part of a concerted effort to conceal money that could damage him politically. To this point Stanchfield argued, "I concede that the failure to report one contribution might be an accident; the failure to report two contributions might be a coincidence; the failure to report a hundred is a crime."[18] Chief Judge Cullen ended the skirmish, agreeing to allow any additional checks to be introduced as evidence not of a new offense but rather to show intent. The court unanimously concurred.[19]

A summary that appeared in the press showed $12,700 in unreported checks and $47,300 in unreported currency. Of that, at least $40,462.50 (of the unreported cash) went directly to Sulzer's brokers.[20]

The testimony was equally incriminating. Cornelius S. Pinkney, a lawyer who donated a check for $200, testified that Sulzer told him, "I do not intend to account for this kind of gift, they must be made to me personally; don't say anything about it; simply between you and myself."[21] There was also testimony from several witnesses that Sulzer asked for—and received—cash wherever possible to "meet traveling expenses."[22]

Notes that Sulzer sent acknowledging the receipt of money during his campaign seemed to back Pinkney's assertion that Sulzer never intended to account for the monies in any formal manner. These notes, in fact, contained no reference to money at all, and instead said things along the lines of "thanking you for all you have done for me" or "thanking you for your letter and enclosure." Sulzer simply did not acknowledge many donations at all.

The prosecution offered a steady stream of witnesses and evidence showing money flowing to Sulzer but not appearing on his sworn report. Many of the witnesses testifying for the prosecution were friendly to Sulzer and sought to "repair" their testimony and thus protect the governor by characterizing their contributions as personal gifts rather than campaign contributions. The defense seized on this characterization, playing up the personal nature of these gifts since presumably personal gifts never needed to be reported or disclosed.

This personal gift defense always seemed a bit of a stretch and might have raised other questions about influencing elected officials, but as the prosecution continued to put on its case, the defense held to this point tenaciously. The strategy failed, as shown by the testimony of Jacob Schiff and Henry Morgenthau, both of whom were extremely prominent financiers and Sulzer supporters.

Jacob H. Schiff was one of the most famous financiers of his time. Sensitive to the discrimination and pogroms against the Jewish people in Russia, he generously loaned an estimated $200 million to the Japanese government, thus allowing them to purchase the munitions necessary to win the Russo-Japanese War. Closer to home, Schiff was affiliated with E. H. Harriman and served as a director of Western Union Telegraph, Wells Fargo & Company, National City Bank of New York, Central Trust Company, and Union Pacific Railroad, among others.

Under direct examination, Schiff testified that Sulzer had personally solicited a campaign contribution and following Sulzer's instructions wrote a check for $2,500 to Sulzer's secretary Louis A. Sarecky. The defense cross-examination elicited that Schiff had placed no conditions on how Sulzer could use the funds:

> Q: "Was anything said in that conversation as to the use which was to be made of that check or the proceeds of that check by Mr. Sulzer?"
> A: "There was nothing said."
> Q: "Did you intend that that should be used for any specific purpose?"
> A: "I think it was the general intent and purpose of the conversation that Governor Sulzer could use this $2,500 for whatever he would please."[23]

One factor complicating Schiff's testimony were the words, "Mr. Schiff's contribution towards William Sulzer's campaign expenses," written on the memorandum line on the face of the cancelled check. This, Schiff testified, had been written at the time he handed the check to the Frawley Committee and then only for identification and not to restrict its use and not to actually describe the gift. The following day, Schiff testified that Sulzer's law partner had offered to refund the $2,500 after the investigation had begun. Schiff refused to accept the money while the matter was under investigation.

Henry Morgenthau was an equally prominent financier and real estate investor. He went on to serve as U.S. ambassador to the Ottoman Empire while his son Henry would serve as Franklin Roosevelt's secretary of the treasury and his grandson Robert as the longtime district attorney of New York County.*

Morgenthau testified that he had not limited the purpose of his "gift" to Sulzer but was forced to concede that it had been his intention to help his friend "in his election" and he would "certainly not" have given the money if Sulzer had not been a candidate for governor.[24]

Others continued this theme. Former judge Conlon testified about a fundraising dinner he had with other members of the Manhattan Club who, believing Sulzer to be in an "impecunious condition," donated money to cover his personal expenses.[25] The prosecution consistently objected, seeking to block any testimony about the intention of the donors as incompetent. The chief judge overruled the objection, opining that Sulzer had the right to prove he was not guilty of larceny even if the other charges could not be refuted. A vote of 33-14 sustained the ruling.[26]

The trial continued to go badly for Sulzer as Morgenthau and Duncan Peck both offered testimony that Sulzer urged them to perjure themselves. Morgenthau, called back to the stand, testified that Sulzer had called him in September, asking Morgenthau to come to Albany immediately. When Morgenthau refused, the governor told him, "If you are going to testify, I hope you will be easy with me." When Morgenthau replied he "would testify to the facts," Sulzer urged him to treat it as a "personal matter" and

---

* Mr. Morgenthau said it was his grandfather who first encouraged him to serve others, telling him, "I couldn't get into public service until I was 55. You don't have to wait that long" ("Looking Back at the Morgenthau Legacy," *City Room* blog, *New York Times*, November 16, 2009).

just between them.²⁷ Morgenthau, although he testified to the phone call, had difficulty figuring out how the managers knew about it.²⁸ He would later say he believed his phone had been tapped.*

More damning testimony came from Duncan W. Peck, state superintendent of public works. A holdover appointment from the Dix administration, Peck had donated $500 to the Sulzer campaign. His reappointment caused some controversy. After the announcement that he would continue to serve, Sulzer said this:

> Mr. Peck was reappointed after a careful investigation of his management of the canals. The report was that he was honest and capable, but not always diplomatic. That is, he has not got along any too well with men working for him, and some contractors do not like him. Those reasons did not militate against him in my judgment. No testimony of persons interested in the canals influenced me in making the appointment. Hereafter he will have nothing to do with the highways. He has all he can do in his department.²⁹

Having been subpoenaed earlier by the Frawley Committee, Peck showed the letter to Sulzer. According to Peck's testimony, the governor said, "Do as I shall; deny it." Peck replied, "I suppose I shall be under oath," to which Sulzer answered, "That is nothing; forget it." Peck faced withering cross-examination but stuck to his story.³⁰

The impeachment managers offered various evidence and witnesses to show that almost $15,000 was deposited into Sulzer's personal account with the Farmers' Loan and Trust Company in September and October 1912—during Sulzer's campaign for governor. And during the period from

---

* The history of telephones dates to 1876, with Alexander Graham Bell's breathtaking invention. By the 1890s, law enforcement agencies were tapping wires on these early telephones, literally an extra set of wires on the line between the switchboard and the telephone that led to a pair of headphones and a primitive recording device.

September 5 through December 31, 1912, just under $15,000 was deposited into Sarecky's account at the Mutual Alliance Trust Company. The defense challenged the authenticity of Sulzer's signature but the Farmers' Loan and Trust Company clerk positively identified the governor's handwriting.

The prosecution offered another series of witnesses and more evidence concerning Sulzer's stock dealings. The testimony clearly established Sulzer as the owner of secret numbered accounts at various brokerages and proved that campaign checks were used to pay for various stocks. Much of this testimony had already been made public by the Frawley Committee. Testimony revealed that Frederick Colwell had handled many of the details of these transactions, from delivering checks and cash and relaying orders to buy or sell, on behalf of Governor Sulzer. Colwell himself failed to answer subpoenas from either the Frawley Committee or the Court of Impeachment.

Colwell's absence had more relevance than just one witness's testimony, no matter how important that testimony. Article Four alleged that Sulzer had suppressed evidence, and Colwell's disappearance could be seen to fit that description.

Where was Colwell? One broker testified that Colwell's last words to him were that he was going to Albany to meet with Sulzer. Despite subpoenas and various other efforts, Colwell was not heard from. Also germane to this count, another one of the stockbrokers, Melvin Fuller, admitted that Sulzer summoned him to a meeting at the Governor's Mansion on the day after he received a subpoena to appear before the Frawley Committee. There the governor told Fuller he could not be compelled to testify, but Fuller insisted that Sulzer did not ask him to withhold information.

To prove the Seventh Article, alleging that Sulzer used his veto power to coerce legislators to vote for his direct primary bill, the managers called two assemblymen, Thaddeus C. Sweet and Spencer G. Prime. Both testified about implied threats but nothing more serious than intimidation. Sweet's testimony concerned a conversation with the governor about a bill providing for construction of a bridge over the Oswego River. According to Sweet, this was their conversation:

Governor Sulzer: Assemblyman, how did you vote on my primary bill?
Assemblyman Sweet: I voted against it.
GS: How are you going to vote in the extraordinary session?
AS: According to the sentiment and in the interest of my district.
GS: See Taylor [Sulzer's legal advisor], smooth him the right way, Assemblyman, and bring your bill to me, but remember, Assemblyman, I take good care of my friends.[31]

Assemblyman Prime's testimony was similar: having visited the governor to urge passage of a $750,000 road expenditure bill for Essex and Warren Counties, Prime was told by Sulzer to reread the direct primary bill, giving it another look. As he was leaving, Sulzer remarked, "You for me, I for you."[32]

The only effort the managers made on Article Eight was a flimsy attempt to connect Sulzer's stock speculation with his message advocating passage of various measures to reform the stock exchange. Sulzer's efforts to increase regulation of the stock market while simultaneously speculating in stocks could not be shown to be more than that.

The managers then took aim at Article Three, alleging that Sulzer bribed witnesses, focusing exclusively on Louis Sarecky. Sarecky was a longtime Sulzer loyalist and his former secretary during the governor's time in Washington and Albany. On the stand, the managers pressured Sarecky to admit that Sulzer had told him not to answer questions from the Frawley Committee. Sarecky stuck to his story, but the managers showed that Sarecky was appointed as deportation agent of the State Hospital Commission only two weeks before he was scheduled to testify before the Frawley Committee. The testimony raised questions about the appointment, because Sarecky was the first nonphysician ever to be hired as a deportation director, and the position almost doubled his salary to $4,000 per year. The managers produced letters from the governor to the Civil Service Commission asking them to waive the qualifications and competitive requirements in order to hire Sarecky. The letter of the Hospital Commission praised Sarecky's "peculiar and exceptional qualifications of educational character" to justify suspending the employment rules.[33] Counsel John B. Stanchfield, who in addition to his career in politics was also credited with throwing baseball's first curved pitch,* presented this as "the strongest possible circumstantial evidence of bribery" for the suppression of Sarecky's testimony.[34]

Following this presentation, the impeachment managers unexpectedly rested their case on October 1. More than a dozen other witnesses were held in reserve, it was reported, ready to take the stand should Sulzer testify.[35]

Austen Fox, opening the case for the defense on October 2, made a formal motion that most of the articles (third, fourth, fifth, seventh, and eighth) be dismissed, as unsupported by the testimony presented. The presiding judge rejected this motion, reminding the Court of the decision that such questions should be determined at the close of the trial.

The trial was adjourned until October 6 to allow the defense more time to prepare their case. Then, when the Court reconvened, the managers asked for — and received — permission to reopen their case to hear additional testimony from a newly discovered witness. The defense objected, but the Court saw fit to allow the additional testimony.

The prosecutors called Allan Aloysius Ryan to the stand. Ryan was the son of Thomas Fortune Ryan, a prominent financier and successful investor. In 1874 the elder Ryan purchased a seat on the New York Stock

---

* According to his obituary in the *New York Times*, as "a pitcher on the Amherst baseball team, Mr. Stanchfield is credited with having thrown the first curved ball. An elderly, strong-opinionated Professor of Physics devoted a portion of his lecture one day citing formulae to prove that a horizontal curve to a hurled sphere violated all laws of nature and physics. 'Your formulae may be correct, Professor,' spoke up young Stanchfield, 'but if you come out on the diamond this afternoon I'll prove that I can throw a curve.' The professor was placed that afternoon behind the end of a brick wall. Near the other end of the wall, out of sight of the physicist and the catcher, Pitcher Stanchfield threw what is known as a 'round house curve' in the catcher's glove. The demonstration filled the professor with the ambition to revise his physics formulae" (*New York Times*, June 26, 1921).

Exchange for his son, making Allan Ryan the youngest member in exchange history. Ryan would also go on to found the New York Cable Railroad, which by 1900 controlled most of New York City's streetcar operations. He also founded the American Tobacco Company, owned large parts of R. J. Reynolds and Liggett & Myers, bought the Equitable Life Assurance Society, and eventually merged his cable car company with the Interborough Rapid Transit Company. Entrepreneurially minded, he owned Royal Typewriter, backed the maker of the Thompson submachine gun, became a Wall Street broker, and developed the diamond fields of the Congo Free States with Leopold II of Belgium, working with Jay Gould and Elihu Root as counsel. Politically, he had been an important advisor to President Grover Cleveland as he was elected to a second term. Later, and more infamously, Ryan cornered the stock of Stutz Motor Car Company and was expelled from the stock exchange.[36] The move took Sulzer's lawyers entirely by surprise.[37]

Allan Ryan's testimony was the most damaging of all. He testified that Sulzer had called him during the campaign and, learning that the elder Ryan was out of the country, had asked Allan to "tell your father I am the same old Bill."[38] Thomas Ryan had sent Sulzer $10,000 in cash, which was also not included in Sulzer's report. A week before the impeachment trial, Sulzer called Allan Ryan, asking him to go to Washington to see Senator Elihu Root. The plan was to convince Root to request that state Republican chairman Barnes, with whom Root had close professional ties, stop the impeachment by voting against its constitutionality.[39]

What followed was like a game of political Ping-Pong: Herrick objected immediately, claiming Ryan's testimony was unrelated to any of the impeachment articles and demanded it be expunged. Following a strict reading of the rules of evidence, Judge Cullen agreed to strike the testimony. Before the Court could either ratify or overturn Cullen's ruling, GOP leader Senator Elon Brown took exception and disputed the ruling. A vote of 32-18 upheld the ruling, and it seemed that the testimony would finally be expunged. However, the next day the Court went into executive session. There is no record of what happened in the executive session, but afterward the Court reversed itself, restoring Ryan's testimony.

Recalled to the stand, Ryan testified that he refused to see Root, although he did reveal that he showed Sulzer a memo by a "certain party," later identified as Lemuel E. Quigg, an old Republican machine stalwart.[40] The memo showed that the Republican organization would do nothing for Sulzer, and the GOP senators would be left to vote their conscious at the impeachment. Hearing this, Sulzer asked Ryan to see DeLancey Nicoll, his father's lawyer, and ask Nicoll to intercede with Tammany leaders. The message to be delivered to Tammany was that Sulzer had had enough, and if the impeachment was called off, Sulzer would "do whatever was right."[41] Ryan testified that he never acted on Sulzer's request. Friedman, in his book *The Impeachment of Governor Sulzer*, captures the effect this disclosure had: "The revelation that the Governor had invoked the powers of the 'invisible government' so bitterly and repeatedly condemned by him in public speech, to save himself from expulsion and disgrace filled even his most loyal friends with consternation."[42]

With that, the managers rested.

THE CASE FOR THE DEFENSE

Harvey D. Hinman, former state senator, opened the case for the defense. He argued that the private life or morals of an elected official are not grounds to impeach that official—as long as they did not affect his performance in office. In other words, said Hinman, high character and integrity were not legal requirements for holding office. Hinman was the right person to deliver this message. He was known as a close advisor of Charles Evans Hughes and the former governor was still held in lofty esteem across the state, especially for his high moral standards.

Hinman then addressed each of the charges individually. Article Eight, concerning the stock market, he dismissed as being unsupported by "even a scintilla of proof."[43] The governor's proposals for the stock exchange, he went on to point out, were made in the interest of the people of the state and would have lowered prices—which ran contrary to Sulzer's interests as an investor—and he would therefore not dignify this charge with any further comment.

Regarding the seventh, or the "big stick," article, Hinman maintained that it was also "absolutely unproved." The conversations with Assemblymen Sweet and Prime were nothing more than the give-and-take of politics, and nothing Sulzer was alleged to have said or done violated the law. As such, the defense would offer no further denial on these charges.

On the third, fourth, and fifth articles—the "bribery" and "criminal suppression of evidence" charges—these, Hinman argued, were based on "insinuations and innuendoes" without any supporting evidence. The prosecution had offered no evidence that Sulzer had even talked to Sarecky about the investigation, which was necessary to prove the charges. The suggestion that Sarecky's appointment and pay raise were in any way connected with the Frawley Committee was only an assumption on the part of the prosecutors. The reticence of Fuller, the stockbroker, was because of his desire to protect his practice and clients, not to help Sulzer. As for Colwell, well, there was no evidence that Sulzer had anything at all to do with his disappearance. Hinman insisted that none of these charges had been proved and no evidence offered to support a conviction. The defense was, therefore, under no obligation to offer any evidence or witnesses to disprove them.

Hinman continued the defense tactic of rejecting Articles One, Two, and Six because they referred to acts that occurred prior to January 1, 1913. At the time of these alleged offenses, William Sulzer was a private citizen, and the Court of Impeachment could take no notice of his actions.

Hinman rejected Article Six, which accused Sulzer of stealing money donated to his campaign, because even if the moneys given to Sulzer were donations, Hinman argued that only the donors themselves could complain if the money had been used for a different purpose. It was not given in trust, and there was no criminal offense involved. "To urge the impeachment of a public official," insisted Hinman, "because he did not use money in aid of his election is so unreasonable as to be almost ludicrous. We venture the assertion that were it not for political exigencies, such a thing would never have been conceived or even dreamed of."[44]

Hinman reiterated the defense's argument that the Public Officers Law did not technically require a sworn statement, and therefore Sulzer's statement was "immaterial," even if it was not accurate. Since the sworn statement was not required, Sulzer was not guilty on Article Two.

As for Article One, Hinman painted a picture of Sulzer as a man without business sense—careless and with a poor handle on money who "trustingly confided the management to the financial details of his campaign to others."[45] He had not filed a false statement, as Article One alleged. Sulzer, Hinman said, was only guilty of trusting people on his office staff. They were the ones who prepared the campaign finance reports and asserted they were true. Sulzer had made the mistake of taking some contributions from friends and well-wishers in the nature of gifts, and thinking they were intended for him. Yes, the defense conceded, Sulzer used some of the money for his stock transactions, but he had never intended to conceal that fact as Sulzer had no wrongful intent.

Then came the key point of the defense's case. These allegations, Hinman asserted, even if they were true, were only minor infractions. What really mattered—in the Court of Impeachment, in government, and in terms of the public trust—was what happened *after* Sulzer took his oath of office. Sulzer, Hinman declared, had been beyond reproach since becoming governor. In fact, the defense insisted, it was his high ethical standards that had actually brought about Sulzer's impeachment.

"Was the proceeding instituted," Hinman asked,

> because of a desire to rid of a public official who was performing his duty? Was the respondent impeached because as they say of "mal and corrupt conduct in office," or because of honest conduct in office? Was he impeached, as they say, for "stealing" the money which his friends gave him, or was it because he was

preventing grafters from stealing the moneys of the taxpayers? Was he impeached because, as they say, he made a false oath, or was it because he refused to violate his official oath of office?[46]

This exact argument had long been made by Sulzer's supporters in the press. Now, it was finally being made in the Court of the Impeachment. Hinman began to call witnesses for the defense.

Samuel A. Beardsley was first on the stand, testifying that he offered Sulzer a $25,000 contribution but that Sulzer refused the money. Unfortunately for the defense, the managers objected to Beardsley's testimony, saying that he had no knowledge of any actual contributions. Judge Cullen agreed. The defense had hoped to show, through Beardsley's testimony and that of others, that Sulzer had rejected large sums of money, casting doubt on the governor's pecuniary greed.[47]

Next for the defense was Herbert H. Lehman, the prominent New York banker. Lehman testified that before Sulzer's nomination for governor, he gave Sulzer $5,000 because he thought Sulzer to be without personal means. Lehman also admitted to spending $6,000 to finance publicity for Sulzer's campaign—the idea being, perhaps, that Sulzer had a history of accepting gifts from friends for his sustenance and that they were not contingent on his being a candidate for governor.

The next witness was Louis M. Josephthal. Josephthal was a top military aide to Governor Sulzer, just as he had been to Sulzer's predecessor and would be to his successor. Josephthal had been dispatched, at the height of the Frawley investigation, to take up Sulzer's brokerage account with the firm of Harris and Fuller. He had been called by the defense to testify about the transaction but ended up doing no favors for Sulzer. Josephthal testified that Sulzer had told him that the stock at Harris and Fuller belonged to Mrs. Sulzer but had to admit that, upon arriving at the brokerage firm, he found that not to be true. Josephthal denied any attempt to influence Sulzer's stock market legislation but did make known to the governor his opposition to increasing the tax on stock transfers. And while Josephthal did not donate to Sulzer's campaign, his firm retained Sulzer's law partner following his reappointment as naval aide to the governor.

Following Josephthal, the defense called Louis A. Sarecky. The impeachment charges dealing with the campaign filings were clearly the strongest charges, and Sarecky, Sulzer's secretary for ten years, was the key to refuting those charges. Sarecky took full responsibility for preparing the campaign filing. Hinman walked the young loyalist through tens of thousands of dollars in contributions and disbursements. Sarecky took full responsibility for the ambiguous "I thank you letters," which made no mention of campaign funds. Every step of the road, he insisted that Sulzer was unaware of the vague letters sent in the candidate's name and completely uninvolved with preparing the sworn statement of campaign receipts.

The prosecution tried every trick, but "calm, self-possessed, and resourceful, [Sarecky] faced the searching cross-examination of Stanchfield without once losing his poise."[48] Sarecky testified that he had prepared the campaign statement with Matthew Horgan—later the secretary of the Frawley Commission. Sarecky described the preparation of the reports: "Is this all right?" he quoted Sulzer as asking. Sarecky replied, "This is as accurate as I could get it."[49] Sarecky also claimed that the commissioner of deeds who witnessed the instrument never read it to Sulzer before affixing his signature. The prosecution had already produced the commissioner of deeds, who testified to having read the entire statement to Sulzer before attesting to it.

Sarecky even took responsibility for writing and signing a letter to the Mutual Alliance Trust Co. authorizing the bank to accept Sarecky's endorsement. The letter to the bank, signed with Sulzer's name, had figured prominently in the Frawley Committee's conclusion that Sulzer had known about the checks. Sarecky refuted this, claiming he had signed the letter just as he had been signing Sulzer's letters for years. Sarecky justified this by an implied "general power of attorney" before proceeding to demonstrate to the Court his proficiency in imitating the governor's signature.

Sarecky went into great detail to explain the discrepancy between the donations and the report of the donations: he had created the report piecemeal from his daily memorandum sheets and deposit slips. He acknowledged that the report was inaccurate and even conceded that it was inaccurate at the time the statement was prepared.

In their cross-examination, the impeachment managers made Sarecky—and his explanation—appear ridiculous. At great length, Stanfield took him through contribution after contribution from the bank records to show that Sarecky reported most contributions on any given day, skipping exclusively and inclusively liquor interests, Tammany district leaders, and Wall Street financiers. These three groups were seriously at odds with both Sulzer's self-projected man-of-the-people image and his constant claims of independence. Although he remained unflappable, Sarecky's only answer was that these must have been the records that had been lost.

Throughout, Sarecky maintained that he had never spoken to the governor about these contributions or about omitting any contributors from the report. He insisted it was his own decision to use some of the campaign money for purposes other than the campaign.

More problematic for the defense, Sarecky said he could not remember whether he had told Sulzer of his subpoena from the Frawley Committee. But under tough cross-examination Sarecky admitted he had notified Sulzer, although he maintained his steadfast denial that the governor had advised him how to handle it. Similarly, Sarecky denied he had conferred with Louis Marshall (one of Sulzer's counsels in the Court of Impeachment) but could not explain his statement to the Frawley Committee that Marshall was his attorney and had advised him not to answer that committee's questions.

Sarecky also testified that he had sent all evidence relating to the campaign contributions, bound in several volumes, to the Governor's Mansion in Albany, just as the Frawley Committee had begun its hearings. He was vague and evasive about who had paid his salary while he worked for Sulzer, essentially claiming not to know the source of his income. Finally, Sarecky seemed ill at ease trying to explain or justify his rapid promotions: first as clerk in the adjutant general's office, then secretary to the governor, and finally as deportation agent. He was especially coy about being appointed as a deportation agent, admitting that he had no special skills or training for the job.

Following Sarecky, the defense turned to a different area, calling Edward P. Meany and Hugh J. Reilly. Meany had loaned $10,000 to Sulzer without asking for collateral and testified it was not a campaign contribution. Reilly, who had previously been associated with Sulzer in an attempt to collect money from the Cuban government, told of loaning Sulzer $26,500, again without security. Apparently these were part of an attempt by the defense to show that many well-wishers simply wanted to help the governor. Instead, they served to raise more questions about the governor's constant need for money. That these loans were made without collateral and offered as evidence without any written proof seriously undermined the testimony and instead may have raised other, equally serious questions.*

The last witness called by the defense was John A. Hennessy. Hennessy was Sulzer's star investigator, and he came to court with a mass of papers that documented graft in government. The defense wanted to show that David Peck, whose testimony had been so damaging to Sulzer and in whose department Hennessy had exposed so much graft and corruption, was tied in with Tammany Hall, leaving the Court—or at least the public—to make the inference that Peck had lied on the stand. Before the attacks on Tammany could even begin, Chief Judge Cullen rejected the line of questioning, ruling that the defense could not discredit the charges by attacking the motives of the accusers or even attack the accusers themselves. This was a big blow to the defense, as their strategy was based in large part on discrediting Sulzer's accusers and, perhaps more importantly, impugning their motives.

And what of Sulzer? "Only a few days after the trial began, [Sulzer]

---

* The managers sought to show that Reilly and his business associates had hired Sulzer while he was a member of Congress to help them collect debts owed by the Cuban government, an apparent misuse of his congressional office, but Judge Cullen ruled this was immaterial and irrelevant, ending the prosecution's attempts to bring Sulzer's congressional career into the trial.

told newspaper men that nothing short of death would prevent him from testifying."[50] The governor had promised "amazing revelations" about prominent Democratic politicians and hinted that those revelations would lead to the indictment of Charles Murphy.[51]

"I'll come out of this with flying colors," Sulzer boasted, "and will show the People, who constitute the highest of all courts, that I am being made a victim of a few little mistakes of mine which are being made to appear in the light of great crimes."[52] "When I make my reply," the governor promised, "and show the real purpose of this move to get me out of the way, I know the People well enough to justify the prediction that they will exonerate me of intentional wrongdoing and will vent their wrath upon Murphy and the other men from whose clutches I have rescued the State."[53]

But William Sulzer never showed up to face the Court of Impeachment. In lieu of his testimony and deprived of the opportunity to put Boss Murphy on trial, the defense abruptly rested its case.[54]

CLOSING STATEMENTS

On October 9 Louis Marshall began the closing statements on behalf of Governor Sulzer's defense with a three-hour-plus speech that set the stage for the final stretch of the impeachment hearings: "We are on the threshold of an event which will make a permanent impression upon the history of our beloved State, which will entail consequences far beyond our ken, which will determine whether or not the reign of law has ceased, and that of passion and prejudice has begun."[55] Falling back on Sulzer's career serving the public, Marshall played up the governor's popularity, his efficient reorganization of government, and his crusading work in exposing graft and corruption. This last attribute proved, said Marshall, that Sulzer was innocent. Marshall asked, why should a man "who wrought all this" be subject to "this awful degradation"? Moving from the general to the specific, he dissected each of the impeachment articles, declaring none of them proved.

Articles One and Two related to actions taken by Sulzer before he entered the office of governor and therefore were, Marshall insisted, not impeachable. He continued, the impeachment itself was inconsistent with the fundamental principles of liberty and justice. It was a dangerous overreach by the assembly, which had assumed an unlimited and arbitrary theory of impeachment. Marshall revisited the history of the state and national constitutions—in great detail and at greater length—arguing that this attempt to impeach Sulzer was without parallel. History, Marshall demonstrated, showed that trying to impeach a governor for anything other than official misconduct *while in office* was equally unprecedented. Rather, he insisted, it was appropriate for ordinary courts to deal with any crime outside the governor's official duties. The justice system could—and should—handle any such complaints or proceedings. Marshall asserted that unless it had been proven that Sulzer had committed a crime, he could not be held guilty under the Articles of Impeachment.[56]

Revisiting the Corrupt Practices Act in great detail, Marshall declared that the statement required by the candidate was not required to include sums contributed to him. Moreover, the act did not require an oath. Therefore, under Marshall's analysis, Sulzer's affidavit was voluntary, extrajudicial, and not perjury. The donors referred to in Articles One and Two testified, Marshall said, that their contributions were neither specifically nor officially campaign contributions. As a result, Sulzer received the monies as gifts, making them available for any purpose he sought fit. Since Sulzer did not intend to use the gifts for election purposes, he could not be guilty of perjury for omitting them from his statement.

Marshall was equally dismissive of Article Three. It was, he argued, indefinite because it did not specify how witnesses were bribed or what testimony was withheld. He pointed out that Fuller did, eventually, testify before the Frawley Committee, attributing his reluctance to testify to his own personal misgivings. As for Colwell, Marshall pointed out that no evidence had been introduced tying him directly to Sulzer, characterizing the testimony that Colwell said he was going to Albany to see Sulzer as trivial. To find Sulzer guilty of bribery or inducing anyone to withhold testimony was, according to defense counsel, "a violent conjecture and an ungrounded suspicion."⁵⁷ On the more damaging instance, the lucrative promotion that Sarecky received, Marshall tried to marginalize the governor's involvement, placing the responsibility for hiring Sarecky with both the State Hospital Commission and the Civil Service Commission, thereby absolving Sulzer of any wrongdoing.

Marshall made quick work of Articles Four and Five. Article Four was too vague, because it offered no specific allegations as to what deceit and fraud were practiced and offered no evidentiary proof. Article Five was also a "blank record," because no evidence had been offered.

Next, Marshall launched his strongest defense of Sulzer, a blistering attack on Peck and his credibility. Noting that Peck's testimony was "a brazen counterfeit and [full] of hypocrisy," Marshall sarcastically marveled at the man's "extraordinary" memory, recounting a conversation word for word almost two months later.⁵⁸ Why, Marshall asked, had Peck not testified before the Frawley Committee? More than simply being false, Marshall dismissed Peck as having an interest in the matter, pointing out that Peck's department had been under investigation and that "irregularities of a very serious nature" had been found. Marshall maintained that these "irregularities" not only threatened Peck's hold on office but also threatened him with criminal prosecution.⁵⁹ This motivated Peck to contribute to Sulzer's destruction. Contrasting Peck's testimony with Morgenthau's, Marshall claimed that Sulzer's discussions with Morgenthau were "easy" and "natural."⁶⁰

Taking up Article Six, Marshall argued that all the contributions to Sulzer had been gifts and, as such, the governor could not be guilty of grand larceny—which, Marshall laid out, was a property crime. Since there had been neither agreement to repay the money, demands for its return, nor any complaint as to how it was used, Marshall insisted there could be no legal basis for a charge of larceny.

Marshall continued his closing argument by dismissing the testimony of Assemblyman Prime and Assemblyman Sweet offered as proof under Article Seven. It was "trivial," claimed Marshall, insisting that the governor had a legitimate right to discuss *any* legislation with *any* member of the legislature. The quote attributed to Sulzer, "You for me, and I for you," was not, Marshall said, malignant.[61] Accordingly, the whole thing should be characterized as simply the fair give-and-take of politics.

Article Eight, Marshall declared, was "if possible, even more contemptible."[62] Characterizing Sulzer's owning stock while simultaneously advocating for regulatory measures on the stock exchange as a crime was the furthest overreach by the prosecution. Elected officials were always a part of the worlds they had to govern. Some conflicts were inevitable, but in this case, Marshall was resolute: Sulzer's proposed regulations would have reduced the value of his own investments. The suggestion that he was guilty of a crime for decreasing the value of his holdings was objectionable.

Having dismissed all of the charges against Sulzer, Marshall turned his attention to the impeachment managers. In their effort to destroy William Sulzer they had "lost all sense of proportion."[63] Although a key part of the defense strategy was to inflame passions against Tammany, Marshall admonished the Court to rise above passions and prejudice: "We are not so much concerned in this case with William Sulzer, the man or the Governor, as we are with the supremacy of the law, with the perpetuity of its principles, with the preservation of orderly government.... Shall ours be a government of laws, or one of passion and caprice?"[64]

It was a well-reasoned speech, one that had many members of the public nodding their heads in agreement, and Marshall would later tell a companion that he was confident it would stave off impeachment. Alton Parker, however, was an equally convincing speaker. His closing statement ran for almost the length of an entire day, from the afternoon session through the morning session of the next day. It focused mostly on the constitutional basis of impeachment and Sulzer's guilt on the perjury, false statement, and larceny charges.

Rising on behalf of the managers, Parker opened by chastising the defense for not answering any of the material facts that the impeachment managers had presented. He went on to describe the origins of the Corrupt Practices Act, asserting it was passed to ensure the publicity of campaign contributions and expenditures. Parker reminded the court that, according to uncontradicted evidence, Sulzer received $37,400 (over $820,000 in 2010 dollars) in unaccounted-for cash and checks. At great length, Parker highlighted Sulzer's refusal to appear and answer any of the charges against him. Instead, and according to Parker this was much worse, Sulzer left the task of defending himself to "so absolutely worthless a character" as Sarecky.[65] How could Sulzer have simply forgotten contributions from the brewers and financiers who would have been out of place in a campaign for a so-called man of the people? How could he have forgotten so many contributions that he had personally solicited? Even if Sarecky had done his best and simply made mistakes (after mistakes after mistakes) on the statement, surely "his master" who signed the statement must have known it was a lie.[66]

Specifically addressing Article Two, Parker slashed at Marshall's interpretation of the election law, making a convincing argument that the law was clear—calling for a sworn statement of all contributions made to a candidate. Ipso facto, Sulzer was a perjurer.

Continuing to attack the defense's case, Judge Parker took issue with Marshall's arguments on Article Six. Being a trustee of the contributions, Parker argued, was not necessary for Sulzer's actions to be larcenous. Citing Section 1290 of the Penal Law, Parker showed that obtaining money by false pretense qualified as larceny. The testimony and evidence showed that the contributions were made for campaign purposes, or at least because Sulzer was a candidate for governor, and Sulzer misappropriated the money for his own personal use. The only plausible explanation for the gift of the monies, according to Parker, was to pay Sulzer's expenses during his campaign for governor. Just because some of the contributors later gave the transaction another name (to save Sulzer from "embarrassment," Parker maintained), it did not change the actual purpose for which the money was given originally. Since Sulzer never informed the donors that he intended to use the money for personal expenses or to purchase stock, Parker declared him guilty of the crime of false representation.[67]

Returning to his discussion of the state constitution, Parker gave a long treatise on impeachment—its origins, evolution, and purpose. That purpose, Parker argued, was not to punish lawbreakers or prosecute crimes but rather to remove a corrupt official from office. Impeachment served not to punish the trespasser but to protect the state from those trespasses. As a result, actions that might not be criminal were still impeachable.

Parker quoted Samuel Tilden at great length. According to the former governor, an officer was impeachable under the constitution and law of New York for acts committed before—or entirely disconnected with—his office. The constitution and laws "do not limit that range of impeachable acts... but leave the whole judgment as to whether or not the disqualification is produced to the supreme and exclusive jurisdiction of the High Court of Impeachment, which is the ultimate agent of the sovereign people in their supervisory power over public office."[68] Election to office, Parker continued, was not "a certificate of any guaranty of fitness to hold that office."[69] However, in this case, Sulzer's offenses were "so closely connected with, and so necessary a condition precedent to his induction into office, that [his offense] constitutes a part of his gubernatorial career."[70]

Parker concluded with a strong denunciation of Sulzer: "Every disguise has been torn from his back, from the petticoat in which he trusted for safety to the armor of defiance in which he threatened to attack and expose a political leadership to which we have found him suing later for merciful obliteration of his misdeeds, and offered the bribe of submission."[71] Parker continued, "With this Court, alone, rests the duty of delivering this State from the menace that like the sword of Damocles hangs above it so long as this man so conclusively demonstrated to be guilty of deliberate and heinous wrongdoing remains in the executive chair."[72]

D-Cady Herrick followed Parker to deliver the final closing remarks for the defense. His themes were reason and fairness. Sulzer, he reminded the Court, "is not on trial for disloyalty; he is not on trial for ingratitude.... He is not on trial for unfitness for office."[73] Herrick reiterated many of Marshall's arguments. Conceding that keeping campaign contributions may not be moral or ethical, Herrick denied that it was illegal and argued that a democratically elected official could not be impeached merely because he had low ethical standards. Herrick also reminded the Court that many notable figures in American public life had received assistance from their wealthy friends.

Responding to Parker's strong attack on Sarecky, Herrick tried to rehabilitate Sulzer's former clerk. He defended Sarecky as "fearless" and "frank" for his story about preparing the campaign statement. There was no reason, Herrick declared, *not* to believe the young clerk's account. Simultaneously, Herrick lambasted Peck, at one point declaring, "The meanest criminal is the man who turns state's evidence."[74]

Herrick then attempted a broader effort at exculpation, offering comprehensive and wide-reaching defenses. He made a vague allusion to Mrs. Sulzer and declared that the governor was acting to protect her honor, at risk to his own dishonor, by not testifying. He justified Sulzer's outreach through Ryan to the political bosses as only natural for a politician. Herrick argued that Sulzer's term would soon end, allowing the voters the opportunity to decide his fate. The defense concluded with an appeal to protect New York State's honor: "The bringing of these impeachment proceedings is lamentable because of the object lesson of what may occur to any man in public life who dares stand and oppose the wishes of those who may know something about his private life and history not known to the general public."[75]

The trial for the managers was closed by former senator Brackett. It included another scathing attack on Sulzer. Brackett accused the governor of using "every art known to the demagogue" to intimidate the members of the Court and the prosecution.[76] Brackett's speech described Sulzer maliciously with words like "faithless" and "criminal" and phrases like "a cringing, miserable craven," "an outcast among men," and many more similarly illiberal representations.[77] Sulzer, Brackett said, had used every weapon in his arsenal of courtroom tricks to have the impeachment charges dismissed without ever addressing their substance. Because Sulzer and his team never contradicted any of the prosecution's evidence, Brackett labeled the governor's general denial of the charges "an infamous lie."[78]

Continuing to evaluate the defense's case, Brackett rejected its contention that the money was given to Sulzer for his personal use, calling it a "sham and pretense."[79] "With regards to these so-called gifts, if the Schiff check was a gift to Sulzer personally, why was it made payable to Sarecky and why was it deposited by Sarecky into Sarecky's bank account?" asked the former senator, describing the clear effort to hide the source of funds and the disposition.

Echoing the doubts many New Yorkers had about Sulzer's transformation from Tammany henchman to unbossed reformer, Brackett mocked the governor's conversion:

> Oh, but on the first of January, like Saul of Tarsus on his way to Damascus, there came a light. Where, before that moment, he was in gall of bitterness and bondage of sin, although prior to that time he had done nothing but serve the forces of evil, yet from the first day of January when the light came to him, William became a consecrated man and devoted himself thenceforth to the service of God and humanity in the People's House. Oh Saul! Saul! Persecutor of the Saints, but, finally the greatest of the Apostles, what foolishness has been attempted through the years because of that sudden conversion of yours on the way to Damascus! There is many a man who tried to liken himself to Paul when the only likeness is to that of Saul.[80]

Brackett contrasted this saint with the man who solicited money from financiers, brewers, and trust magnates. "Can you imagine," Brackett asked, "Paul telephoning to Gamaliel that he was 'the same old Saul,' and 'Can't you make it more than $7,500?'"[81] Regarding Sulzer's request to Morgenthau "to go easy" on him, Brackett asked, "Do criminals find it necessary to solicit witnesses to tell the truth?"[82]

Seeking to rehabilitate Peck, Brackett pointed out that despite all the attacks on Peck's professional life and his work at the Highway Department, no one from the defense and not a single witness said anything to specifically contradict his testimony. The same was true of Ryan's testimony: no witness said anything to challenge its essentials. Both collectively, and individually, these witnesses proved that Sulzer had encouraged and suborned perjury.

In fact, Brackett argued, the defense's chief witness, Sarecky, had "sworn himself a criminal" when he admitted to forging Sulzer's name on countless occasions.[83] And how did that great reformed Saint Sulzer react? Instead of admonishing or disciplining Sarecky, Sulzer promoted him. The fact that Sarecky had intentionally destroyed every shred of evidence—Sarecky testified that, other than the information he sent to the Executive Mansion, he had shredded or burned any other records—was proof of guilty intent. With this, the closing statements ended.

FURTHER TRIAL MOTIONS

The Court then adjourned until October 13, a full four days, under strict instructions from the chief justice to refrain from discussing the case. Upon reconvening there was another recess before both sides argued a technical point: Did the testimony of Morgenthau, Ryan, and Peck fall under Article Four? That article charged Sulzer with suppressing evidence (violating Section 814 of the Penal Code) in that he had "practiced deceit and fraud and used threats and menaces, with intent to prevent said committee and the people of the State from procuring the attendance and testimony of certain witnesses, to wit: Louis A. Sarecky, Frederick L. Colwell and Melville B. Fuller, and *all other persons?*" (emphasis added). And if not, did the Court have the power to amend the articles? Or did they need to be returned to the assembly in order to be revised? It was another attempt by the defense to find help in a technicality.

Stanchfield, speaking for the impeachment managers, argued that although the assembly alone had the power to impeach, the Court of Impeachment, being an extraordinary court, had the power to modify the articles as necessary in light of the proof in front of them. Moreover, since the charge included the catch-all "all other persons," that covered, well, just about anyone. After formally asking the court to include those charges, Stanchfield offered an additional opportunity to Sulzer to take the stand or offer new witnesses to meet the new accusation.

Herrick and Marshall offered compelling arguments for the defense. Arguing that an impeachment trial and criminal trial are analogous, they offered the criminal justice standard that the accused could only be tried for the specific offenses brought against him. Moreover, the conversations with Morgenthau, Peck, and Ryan all happened *subsequent* to the adoption of the impeachment articles. Article Four spoke specifically to the Frawley Committee, and each of these conversations happened after that committee had offered its report to the legislature.

The Court of Impeachment spent a day in private, closed consultation. Afterward, the chief justice announced the rejection of the application to amend the articles. However, the Court also ruled that Article Four was sufficiently broad to include Peck's testimony as substantive proof. Morgenthau and Ryan could be considered not on their own but instead as corroborative evidence to the other allegations.

Following this pronouncement, the Court returned to executive session for another thirty-six hours. There is no record of those proceedings, but credible observers offered that the nonlawyers among the senators were being instructed as to the value in a legal context of the evidence submitted for and against the governor.[84]

Sulzer and many of his supporters knew the damage that had been done and recognized that the Court was aligned against him. Nevertheless, they expressed the fervent hope that the Court would only consider the charges that occurred subsequent to his inauguration, disregarding every other charge against him.[85]

There was also a widespread sense that the senators, mindful of the gravity of their decision and the potential for precedent, would be fair and objective. Even the most loyal Tammany senators were adamant that their judgment would be guided by a judicious interpretation of the law. The press reported that "no orders" had been issued by Boss Murphy.[86] "The only suggestion made by Murphy," said a senator who insisted on anonymity but made no effort to downplay his allegiance to the Tammany Hall, "is that we vote according to the facts and take our law from the Judges of the Court of Appeals."[87]

In the absence of orders from Boss Murphy, would the law and facts of the case be enough to save William Sulzer?

22

THE VERDICT

LATE IN THE AFTERNOON ON OCTOBER 16, after a twenty-one-day trial with hundreds of hours of testimony, the Court ended its executive session and proceeded to a public vote on the governor's impeachment. The atmosphere was tense and hushed. Whatever happened next, whether exoneration or removal from office, history would be made. First, the clerk read each article in turn. Then, as he called each member of the Court by name, the presiding judge asked, "How say you? Is the respondent guilty or not guilty?"

Many members took the opportunity to explain their votes. Those voting for acquittal for the most part reported that, yes, the managers had proved beyond a doubt that Sulzer's actions were unethical and immoral, but those acts were nonetheless technically not impeachable.

Chief Judge Edgar Cullen, a man of sterling integrity and benign impartiality who commanded universal respect and whose handling of the case was widely praised, also voted no[1] — not because he thought Sulzer innocent; rather, the chief judge thought that the impeachment power of the legislature only applied to acts that occurred during the accused's term of office. Cullen said of Sulzer's actions, "They displayed such moral turpitude and delinquency that, if they had been committed during the respondent's incumbency of office, I think they would require his removal."[2]

Cullen believed the accusations of the First Article to have been proved. The sum received by Sulzer was "so grossly in excess" of what had been reported that the error could not have been a simple mistake. Even if Sarecky's testimony was to be believed, it did not, in Judge Cullen's view, relieve Sulzer of the responsibility since most of the money had been personally received by Sulzer. Judge Cullen found that the statement Sulzer signed (and to which he had sworn) was false, but that *technically* it was not required by the Election Law and was therefore not perjury, and that *technically* the Penal Law did not require an accounting of his contributions. Nevertheless, Cullen declared, the "moral guilt remained the same."[3] Damning Sulzer even more, Cullen announced that he found Sulzer guilty of asking Peck to perjure himself, but since *technically* Peck was not a part of the charged offense and since the Court had no power to amend the Articles of Impeachment, he therefore could not vote to remove the governor from office.

Cullen acknowledged that these were all technicalities and said as much: "The point here urged may be criticized as technical, but if so I hope that technicality will always be respected to the extent of preventing the trial of a man for one offense and convicting him of another."[4] "As has been often expressed," Cullen said, "the object of impeachment is to remove a corrupt and unworthy officer. But a corrupt and unworthy officer is an entirely different thing from an officer who has, before his office, been unworthy and corrupt."[5] In conclusion, Cullen argued that "[such a] rule contended for amounts in reality to an ex post facto disqualification from office for an offense which had no such penalty when committed, without affording an opportunity for showing repentance or atonement."[6]

On the other hand, Judge Frank Hiscock dismissed those objections. Hiscock, who would serve as chief justice from 1917 until his mandatory retirement in 1926, said, a "fair and reasonable interpretation of the Constitution did not arbitrarily prohibit the impeachment of an official for an act performed before entering into his office," and that Sulzer's conduct between his election and inauguration with respect to campaign contributions had "such a relation to his office, his official tenure, and the discharge of his official duties that it reasonably came within the spirit of the Constitution."[7] It is worth noting that Hiscock was a Republican and not allied in any way with Murphy or Tammany Hall.

Perhaps the best summary of the case is this: "With the facts before it, even a friendly court could hardly have failed to condemn him on the merits, and this court was not friendly."[8]

In the final analysis, the judges of the Court of Appeals were divided on the technical legal aspects of the case (Judge Werner, unable to reconcile the legal impeachability of Sulzer's bad acts, said he gave Sulzer "the benefit of the doubt"[9]), the most grave of which was the doubtful and difficult question of impeachment for acts not committed in office, though related to his position as governor. Yet none of the judges questioned the seriousness of his delinquency.[10] "Although there was a division on the question of Sulzer's legal guilt, there was practically no division of opinion about his moral guilt."[11] Justice William Werner said, "We know that he had committed acts which are so morally indefensible that they can hardly be described in language of judicial air and form."[12] Judge Nathan Miller (later elected governor) said, "A grave offense committed before induction to office may constitute cause for impeachment provided it so touches the office and bears such a relation to the discharge of its duties as to unfit the offender to discharge those duties."[13] Four judges of the Court of Appeals shared Judge Miller's views: Hiscock, Collin, Cuddeback, and Hogan (Miller, Hiscock, and Collin were Republicans, and Cuddeback and Hogan were Democrats).

While there existed among Murphy's critics a feeling that Sulzer had in fact been punished not for his vices but for his virtues, nevertheless he had "so discredited himself that his removal was approved by most thoughtful men."[14]

Succinctly, one observer summed it up thus:

> Sulzer was a dreamer, erratic and egotistical, inspired by a desire to serve the public, but also by an overwhelming ambition for leadership and distinction. He had studied the examples of Roosevelt and Hughes as champions of moral issues, and he sought to follow in their footsteps, but he had neither the ability, equipment, nor character for such a part. He failed to realize that the Galahad of politics must be beyond reproach. With incredible levity for one dreaming of the high mission that he had set for himself, he gave hostages to his enemies and put himself in their power by acts that any circumspect politician would have avoided from policy if not from principle.[15]

The biggest surprise of the trial was not what had happened in the Court but what *had not* happened. In spite of his boasts, Sulzer never showed up, nor had he attempted to tell his side of the story, at least under oath. Even as late as two weeks before the end of the trial Sulzer continued to declare, "I have fully decided to go on the witness stand. Nothing can prevent me from going on the stand and telling everything that I know if the Judges give me the opportunity."[16]

Sulzer's silence completely changed public perception, negating all the gains that had been made in his favor when his impeachment proceedings had been rushed through in the middle of the night. As long as Sulzer promised to destroy Murphy, expose Tammany, and shine the light of truth on the evils of government under boss rule, he maintained a strong following across the state, an unfairly persecuted champion of "the People."

However, his silence during the trial was louder than his usual loquaciousness, and his reticence was interpreted as guilt, not resolve. In one analysis, "His sinister silence put the seal of accuracy upon the cumulative testimony of Morgenthau, Peck, and Ryan, and led to a decided change of sentiment even among his most devoted followers. Sulzer's failure to come before the Court under oath and make an effort to vindicate himself simply meant that he had no defense to offer, other than that he was not personally responsible for the violation of the Corrupt Practices Act."[17] Even worse, said the *World*, the governor's case rested on "the unsupported and ridiculous testimony of a scapegoat stenographer."[18]

Another analyst said, "Indeed, he probably would have taken the witness stand and denied everything had it not been for the appearance of Allan Ryan, son of Thomas F. Ryan, who was called as a witness on the trial and testified that he had been appealed to by Sulzer to save him. The result was an unrelieved picture of petty dishonesty and futile intrigue, and the defense was driven to reliance on legal technicalities."[19]

The only explanation offered by Sulzer's counsel was that he did not want to "drag his wife into the situation."[20] "There would have been no end of condemnation and a well-nigh unanimous demand for his removal if Mr. Sulzer had resorted to such a cowardly act as hiding behind a woman's skirts," said Herrick.[21] Considering that none of the witnesses who did appear, including Sarecky, made any efforts or offered any testimony that even remotely implicated Mrs. Sulzer, it is difficult to credit Herrick's contention. Even if Sulzer himself was too gentlemanly to implicate his wife, it is difficult to believe that the other witnesses, especially those involved with the shares, would not have offered any connection to Mrs. Sulzer or any plausible trail that could have implicated her as responsible for the scandal if they could have done so. One loyalist, Samuel Bell Thomas, offered a different explanation in his polemic. Sulzer "had an absolute defense to the 'framed-up charges' of Mr. Murphy. His defense was carefully gone over by his lawyers and they knew that should he take the stand, the revelations he would make would bring about the Governor's complete vindication." But when the "packed" court ruled out the testimony of Hennessy, Thomas claimed, it was apparent that it would also do the same to any testimony Sulzer might offer relating to the difficulties he had with Murphy."[22] Yet it is very difficult to credit this account. The Court rejected Hennessy's testimony because it was about another witness's alleged corruption. It is hard to believe that the Court would have not allowed Sulzer the opportunity to tell his story. While the majority of the Court may have been disinclined to support Sulzer, Cullen was credited by all objective observers with presiding over a fair trial.

The truth is more difficult to ascertain. The *Times* stated "on excellent authority" that neither the counsel nor the managers would have objected to Sulzer telling his story, especially since it would have given the managers the opportunity to cross-examine him.[23] They were prepared to make sensational disclosures, hitherto unsuspected, dealing with his private business activities while serving as governor.[24] "If Sulzer doesn't go on the stand, his failure will be interpreted as a confession; if he does go on, it will be suicide."[25] It seems likely that Sulzer avoided testifying, not because he was protecting his wife, but because he was avoiding the merciless cross-examination. His legal team preferred to rest its case on the ground that the prosecution failed to prove the charges rather than risk putting Sulzer on the stand where every scandal—from the breach of promise charges, to allegations of corruption in Congress, and so on—would be used to destroy his credibility.[26]

Without Sulzer's testimony, the Court of Impeachment was left to make a decision on the evidence that had been presented.

On Article One, making and filing a false statement, Sulzer was found guilty. Judges Collins, Cuddeback, Hogan, Hiscock, and Miller along with twenty-three Democratic senators and eleven Republican senators voted guilty. Had the four senators whose votes were challenged at the beginning of the trial been disqualified, Sulzer would have survived; the guilty vote was just one vote more than the two-thirds necessary to convict.

On Article Two, perjury in filing the campaign finance statement, Sulzer was found guilty by the same vote. At this point, Chief Justice Cullen made a speech to the point that the law did not require the sworn statement. Senator Blauvelt challenged him, arguing that "measured by legal standards" Sulzer's offense was just as bad since the intent to deceive was there.[27]

The third article accused Sulzer of bribery in trying to influence witnesses. On this count, the court unanimously acquitted Sulzer. There was no discussion, and Judge Cullen dispensed with the formality of asking each senator if he wanted to explain his vote.

On the fourth article, that of suppressing evidence, Sulzer was found guilty by a vote of 43-14. Three judges—Werner, Chase, and Bartlett—and three senators joined the guilty votes, while two judges who had voted guilty on counts one and two voted not guilty on this count. That is, six of the judges voted to sustain this count. Most of the explanations centered on Peck's testimony. Justice Cullen forcefully dissented on the grounds that Peck's testimony did not fall under the scope of the original article. "It seems to me," said Judge Werner, "to require the narrowest kind of technical reasoning to hold that, because Peck was not mentioned by name in the fourth charge, it must be regarded as insufficient to charge the offense established by his testimony." The threat need not be by word of mouth "but may be fairly implied when the relations of the parties to such a transaction, as was testified to by Peck, are such that the very request carries with it the menace in case of non-compliance."[28]

Out of the nine judges, presumably more independent or at least less partisan than legislators, seven found Sulzer guilty of at least one count.

Sulzer was acquitted of the other counts, Articles Five and Six, unanimously. By the senators' remarks, it was clear that "the general attitude was that on the evidence adduced, Sulzer had unquestionably taken advantage of his nomination to obtain large sums of money for his own enrichment, but that the misappropriation of campaign contributions could not be regarded as larceny in the legal sense. Even though the senators voted to acquit him, every judge or senator who explained his vote took the opportunity to condemn Sulzer. Senator Bussey called Sulzer's actions "panhandling."[29] Judge Cullen, who voted throughout to acquit, said Sulzer was guilty of "such moral turpitude and delinquency that if they had been committed during the respondent's incumbency of office I think they would require his removal."[30]

By a margin of 43-12, the Court of Impeachment voted to remove William Sulzer from the office of governor of the state of New York.

PART FIVE

23

AFTERMATH

IMPEACHMENT. REMOVAL FROM OFFICE. The enormity of these actions in October 1913 cannot be overstated. In the 124 years since the adoption of the U.S. Constitution, the impeachment of a chief executive was extremely rare—and conviction and removal from office even less common. Five states had experienced the impeachment of their chief executive, and each case was in the midst of the turmoil of Reconstruction following the Civil War or the chaos leading up to it, as in Bloody Kansas. And only two of those governors had their impeachment sustained and were removed from office.

- In 1862 the first governor of Kansas, Charles L. Robinson, was impeached. Originally from New England, Robinson was a fierce advocate of the Free-Staters when the state was called "Bleeding Kansas" because of the bloody struggle with proslavery advocates. This advocacy led to his impeachment, but he was acquitted and served the remainder of his term.

- William Woods Holden was appointed as governor of North Carolina by President Andrew Johnson and later elected in large part by African American voters newly freed from slavery and grateful for the Republican Party's candidates. Holden was aggressive in challenging the Ku Klux Klan, but that group's suppression of the black vote cost the Republican Party its majorities in the legislature. Newly emboldened Democrats impeached and removed Holden from office in 1870 based on charges resulting from the conduct of the militia in combating the abuses of the Klan, including the assassination of a state senator and the lynching of an African American police officer. In 2011 the North Carolina Senate pardoned Holden by a vote of 48-0.
- David Butler was the first governor of Nebraska and the only one to be impeached. Elected governor in 1866 he moved the state's capital from Omaha to Lincoln. In the spring of 1871, in his third term, Butler was accused of misusing money from the state school fund (a sum of $16,000) and other offenses. Impeached and convicted of this charge, he was removed from office. In 1877 the state legislature expunged the impeachment proceedings from the record. Ten years later, Butler was elected to the state senate for two terms.
- The year 1872 saw Louisiana governor Henry Clay Warmoth impeached. Warmoth arrived in New Orleans as a carpetbagger following the Civil War. His support of civil rights legislation earned him the support and votes of newly enfranchised African American voters and Radical Republicans, and he was elected governor at the age of twenty-six. His less fierce advocacy in office lost him the support of this political base. Elected as a Republican, he

campaigned hard for the Democratic ticket in 1872, an election that had the results disputed. He was impeached for these actions, but only thirty-five days remained before the end of his term. No impeachment trial was ever held.

- Adelbert Ames, a distinguished soldier, served as military governor of Mississippi and, after serving in the U.S. Senate, was elected to governor. A carpetbagger himself, he was locked in a vicious battle with the scalawag faction for control of the state's Republican Party. A close election in 1876 led to riots in Vicksburg and the so-called Mississippi Plan, whereby feuding factions of Democrats laid aside their differences to unite against the GOP. The results were marred by widespread election fraud and voter intimidation. Ames's call for the intervention of the U.S. Congress caused the legislature to vote to impeach him. Before the vote to convict him, Ames struck a deal with the legislature: he resigned and the impeachment articles were dropped.

Now the governor of New York State had been removed from office. The verdict was headline news across the nation. Major cities — with political machines of their own — had certainly followed the story. The banner headline in *The Day Book* of Chicago was, "SULZER IS OFFICIALLY OUSTED FROM THE GOVERNOR'S CHAIR — GLYNN SWORN IN." San Francisco's *The Call* led with "War Balloon Explodes, 27 Are Killed," but just below, in equally large type, the "Clean, Wholesome Paper for California Homes" headlined, "SULZER, DENOUNCED, REMOVED," with the subheading, "Governor Thrown Out of Office: Even Former Friends Score Executive for Acts." In Washington, DC, the *Washington Times* published, "SULZER VOWS TO BREAK TAMMANY; WILL RUN AGAIN: Deposed Official Declares He Will Redeem Himself Before People In November."

And the *Washington Herald* printed, "'GUILTY' IS VERDICT OF JUDGES IN SULZER CASE," along with an enormous picture of "New York's Guilty Governor and 'Boss' Who Unmade Him."

New York State was so central to the entire union and the trial was so compelling that the impeachment was also front-page news in every corner and in every small town. *The Ogden Standard*, the "Fearless, Independent, Progressive Newspaper" of Ogden City, Utah, declared, "SULZER REMOVED FROM OFFICE: Deposed Governor Receives News at Executive Mansion in Absolute Silence." The *Bismarck Daily Tribune* reported, "SULZER FOUND GUILTY ON THREE COUNTS BY HIGH COURT'S VERDICT," along with "Latest Pictures of William Sulzer, Governor of New York, Declared Guilty By Impeachment Court." Even the *Rogue River Courier*, from Grant's Pass in Josephine County, Oregon, featured the headline, "GOV. SULZER IS FOUND GUILTY."

With the impeachment verdict known, the attention of the press turned to the victor in that struggle for supremacy in the state democracy: Charles Francis Murphy, the grand sachem of Tammany Hall. The day after the verdict, the *New York Times* wrote that Murphy had "established himself securely as the Dictator of Democratic policies in the State."[1]

Sulzer, of course, blamed Murphy exclusively. The now former governor said, "I was impeached not because of the offenses with which I was charged, but because I refused to do Charles F. Murphy's bidding, and because, as the records show, I have relentlessly pursued Mr. Murphy's corrupt henchmen in office."[2]

The biggest shock after Sulzer's impeachment was that the Tammany Hall boss actually spoke to the press. Murphy basically tried to turn the tables, asking, if Sulzer was innocent (or even not guilty), why did he not appear in the Court of Impeachment and say so? If the charges were not true, surely Sulzer would have taken the stand and under oath said as much. Sulzer's failure to speak up for himself, said Murphy, was damning. "The only man responsible for the disgrace and downfall of Governor Sulzer is William Sulzer himself."[3]

Sulzer's constant attacks—on the Court of Impeachment, Tammany Hall, and Boss Murphy—included an often repeated remark in his own defense, namely that he wanted to take the witness stand but was "dissuaded by his lawyers." It might stretch the author's prerogative to say it was untrue, but contemporary reporters called the claim "astonishing."[4] The *New York World*, under the headline, "Lawyers Said to Have Pleaded With Him to Testify," reported, "While D-Cady Herrick and Harold Hinman, of Mr. Sulzer's counsel, have no desire to engage in any controversy with him involving veracity, it is said that under pressure they would say that they not only advised him to take the stand but pleaded with him to do so and that he refused at the last minute."[5] Whether the impeachment managers held more damaging evidence in reserve to challenge Sulzer or whether he simply feared the inevitable ferocious attacks under cross-examination, William Sulzer clearly made the conscious choice not to appear in front of the Court of Impeachment to argue his own case. He preferred, it seemed, the court of public opinion, where many were so blind with hatred at Tammany Hall that they could overlook the former governor's own sins—including his longtime complicity in Tammany Hall's transgressions.

However, many New Yorkers were willing to see in Sulzer the best hope to defeat Tammany Hall. As a longtime creature of the Tammany machine, he knew their tactics and, presumably, their weaknesses. This knowledge and experience were why so many gave credit to Sulzer's attempt to blame Murphy—if not for the former governor's own conduct, then at least for having the temerity to expose that behavior.

Sulzer himself put the best face forward in regard to his removal from office. The *New-York Tribune* reported, "Governor Sulzer appeared to be entirely unaffected by the news of his defeat when seen to-night at the Executive Mansion. 'I have a lot of fight left yet,' the Governor said, 'and they'll find the fight has just begun.'"[6] In fact, as the vote was being taken and reports were trickling back to Sulzer, he and Mrs. Sulzer hosted a small dinner party for close friends. Samuel Bell Thomas said, "Governor Sulzer ate a good, hearty dinner; in fact, an exceptionally hearty dinner and he seemed to enjoy himself throughout."[7] There was talk of a tour of the Midwest, stumping for progressive, unbossed candidates, and of various magazine articles to tell his story before going on the "Chautauqua platform" or speaking circuit.

Instead, Sulzer went home to the East Side of Manhattan to the Sixth Assembly District. This district had been the former governor's home for almost thirty years and had formed the base of his political support as a member of both the assembly and Congress.

The political climate in 1913 was not strikingly dissimilar from that of 1912, when Sulzer was elected governor with voters divided fairly equally between the Democratic, Republican, and Progressive Parties. In an attempt to capitalize on the anti–Tammany Hall sentiment inflamed by Sulzer's impeachment, Republican and Progressive leaders had agreed to a fusion pact. In some districts, the Republican candidate would stand down, and the local party would endorse the Progressive, and vice versa. By not splitting the votes of reform or anti-Tammany voters between different candidates, the hope was that both parties could gain seats in the state legislature at the expense of the Democrats—and not each other.

For this reason, the original Progressive candidate, Otto Lorence, had declined the nomination with the understanding that the Progressive organization in the Sixth District would throw its support behind the Republican candidate, incumbent Harry Kopp. But these were extraordinary times, and many in the Sixth District would always be loyal to William Sulzer. He was convicted by two-thirds of the Court of Impeachment. He was convicted by most in the court of public opinion. Yet many in his community would always love Plain Old Bill. These were his neighbors and friends—the beneficiaries of his representation in Albany and Washington in happier days.

Sulzer's motivation for returning to electoral politics was threefold. First and foremost, the former governor was looking for vindication. Being elected by the people—to any office—would afford him the ability to say that the people supported him, that they forgave his past indiscretions in favor of his progressive accomplishments, and that they took his side over that of Tammany Hall. An election victory would also cast some discredit on the verdict of the Court of Impeachment, as it clearly has in the last century. Second, electoral success would allow him to continue his fight against Murphy and Tammany Hall, giving him a platform and keeping him relevant to the press—more relevant than the "Chautauqua platform." Finally, and certainly not least, Sulzer had a dream: to be the first U.S. senator from New York chosen by direct election or the votes of the people. To run for senate, he had to show he could still win support, and where better to start than the old neighborhood?

In the Sixth District, the voters were ready. Rabbis from every synagogue in the district, along with a "number of old friends," pleaded with Mrs. Sulzer for more than two hours to earn her support for his candidacy. It worked. She said to her husband: "Accept / The people call you. Fight for the cause—win or lose." The deck was stacked. Even Harvey Kopp, the Republican incumbent, promised to retire in favor of Sulzer's candidacy.[8]

In light of his unsatisfied ambitions, the choice was an easy one for the former governor: "In view of urgent pleadings from lifelong friends... begging me to accept the nomination for member of Assembly to further the cause of honest government, I have consented to come back to Albany for the good that I can do."[9]

Many people, including many Progressive leaders, were adamantly against endorsing the former governor. They recognized that he could win the assembly seat but felt that Sulzer's corruption (and their doubts about how far that corruption was in his past) was anathema to the values of the Progressive Party. They also envisioned Sulzer as a distraction to their larger goals. The opposition was led by the chair of the Progressive national executive committee, the New York City chairman, and many other leading members of the party. Unfortunately for them, the power to nominate in an individual assembly district was solely vested in the local committee. Despite strong pressure, these leaders were only able to delay the nomination, not stop it, and the local committee decided to go forward.

Sulzer accepted the nomination and immediately took his campaign to the streets, offering a new twist on an old aphorism: "Hell hath no fury like a governor impeached." Sulzer's campaign was tireless and unsparing. He savaged Tammany and Murphy, and the results showed that Tammany paid full price. The 1913 election was a disaster for the boss and his troops. Nine Organization Democrats lost their seats in the assembly. Tammany's allies in Buffalo, under William Fitzpatrick, lost assemblymen and the mayoralty. Statewide, it was a Republican landslide with the party picking up twenty-five seats in the assembly for a total of seventy-four Republicans, forty-one Democrats, twenty-four Progressives, and eleven members elected on both the Democratic and Progressive tickets (leaving the GOP two votes short of an outright majority). In the biggest blow to Boss Murphy, Fusion candidate John Purroy Mitchel was elected mayor of New York City.[10]

The situation was bad. The *Sun* declared, "Tammany Rout Now Complete." The mayor-elect had been a foe of Murphy's as president of the Board of Aldermen before President Wilson had appointed him as the collector of the Port of New York, and he had campaigned on an anti–Tammany Hall platform. An analysis of city records showed that more than 250 positions served at the pleasure of the mayor, with an aggregate salary of over $1 million. This patronage had been controlled, in large part, by Charles Murphy and had served as the foundation of much of the boss' power. Now it was gone, and already some called for Boss Murphy's head. The *New-York Tribune* headline the morning after election day screamed, "PATRONAGE GONE; MURPHY MUST GO."[11] Although some of Tammany's loyal soldiers were wavering, fear of Murphy kept them quiet. "On the question of a revolt against Murphy they shy like a colt from an automobile." The only leader willing to go on the record, "Big Percy" Nagle, from the uptown's East Side, insisted, "There's nothing to this talk about Murphy's overthrow. Why, any Tammany man who talks about putting Murphy out is a traitor and a cur. Murphy isn't to blame for this. Any man we nominated would have been defeated—it wasn't our year, that's all. The Sulzer thing was too deep. The opposition was united, but we did the best we could."[12] John McCooley, Murphy's counterpart in Brooklyn, was in trouble, but any would-be challengers to Silent Charlie Murphy know "that Murphy will and can fight... As soon as one leader shows his hand, they know that Murphy will set up a new leader in his district and a fight will be begun."[13]

The press and conventional wisdom suggest that these losses were Sulzer's revenge—that the public was so outraged at Tammany's treatment of Sulzer that they turned Murphy's allies out in every part of the state.

This viewpoint is almost universal among those few who know anything about William Sulzer and his story. The Sulzer chapter is a dark one in the history of Tammany Hall and a stain on the impressive records of great New Yorkers like Al Smith and Robert Wagner—a black mark for them, no matter Plain Bill's clear guilt and complicity. However, Sulzer's impeachment was merely a small part of the reason for Tammany's electoral defeat in 1913.

Gambling, gangsters, and murder were the real cause.

On July 16, 1912, a small-time bookmaker named Herman Rosenthal was shot dead in front of the Hotel Metropole near Times Square in midtown Manhattan. The Metropole was a "swell" hotel and the first in the city to have running water in each room. Nevertheless, it was not unusual for men to loiter in front of the hotel, and few noticed anything remarkable about the men gathered there that July morning until just before 2:00 a.m., when Rosenthal stepped out of the dining room. Acting as one, six men pulled revolvers from their pockets and fired. Rosenthal's face was "so spattered with blood and torn by the bullet or bullets that none could be certain how many of the several shots had hit him."[14] The killers leaped into a waiting car that sped away.

The murderers were members of the Lennox Avenue Gang. A violent group of muggers, robbers, and occasional murders, the gang had operated out of Manhattan's Lower East Side since the early 1900s. In a city riddled with gang activity, the Lennox Avenue contingent was considered one of the most violent, with membership that included some of the early twentieth century's most notorious criminals.

This was an era in which crime and police corruption went hand in hand; in eleven years, New York City ran through eight police commissioners alone. But Manhattan district attorney (and future New York governor) Charles Whitman refused to look the other way. Determined to get to the bottom of Rosenthal's murder, he ordered his office to conduct a thorough investigation. What he discovered would rock city politics.

It all began on April 15, 1912, when a squad of policemen, led by Lieutenant Charles Becker, raided Herman Rosenthal's gambling house on West Forty-Fifth Street. This action began a chain of events that culminated on July 11 when Rosenthal went to the West Side Police Court to protest the "oppression" of the police stationing a uniformed man on continual duty inside his venue. He also made a shocking accusation in a signed affidavit that appeared in the New York *World* on July 14. In it, he named Lieutenant Becker as his partner in this gambling operation.* Two days later, Rosenthal was riddled with gunfire. Eyewitnesses reported seeing the gunmen flee in a speeding automobile. Eventually, four of the gunmen—Bald Jack Rose, Bridgie Webber, Harry Vallon, and Sam Schepps—were apprehended and arrested.**

The crime sparked public outrage. A mass meeting was held at Cooper Union on August 14, and a Citizens' Committee was appointed to urge local law enforcement to prosecute to the fullest extent of the law. The Citizens' Committee report, issued in late February 1913, read in part,

---

* "Partner" may be a strong word for what appears to have been a system of levying tribute on unraided gangsters. There was also a story that Becker was angry at Rosenthal for refusing to pay for the legal defense of Becker's press agent, who had been charged with killing an African American in a "raid" on a crap game.

** The informers who tipped police off and later testified were named Louis Rosenberg (alias Lefty Louie), Harry Horowitz (alias Gyp the Blood), Jacob Seidenshner (alias Whitey Lewis), and Frank Cirofici (alias Dago Frank).

Evil thus breeds new maggots of evil. The sums collected by the police excite the greed of certain politicians; they demand their shares, and in their turn they protect the criminal breaches of the law and the police in corruption. The presence of "politics" brings strength and complexity to the "system" and makes it harder to break up. The city, we believe, is convinced that it is time for more radical efforts at improvement.[15]

Reacting to public opinion, the Board of Aldermen got into the act, holding eighty public sessions and taking over 4,800 pages of testimony. Meanwhile, District Attorney Whitman continued his investigation and leaked a report to the press that he had set up a meeting with Rosenthal to discuss the bookie's accusations, not only against Charles Becker, but also three other senior New York City police officials. Rosenthal, however, was gunned down before that meeting could take place, an act that convinced Whitman that Charles Becker had ordered the murder.

The complicated and lengthy investigation dominated the New York papers for the duration. When the dust finally settled nearly two years later, Whitman's office had convicted four police inspectors of bribery, one police captain and one lieutenant of extortion, one patrolman of perjury, and two of extortion. Rosenthal's murderers were electrocuted at Sing Sing on April 13, 1914. Lieutenant Becker met the same fate.[16]

The outcry over Rosenthal's killing built throughout 1913, growing as the hearings were held and as politicians fell over themselves to expose and denounce the corruption and criminal conduct that was not only widespread but had reached the upper echelons of the Police Department.

District Attorney Charles Whitman's determination to see justice prevail would serve him especially well. In 1914 he defeated acting governor Martin Glynn in a landslide, returning the Republican Party to the Executive Mansion and dealing another blow to Charles Murphy and Tammany Hall.[17] Contrary to public opinion today, which ascribes Tammany's losses entirely to the impeachment, the scandal that rocked New York City law enforcement played at least as large a role in Tammany's defeat. In fact, if Tammany was punished by the voters for the Sulzer affair, it was just as much for backing Sulzer in the first place and "getting him in" as it was for impeaching him. The public felt that every part of the William Sulzer experience was a debacle.

Ironically, less than a month after Sulzer was impeached and thrown out of office, he was elected back to Albany as a member of the assembly. In the legislature he was not a factor, but in 1914 he was chosen by both the Prohibition Party and the American Party as their candidate for governor. From both ballot lines, Sulzer garnered 125,844 votes (70,655 on the American line and 54,189 on the Prohibition line). That was about the same that his lieutenant governor, Martin Glynn, received on the Independence League ticket (125,252). But Glynn was also on the Democratic line, where he received 412,253 votes. The end result was Charles Whitman (Republican), 686,701 votes; Glynn, 537,505 votes; and Sulzer, 125,844 votes. Even with Sulzer's votes Glynn would have lost, albeit narrowly, to Whitman. In other words, Sulzer's votes hurt his successor electorally but Glynn would have lost anyway. Sulzer was not a factor in the election.

24

THE CAMPAIGN OF 1917

AT FIFTY-FOUR YEARS OLD, Sulzer continued to be active in politics, especially in New York City municipal elections. In 1917 he campaigned actively for John Purroy Mitchel's reelection as mayor. But, it seems, Sulzer simply could not avoid scandal and controversy.

A leader in the reform movement (especially of the Police Department), Mitchel had still earned the enmity of William Randolph Hearst, allegedly for refusing to appoint Hearst's wife as head of a Women's War Service Committee. Hearst lined up all of his not-inconsiderable resources against Mitchel, attacking him most vociferously as an enemy of the poor.[1] Instead, Hearst found common cause with Charles Murphy, who was desperate enough to return to power that he was willing to work with Hearst. Tammany Hall endorsed Supreme Court judge John Hylan, and Hearst put his media empire behind Hylan's campaign.*

---

* After losing his re-election bid, Mitchel was commissioned a major in the Aviation Section of the Signal Corps. On a training flight, just before his thirty-ninth birthday, Mitchel slipped out of his aircraft, falling 500 feet to his death. He was not wearing his seat belt.

Although Sulzer had spent much of his time as governor trying to ingratiate himself with Hearst, the former governor continued to back Mitchel and was in fact paid the handsome sum of $5,000 to support Mayor Mitchel.

In a move reminiscent of Sulzer's impeachment, the payment to William Sulzer did not appear on the Fusion Committee's election filings. The 1917 campaign was just as raucous and freewheeling as other campaigns in this era, and an extraordinary grand jury was appointed by Governor Whitman to investigate various campaign practices, especially the role that money played in the election. After several months of investigation and hearing testimony, the grand jury indicted Sulzer, William Hamlin Childs (chairman of the Executive Committee of the Fusion Committee of 1917), and former state senator Josiah T. Newcomb on misdemeanor violations of Section 751 of the Penal Law, which required requiring reporting of all campaign expenditures to the Secretary of State.[2] It seemed that these three men concealed under a general item two expenditures—Sulzer's $5,000 payment and a check for $6,500 to Misha Appelbaum of the Humanitarian Cult—which were lumped together as a $11,500 expense "for rent of halls, speakers, taxicab hire, and expenses of meetings."[3]

Childs was a wealthy New Yorker involved with many causes, including the settlement movement, epitomized by the Hull House in Chicago. Childs had been particularly active for Seth Lowe, the Citizens' Union reform candidate for New York City mayor in 1897, and Otto T. Bannard, the Republican candidate for mayor in 1909. Along with George Perkins, Childs was among the largest contributors to President Theodore Roosevelt's campaign when he ran unsuccessfully for president in 1912.[4] Childs was a member of the Merchants Association of New York and a principal in Childs & Childs and Bon Ami, making most of his money through the manufacture of various soaps.

Before the indictment, the grand jury foreman expressed doubts about the case, concerned that the actions were only minor technicalities. The judge presiding over the special term offered a different view. "I charge you that there is no such thing as a technical offense known to law." Judge

Goff continued, "Technicalities may depend upon matters of procedure, which the Court within its discretion is empowered to regard or disregard as the interests of justice prompt. In so far as a plain violation of law is concerned, if that law be violated by a rational person, that is a violation of the law and the person committing it is responsible."[5]

Sulzer's response when reporters notified him of the indictment was predictable: "I had not heard of it. It is a Tammany frame-up, that is all I've got to say."[6]

District Attorney Swann described the entire situation as "bizarre," telling the press that Newcomb had volunteered to the district attorney's investigators the information that the campaign filing was inaccurate and that some expenditures had been hidden under different headings. In the same press conference, Swann said it was Childs who testified that Sulzer solicited a job with the Campaign Committee and estimated the expenses of his American Party at $20,000. Sulzer admitted he got the money but denied it was for "expenses"; instead, he insisted that it was a direct payment for speeches on Manhattan's East Side. In testimony, others "contended that it was on [Sulzer's] own initiative that the payment to him was concealed." Swann concluded by noting that a crime was committed when anyone "willfully omits, refuses, or neglects to do any act required by the election law."[7]

The special grand jury ranged far beyond this violation in its two-month-long inquiry. Before concluding, the grand jury had also indicted former state senator William H. Reynolds and others for a corrupt land sale in Seaside Park as well as sixty election inspectors for making false returns of the ballot in the Republican primary.[8] They indicted former coroner Timothy Healy, president of the International Brotherhood of Stationary Firemen, for attempted bribery, petit larceny, and forgery.[9] Finally, they indicted three motorcycle police officers for extortion and three other officers for neglect of duty in a murder case.[10] The jury foreman was a Republican who had personally made two contributions to the Fusion fund.[11]

According to the investigation, the Fusion campaign fund totaled

$1,610,802.58 or the equivalent of over $27 million in today's dollars—a staggering amount of money at any time. Even more impressive is that $170,851.42 was spent on Election Day itself by district leaders and other functionaries in an effort to find and influence votes. In addition to the indictments and a report, the special grand jury also offered recommendations: "The evidence before the Grand Jury as to the campaign conducted by the Fusion Committee of 1917 as regards the amount of money expended seems so detrimental to the purity of the ballot as to warrant the strongest condemnation, and it most earnestly recommends that a recurrence should be prevented without delay by remedial legislation."[12]

Judge Goff echoed their call:

> You have touched the vital spot. The foundation of our political institutions, irrespective of party affiliations or of leaning, and their existence and maintenance, we must all recognize, must depend upon the purity of the ballot box, and no more important presentment has ever been handed up to this Court in this county than the one you have handed up. For the service which you have rendered the People of the City should be deeply appreciative, and the Court adds to that appreciation its own expression of grateful recognition.[13]

Noting that the law prescribed limits on spending by candidates but no limits on spending by the parties on behalf of candidates, the grand jury recommended limits to prevent the use of unlimited funds by any political party. To impose accountability, they also advocated one responsible officer for political committees instead of the three then in place. The new rules would also provide for a fixed compensation for all poll workers; make the payment of an above fair and reasonable rate prima facie evidence of corrupt intent; prohibit special "election rates" by newspapers; prohibit any payments to societies, cults, or organizations with the intent of influencing voters; and require that committees file the names of election workers in a delineated period before the election. As the *Times* noted, "The campaign funds are a source of evil and should be remedied."[14]

Before any new rules could take effect, however, the accused had to answer the grand jury's indictment. The lawyers for Sulzer et al. raised questions about the validity of the charges on the grounds that the court was not legally constituted in conformity with the proclamation of Governor Whitman. In a strange twist of fate, the defense attorneys were former impeachment managers John B. Stanchfield and Isidor J. Kresel. Their argument: Justice Goff's authority to impanel a grand jury came from Governor Whitman's proclamation convening an extraordinary term of the Supreme Court and designating Goff to preside. The governor's proclamation provided that notice be given by publicizing the proclamation in two newspapers (the *Sun* and *New York Morning Telegraph*), once each in two successive weeks. However, instead, the proclamation was published in the *Morning Telegraph* twice in one week, and not in two successive weeks, as was required.[15]

That argument was good enough for the Supreme Court, Appellate Division, to grant a writ of prohibition restraining Justice Goff from proceeding with the indictments of the extraordinary term.[16] Split 3-2, the Court ruled, "It is our duty to enforce the statute as we find it and not substitute our judgment for that of the Legislature as to what is or is not essential in the way of notice." In dissent, the minority said, "The point as I view it is the merest technicality. If sustained, it would subject the formal and deliberate action of the Governor and his Secretary, performed in the exercise of the highest executive prerogative, with the strictest regard for statutory provision, to nullification by a printer's error. In my opinion, the time has long passed in this State for formal court proceedings to be nullified by such matters."[17]

Childs brought a habeas corpus proceeding alleging that he was illegally detained and that there was no ground for his indictment. His lawyers argued, "He has done nothing for which he is indictable, even assuming that the facts are true, and the Grand Jury was without jurisdiction." The rules were that the Court had to first require the defendant to file a correct statement of expenditures, and if he failed to do so, he could be punished by a fine of $1,000 or one year in prison.[18] Of course, the defendants saw the whole prosecution as politically motivated. Childs wrote a letter to the Fusion Committee of 250 (basically the ruling body of the Fusion Party) that said in part, "The whole investigation has been a sinister political propaganda in the personal interest of the Hearst-Swann combination, as a ground work for this Fall's State election." Childs's letter continued, "[The indictments were] based solely upon the contention of the District Attorney that the names of Messrs. Sulzer and Appelbaum should have been mentioned in connection with this item. There was no charge of misappropriation of money or of improper expenditure of funds."[19]

There was some validity to this accusation. The district attorney seemed to have focused almost exclusively on the Fusion campaign. Much more serious allegations had been made about the finances of the Democratic ticket, and there was circumstantial evidence of at least technical, if not serious, irregularities forbidden by law.

Childs concluded his defense by cautioning others. "I warn the public-spirited citizens of New York," he continued, "that this attack ... was aimed not at me, but at them." The prosecution was, Childs alleged, intended to frighten and chill.[20]

District Attorney Swann announced immediate plans to appeal. The mayor approved and for some strange reason sent Swann a public letter commending him on his decision to appeal.[21]

The Court of Appeals ruled, by a vote of 4-1, that the defendants must still stand trial, as the indictments were valid, holding that the grand jury was properly constituted even though the special term was not. The Court decision said, "Sufficiently charge [sic] the relator [Childs] and his co-defendants with a conspiracy to prevent a compliance with the requirements of the election law by Clarke as Treasurer." The Court continued, "As to the argument that the election law was intended to provide an exclusive remedy, thus barring recourse to the penal law, I think it is without force." They concluded with the point that habeas corpus was not the proper course to pursue.²² The appeal by District Attorney Swann from this writ of habeas corpus was sustained by the court, which "ordered, that the order sustaining the writ of habeas corpus appealed from be and the same is hereby reversed. The said writ is dismissed and the relator remanded to custody."²³

Childs, serving as the test case for Newcomb and Sulzer, then took his case to the public. He reminded people that he was not actually a member of the committee that filed the report and, furthermore, claimed never to have seen it before it was filed. "I mean to fight this thing out to its conclusion not only in my own interest," said Childs, "which of course, I am bound to do, but in the interests of public-spirited men of affairs, who it is sought to drive out from participation in matters of municipal government."²⁴

Ironically, Supreme Court Justice (and former senate majority leader) Robert Wagner dismissed the case. Between indictment and trial, a key prosecution witness, Frank M. Loper, changed his mind about cooperating with the district attorney's office and became a "hostile" witness. As a result, Swann decided it would be "futile to proceed to trial" and asked Justice Wagner to dismiss the case.²⁵

Childs, sounding much like Sulzer, claimed, "It was an attempt by Tammany Hall to punish him. The Democratic District Attorney probed the Mitchel campaign fund assiduously for months to find illegalities in expenditure, eager to charge that the wealthy were attempting to buy the election. Although the expenditures of the Mitchel campaign fund were correctly reported, technicalities were seized upon to indict."²⁶

All good points. Regardless, the implications of wrongdoing irreparably harmed Mitchel's campaign. Supreme Court judge John Hylan, backed by both Hearst and Tammany, won the mayoral election by a vast majority of the vote.

25

A GHOST BEFORE HE DIED

THE AMERICAN PARTY, a party whose ideology was based primarily on support for William Sulzer and opposition to his enemies, offered Sulzer the nomination for president in 1916. He declined. The party, which had adopted the Liberty Bell as its symbol on the ballot, received enough votes during Sulzer's campaign in 1914 to receive automatic ballot access, and the party ran a full statewide slate in 1916. An interparty dispute resulted in a primary for governor pitting Republican incumbent, Charles Whitman, against his Democratic challenger, Samuel Seabury. In the statewide primary, Whitman won by the vote of 38-37 (Robert Bacon, a Republican, lost the primary for senator to Democrat William F. McCombs, 23-22). The small number of participants in the primary shows how few people supported the party. It would not receive automatic ballot access again.

Sulzer's impeachment and Rosenthal's murder were the beginning of a dark period for Charles Murphy and Tammany Hall, but those times did not last. Soon Tammany was back, bigger than ever. Judge Hylan had been elected as mayor of New York City in a landslide in 1917, and the next year, Al Smith, the Speaker of the assembly who had rallied the troops and forced an impeachment vote in the middle of the night against Sulzer, was elected governor.

As chief executive, Smith would build a decidedly progressive agenda, continuing his work with Sulzer on the Triangle Fire Committee to strengthen labor laws, especially for working women and injured workers, and create the social programs while also radically reorganizing and professionalizing state government. Smith's social reforms would become the underpinnings of much of the New Deal while his state reorganization would be replicated in states across the nation. Smith would serve four terms as governor before being nominated for president.

Robert Wagner, who had been one of Sulzer's fiercest critics—especially on the direct primary fight—was elected to the New York State Supreme Court.[*] From the bench he would be elected to four terms as a U.S. senator. A close ally of President Franklin Roosevelt, Wagner formed part of the president's "brain trust" and was the sponsor of many facets of Roosevelt's New Deal agenda, notably the National Labor Relations Act (also known as the Wagner act) and the Social Security Act.

Boss Murphy engineered these elections and much more. All told, under Murphy's leadership, Tammany Hall elected three governors, three mayors, two U.S. senators, and numerous protégés, including Mayor Jimmy Walker. In 1923, only ten years after Sulzer's impeachment and the gambling/police scandals, Tammany men held the governorship, the mayoralty, and numerous other elected offices. No other Tammany leader ever had or would ever again enjoy such power.

Maybe Murphy had learned a lesson from the Sulzer debacle?

Al Smith was the best of many promising Tammany Hall politicians, and Murphy acted to inoculate him from the same challenges that William

---

[*] Wagner presided over the only court case ever involving Charlie Murphy. The case revolved around a partnership between an arms manufacturer and the company in New York that mined the minerals needed to make their munitions. Murphy, worried that he was making "too much money" and that the perception of war profiteering would damage Tammany Hall, broke the contract (Allen, 299).

Sulzer faced.* In 1915 Murphy and Tammany Hall nominated Al Smith for sheriff of New York County. Smith resisted the nomination, having no desire to serve as sheriff. However, the position was paid on a fee basis and was estimated to be worth over $50,000 per year, a quite substantial sum, and Murphy urged Smith to take the job, telling his earnest protégé, "Al, I'm making you sheriff so you can make some money. Then you can afford to be an honest man."

More importantly, when Smith was elected governor, Murphy was reported to have said, "I shall be asking you for things, Al, but if I ever ask you for anything which you think would impair your record, just tell me so and that will be the end of it."

The boss also knew when to fight ... and when not to fight. Throughout 1913 he had fought tooth and nail with William Sulzer over direct primaries. In 1914 Charlie Murphy announced his support for open primaries.[1]

Governor Smith would go on to be the Democratic nominee for president in 1928, but Smith would have to run the national campaign without Charles Francis Murphy's counsel. The boss died suddenly at his home in 1924 from an attack of "acute indigestion" that affected his heart.

Murphy was buried out of St. Patrick's Cathedral and passed along streets lined with over sixty thousand people. According to one observer, it was the most impressive funeral in New York City since the death of General Grant.[2]

William Sulzer would live until the age of seventy-eight, dying after a short illness in November 1941. A small funeral was held and attended by close friends. The former congressman, Speaker of the assembly, and governor merited only a half-column obituary in the *New York Times*. That newspaper editorialized, "William Sulzer may be said to have been a ghost

---

* Court of Appeals judge Samuel Seabury declared, "Mr. Smith is the best representative of the worst element in the Democratic party in this State." Seabury would later chair the investigation of Mayor Jimmy Walker's administration and cause Beau James (as the mayor was known for his carousing) to flee to Europe. He was also the only dissenter at the 1918 Democratic convention that nominated Smith for governor.

long before he died. Save in his own immediate neighborhood he must have been pretty well forgotten. To the new generation he is unknown." Their conclusion may also be ours:

> In his campaign [Sulzer] received certain fat contributions which were not acknowledged. He was hard up, as he told Theodore Roosevelt in a private letter. He broke the law, apparently embezzled those contributions and capped the performance with perjury. But there is irony in the thought that if Sulzer had been duly docile to Charles F. Murphy, that is, if he had included the greater guilt, the less would probably never have been heard of, and he might have lived and died in public honor.[3]

ACKNOWLEDGMENTS

This book owes much to many.

It would not have happened without the forbearance of Alfred S. Konefsky, a Distinguished Professor at the State University of New York at Buffalo Law School. Fred gave me the time to study William Sulzer's impeachment trial and find the law in that history. He also gave me a couple of good grades, helping me make it to graduation.

Dr. Jacob Alexis Friedman's *The Impeachment of Governor William Sulzer* was an invaluable guide throughout this process. His book is an excellent standard to which this one can only aspire.

My editor, Rena Distasio, and my publisher, Edwina Woodbury, at Chapel Hill Press, helped make this book better and made it possible to publish.

Special thanks go to the New York State Archives, the Buffalo & Erie County Public Library, the State University of New York at Buffalo Law School, the 39 Steps, and Whitney and Laney Kemp for finding the lost (to me at least) transcripts of the Court of Impeachment.

Appreciation is also due to my friends and colleagues at Canisius College: Walt Sharrow, Dick Thompson, and Reverend Edward Dunn, S.J. from my student days; Peter Galie for his help with research and editing; and Mike Haselswerdt, who was a great teacher and a better friend.

NOTES

EPIGRAPH

1. Edgar L. Murlin, *The New York Red Book* (New York: J. B. Lyon Co., 1913), 44.

FOREWORD

1. Jacob Alexis Friedman, *The Impeachment of Governor William Sulzer* (New York: Columbia University Press, 1939), 11.
2. Woodrow Wilson, *A History of the American People* (New York: Harper & Brothers, 1901).
3. C-SPAN, "Survey of Presidential Leadership 2009," www.c-span.org/PresidentialSurvey.
4. C-SPAN, "Survey of Presidential Leadership 2009," www.c-span.org/PresidentialSurvey.
5. Friedman, *Impeachment of Governor William Sulzer*, 12.
6. Paul F. Boller, *Presidential Campaigns* (New York: Oxford University Press, 1996).
7. United States Census Bureau, Annual Estimates of the Resident Population for the United States, Regions, States, and Puerto Rico: April 1, 2000, to July 1, 2008, http://www.census.gov/popest/states/NST-ann-est.html.

CHAPTER 1

1. *New York Times*, January 2, 1913.
2. Murlin, *New York Red Book*, 33.
3. Murlin, 33.
4. Alaska Mining Hall of Fame, http://alaskamininghalloffame.org/inductees/sulzer.php.
5. Murlin, 33.
6. Murlin, 33.
7. Herbert Asbury, *All around Town* (New York: Basic Books, 2003).

CHAPTER 2

1. L. T. Myers, *Great Leaders and National Issues of 1912* (New York: J. C. Winston), 1912, 266.

CHAPTER 3

1. Murlin, 44.
2. Murlin, 47.
3. Murlin, 46.
4. Murlin, 46.
5. *New York Times*, December 22, 1912.
6. Alaska Mining Hall of Fame.
7. Congressional Biography Service, www.Thomas.gov.
8. Murlin, 33.
9. Friedman, 15.
10. Friedman, 16.
11. *New-York Tribune*, January 2, 1893, cited in Friedman, 17.
12. Alfred E. Smith, *Up to Now* (Garden City, NY: Garden City Books, 1927), 169.
13. Smith, 155–56.
14. *Harper's Weekly*, August 23, 1913, 25, quoted in Friedman, 19.
15. *New York Times*, February 7, 1886.
16. Friedman, 16.
17. Friedman, 16.
18. Friedman, 16.
19. Murlin, 35.
20. *New York Times*, April 3, 1890.
21. *New York Times*, March 28, 1890.
22. Friedman, 17.
23. Friedman, 17.
24. Friedman, 17.
25. *New-York World*, April 25, 1893, quoted in Friedman, 17.
26. *Cosmopolitan Magazine*, July 1912, 248–49, quoted in Friedman, 17.
27. Friedman, 12.

CHAPTER 4

1. Friedman, 19.
2. Library of Congress, www.Thomas.gov.
3. Friedman, 24.
4. Friedman, 19.
5. *New York Evening Post*, October 3, 1912, quoted in Friedman, 20.
6. William Sulzer, *Sulzer's Short Speeches* (New York: J. S. Ogilvie, 1912), 38–39.
7. Friedman, 23.
8. Congressional Record, 62nd Congress, 2nd Session, Vol. 48, Part V, 4364.
9. *New York Times*, October 4, 1912.
10. *New-York Tribune*, July 24, 1896.
11. *Harper's Weekly*, August 23, 1913.

CHAPTER 5

1. *New York Times*, August 8, 2010.
2. *New York Times*, August 8, 2010.

CHAPTER 6

1. Roscoe C. E. Brown, *History of the State of New York: Political and Governmental*, vol. 4, *1896 to 1920* (Syracuse: Syracuse Press, 1922) 144.
2. Brown, 146.
3. Charles Elliot Fitch, *Encyclopedia of Biography of New York: A Life Record of Men and Women of the Past*, vol. 4 (New York: American Historical Society, 1916), 445.
4. Fitch, 24.
5. Brown, 145.
6. Brown, 146.
7. Brown, 146.
8. *Times*, December 1, 1910.
9. Gustavus Meyers, *History of Tammany Hall* (New York: Boni & Liveright, 1917), 352–53.
10. Fitch.
11. Brown, 174.
12. Brown, 184.
13. Brown, 184.
14. Brown, 185.

[15] *New York Times*, March 21, 1911.
[16] Meyers, 353.
[17] *New York Times*, July 29, 1911.
[18] Brown, 174.
[19] Brown, 175.
[20] Brown, 185.
[21] Brown, 185.
[22] Meyers, 353.
[23] Meyers, 353.
[24] Meyers, 354.
[25] Brown, 184.
[26] Brown, 185.
[27] Meyers, 355.

CHAPTER 7

[1] *New York Press*, October 28, 1998.
[2] *New York Press*, October 28, 1998.
[3] A. Maurice Low, *Tammany Hall: Its Boss, Its Methods, and Its Meaning*, ed. Henry Norman, vol. 2: *World's Word and Play*, June–November 1903.
[4] Low, 379.
[5] Low, 380.
[6] *New York Times*, October 2, 1912.
[7] Jay W. Forrest and James Malcolm, *Tammany's Treason: Impeachment of Governor William Sulzer (The Complete Story Written from behind the Scenes, Showing How Tammany Plays the Game, How Men Are Bought, Sold and Delivered)* (Albany: Fort Orange Press, 1913), 21.
[8] *New-York Tribune*, October 18, 1913.
[9] A speech delivered in Tammany Hall, February 13, 1902, reprinted in pamphlet form and included in Sulzer, *Sulzer's Short Speeches*.
[10] *New-York Tribune*, September 17–18, 1896.
[11] Forrest and Malcolm, 20.
[12] Forrest and Malcolm, 22.
[13] Oliver E. Allen, *The Tiger: The Rise and Fall of Tammany Hall* (New York: Addison-Wesley, 1993), 48.
[14] Allen, 48.
[15] Allen, 49.
[16] Allen, 53.
[17] Allen, 53.
[18] Allen, 54.
[19] Allen, 55.
[20] Allen, 54.
[21] *New York Times*, October 2 1912.
[22] Brown, 223.
[23] *New York Times*, October 3, 1912.
[24] *New York World*, October 3, 1912.
[25] *New York Times*, October 4, 1912.
[26] Friedman, 28.
[27] Friedman, 28.
[28] *New York Evening Post*, editorial, October 7, 1912.
[29] *New-York Tribune*, October 18, 1913.
[30] *New York World*, October 3, 1912.
[31] *New York Times*, October 4 1912.
[32] *New York Times*, October 11 1912.
[33] *New York Evening Post*, October 3 1912.
[34] *New York Evening Post*, October 10, 1912.
[35] *New York Times*, October 17, 1912.
[36] *New-York Tribune*, Editorial, October 4, 1912.
[37] *New York Times*, October 4, 1912.
[38] Murlin, 38.
[39] Murlin, 40.
[40] Murlin, 40.

CHAPTER 8

[1] *New York Times*, January 2, 1913.
[2] Friedman, 35.
[3] *New York Times*, January 2, 1913.
[4] Allen, 88.
[5] *New York Times*, January 2, 1913.
[6] *New York World*, January 1,19136.
[7] *New York Times*, January 1, 1913.
[8] Friedman, 35.

⁹ *New York Times,* January 2, 1913.
¹⁰ Friedman, 35.
¹¹ *New York World,* January 1, 1913.
¹² *New York Times,* December 26, 1912.
¹³ *New York Times,* January 2, 1913.
¹⁴ William Sulzer, *Public Papers* (Albany: J. B. Lyon Co., 1914), 21–39.
¹⁵ *New York Times,* January 1, 1913.
¹⁶ *New York Times,* January 1, 1913.
¹⁷ *New York Times,* January 1, 1913.
¹⁸ *New York Times,* January 1, 1913.
¹⁹ *New York Times,* January 2, 1913.
²⁰ *New York Times,* January 1, 1913.
²¹ *New York Times,* January 1, 1913.
²² *New York Times,* January 1, 1913.
²³ *New York Times,* January 1, 1913.
²⁴ *New York Times,* January 1, 1913.
²⁵ *New York Times,* January 1, 1913.
²⁶ *New York Times,* January 1, 1913.
²⁷ *New York Times,* January 1, 1913.
²⁸ *New York Times,* January 1, 1913.
²⁹ *New York Times,* January 1, 1913.
³⁰ *New York Times,* January 1, 1913.
³¹ *New York Times,* January 1, 1913.
³² *New York Times,* January 1, 1913.
³³ *New York Times,* January 1, 1913.
³⁴ Murlin, 40.
³⁵ Murlin, 41.
³⁶ *New York Times,* January 2, 1913.
³⁷ Murlin, 41.
³⁸ Murlin, 42.

CHAPTER 9

¹ Robert A. Slayton, *Empire Statesman: The Rise and Redemption of Al Smith* (New York: Free Press, 2001), 112.
² Brown, 224.
³ Allen, 181.
⁴ United States Senate, "Featured Biography," www.Senate.gov.
⁵ Allen, 130.

CHAPTER 10

¹ Friedman, 38.
² Friedman, 38.
³ *New-York Tribune,* January 22, 1912.
⁴ *New York Times,* December 22, 1912.
⁵ *New York Times,* December 22, 1912.
⁶ *New York Times,* December 22, 1912.
⁷ Brown, 294.
⁸ *New York Evening Mail,* October 20, 1913; October 21, 1913.
⁹ Slayton, 141.
¹⁰ Allen, 203.
¹¹ *New York Times,* December 28, 1912.
¹² Brown, 295.
¹³ *New York Times,* January 2, 1913.
¹⁴ Brown, 297.
¹⁵ *New York Times,* March 19, 1913.
¹⁶ *New York Times,* March 19, 2013; March 20, 1913.

CHAPTER 11

¹ *New York Times,* January 28, 1913.
² *New York Times,* January 3, 1913.
³ Allen, 145.
⁴ *New York Times,* January 3, 1913.
⁵ *New York Times,* January 28, 1913.
⁶ *New York Times,* January 3, 1913.
⁷ *New York Times,* January 24, 1913; Friedman, 39.
⁸ *New York Times,* January 3, 1913.
⁸ Friedman, 39.
¹⁰ Friedman, 40.
¹¹ *New York Times,* January 13, 1913.
¹² *New York Times,* December 31, 1912.
¹³ *New York Times,* January 13, 1913.
¹⁴ Brown, 296.
¹⁵ *New York World,* February 4, 1913.
¹⁶ *New York World,* February 4, 1913.
¹⁷ *New York World,* editorial, February 4, 1913.
¹⁸ *New York Times,* editorial, February 5, 1913.

19. Allen, 188.
20. Brown, 295.
21. Allen, 190.
22. Friedman, 46.
23. Samuel Bell Thomas, *The Boss, or the Governor: The Truth about the Greatest Political Conspiracy in the History of America* (New York: The Truth, 1914), 99.
24. *New York Times*, February 12, 1913.
25. Friedman, 48.
26. Friedman, 49.
27. *New York World*, March 14, 1913.
28. *New York Times*, March 25, 1913.
29. *New York Times*, April 28, 1913.
30. *New York Times*, Mary 25, 1913.

CHAPTER 12

1. Friedman, 50.
2. *New York Times*, March 11, 1913.
3. Allen, 194.
4. Allen, 195.
5. *New York World*, March 17, 1913.
6. *New York Times*, March 12, 1913.
7. Friedman, 51.
8. *New York Times*, March 18, 1913.
9. *New York Times*, March 13, 1913.
10. *New York Times*, March 13, 1913.
11. *New York Times*, March 13, 1913.
12. *New York World*, March 18, 1913.
13. *New York Times*, March 18, 1913.
14. *New York Times*, March 18, 1913.
15. Henry Morgenthau, interview, quoted in Friedman, 58.
16. *New York World*, March 19, 1913.
17. *New York Times*, March 19, 1913.
18. *New York World*, March 20, 1913.
19. Friedman, 56–57.
20. *The Nation*, editorial, March 20, 1913, 276.
21. Friedman, 57.
22. *New York World*, March 17, 1913.

23. *New York Times*, March 25, 1913.
24. Sulzer, *Personal Papers*, 1088.
25. *New York Times*, March 29, 1912.
26. Sulzer, *Public Papers*, 1128.
27. *Senate Journal* 1913, 1:1063–64.
28. *New-York Tribune*, May 3, 1913.
29. *New York Times*, April 3, 1913.
30. Forrest and Malcolm, 183.

CHAPTER 13

1. *New York Times*, April 18, 1913.
2. *New York Times*, April 18, 1913.
3. *New York World*, April 22, 1913.
4. Friedman, 70.
5. Friedman, 70.
6. Friedman, 72.
7. *New York Times*, May 13.

CHAPTER 14

1. Allen, 197.
2. Brown, 320.
3. Friedman, 73.
4. Friedman, 73.
5. *New York Times*, January 21, 1913.
6. Friedman, 74.
7. Friedman, 75.
8. *New York Times*, April 12, 1913.
9. *New York Times*, April 12, 1913.
10. Allen, 203.
11. Allen, 203.
12. Friedman, 77.
13. *Senate Journal*, 2:1399.
14. *Assembly Journal*, 3:2773.
15. Allen, 204.
16. Friedman, 77.
17. Friedman, 78.
18. *New York Times*, April 30, 1913.
19. *New York World*, April 30, 1913.
20. *New York World*, April 30, 1913.
21. Allen, 212.
22. Allen, 212.

23. *New York Times*, April 27, 1913.
24. *New York Times*, April 28, 1913.
25. *New York Times*, April 28, 1913.
26. *New York Times*, April 29, 1913.
27. *Senate Journal*, 2:1825.
28. Friedman, 82.
29. *New York Times*, May 1, 1913.
30. *New York World*, May 1, 1913.
31. *New York Times*, May 1, 1913.
32. *New York Times*, May 2, 1913.
33. *New York Times*, May 2, 1913.
34. *Senate Journal*, 2:2009; *Assembly Journal*, 3:3301.
35. *New York World*, May 3, 1913.
36. *New York Times*, May 3, 1913.
37. *New York Times*, May 3, 1913.
38. *New York Times*, May 3, 1913.
39. *New York Times*, May 2, 1913.
40. *New York Times*, May 2, 1913.
41. *New York Times*, April 29, 1913.
42. *New York Times*, May 18, 1913.
43. *New York Times*, May 18, 1913.
44. Friedman, 85.
45. *New York Times*, May 5, 1913.
46. *New York Times*, editorial, May 20, 1913.
47. *New York World*, May 8, 1913.
48. *New York Times*, May 8, 1913.
49. *New York Times*, May 8, 1913.
50. *New York Times*, May 8, 1913.
51. *Review of Reviews*, June 13, 1913. 686.
52. *New York World*, May 17, 1913.
53. *New York World*, April 30, 1913.
54. *New York Times*, June 12, 1913.
55. *New York World*, August 4, 1913.
56. *Morning Telegraph*, July 1, 1913.
57. *New York Times*, July 20, 1913.
58. *New York Times*, July 20, 1913.
59. *New York Times*, May 29, 1913.
60. *New York Times*, May 29, 1913.
61. *New York Times*, May 18, 1913.
62. *New York Times*, May 18, 1913.
63. *New York World*, October 12, 1912.
64. *New York World*, May 19, 1913.
65. *New York Times*, May 20, 1913.
66. *New York Times*, May 20, 1913.
67. *New York Times*, May 20, 1913.
68. Friedman, 94–95.
69. *New York Times*, May 20, 1913.
70. *New York World*, May 20, 1913.
71. *New York Times*, May 20, 1913.
72. *New York Times*, May 21, 1913.
73. *New York Times*, May 21, 1913.
74. *New York Times*, May 21, 1913.
75. *New York World*, May 22, 1913.
76. *New York Times*, May 22, 1913.
77. *New York Times*, May 22, 1913.
78. *New York Times*, May 23, 1913.
79. *New York Times*, May 23, 1913.
80. *New York Times*, May 23, 1913.
81. *New York World*, May 22, 1913.
82. *New York Times*, May 29, 1913.
83. *New York Times*, May 31, 1913.
84. *New York Times*, May 30, 1913.
85. *New York Times*, December 31, 1912.
86. *New York Times*, June 1, 1913.
87. *New York World*, June 5, 1913.
88. *New York Times*, June 5, 1913.
89. *New York Times*, June 9, 1913.
90. *New York World*, June 5, 1913.
91. *New York World*, June 9, 1913.
92. *New York Times*, June 11, 1913.
93. *New York World*, June 15, 1913.
94. *New York World*, June 15, 1913.
95. *New York Times*, June 16, 1913.
96. *New York Times*, June 16, 1913.
97. Friedman, 106.
98. *New-York Evening Post*, July 26, 1913.
99. *New York World*, August 31, 1913.
100. *New York Times*, June 17, 1913.
101. *New York Times*, June 17, 1913.
102. *The Sun*, June 17, 1913.
103. *New York Times*, June 17, 1913.
104. Sulzer, *Public Papers*, 1466–70.
105. *New York Times*, June 18, 1913.

106 *New York Times,* June 19, 1913.
107 *New York Times,* June 20, 1913.
108 *New-York Tribune,* June 16, 1913.
109 Sulzer, *Public Papers,* 117–35.
110 *New York Times,* June 17, 1913.
111 *New York Times,* June 17, 1913.
112 *The New York Press,* June 25, 1913.
113 Friedman, 114.
114 *The New York Press,* June 25, 1913.
115 *New York World,* June 25, 1913.
116 *The New York Press,* June 25, 1913.
117 *New York Times,* June 26, 1913.
118 *New York Times,* June 26, 1913.
119 *New York World,* June 26, 1913.
120 *New York World,* August 4, 1913.

CHAPTER 15

1 *New York Times,* June 21, 1913.
2 *New-York Evening Post,* June 23, 1913.
3 *Evening World,* June 23, 1913.
4 Friedman, 118.
5 Forrest and Malcolm, 71.
6 *New York World,* June 22, 1913.
7 *New York World,* July 2, 1913.
8 *New York Times,* July 3, 1913.
9 *New York World,* July 3, 1913.
10 *New York Times,* July 3, 1913.
11 *New-York Evening Post,* October 23, 1913.
12 *New York Times,* October 23, 1912.
13 *The Sun,* July 22, 1913.
14 *The New York Press,* July 27, 1913.
15 *New York Times,* July 26, 1913.
16 *The Sun,* June 17, 1913.
17 *The American,* June 18, 1913.
18 *New York Times,* August 23, 24, 1913.
19 *New York Times,* August 23, 1913.

CHAPTER 16

1 Forrest and Malcolm, 77.
2 Forrest and Malcolm, 108.

3 *New York Times,* June 12, 1913.
4 *New York Times,* July 2, 1913.
5 *New York World,* July 26, 1913.
6 Assembly Documents, Session 1913, Vol. 35, No. 2, 136.
7 Assembly Documents, 169–205.
8 Assembly Documents, 87.
9 Assembly Documents, 81–83.
10 Assembly Documents, 163.
11 *New York Times,* July 17, 1913.
12 Assembly Documents, 23.
13 Assembly Documents, 138.
14 Sulzer, *Personal Papers,* 984.
15 Friedman, 128.
16 *New York World,* June 4, 1913.
17 *New York Times,* April 24, 1913.
18 *New York World,* July 9, 1913; July 10, 1913.
19 Assembly *Journal,* 4:88–91.
20 *New York Times,* July 24, 1913.
21 Sulzer, *Life and Speeches of William Sulzer.* Albany: Nabu Press, 2010.
22 *New York Herald,* July 30, 1913.

CHAPTER 17

1 Assembly *Journal,* 4:358.
2 Slayton, 122.
3 *New York Times,* August 1, 1913.
4 Assembly *Journal,* 4:364.
5 *Evening Sun,* July 21, 1913.
6 *New York Herald,* July 30, 1913.
7 *American,* July 20, 1913.
8 *American,* July 20, 1913.
9 *New York World,* August 1, 1913.
10 *New York Times,* October 8, 1912.
11 Assembly *Journal,* 4:367.
12 *New York Times,* August 1, 1913.
13 Assembly *Documents,* 371, 381.
14 Assembly *Documents,* 377.
15 United States Department of Labor, CPI Inflation Calculator (data.bls.gov/cgi-bin/cpicalc.pl).

16. Meyers, 346–48.
17. *Outlook*, October 18, 1913, 357.

CHAPTER 18

1. *New York Times*, August 8, 1913.
2. Brown, 298.
3. Allen, 243.
4. *New York Times*, August 10, 1913.
5. *New York Times*, August 8, 1913.
6. *New York Times*, editorial, August 9, 1913.
7. *New York World*, August 9, 1913.
8. *New-York Tribune*, editorial, August 8, 1913.
9. *New York Evening Post*, editorial, August 8, 1913.
10. *American*, editorial, August 9, 1913.
11. *New York Times*, August 11, 1913.
12. *New York Times*, August 12, 1913.
13. *New York Times*, August 11, 1913.
14. Assembly *Journal*, 4:94.
15. *New York Times*, August 12, 1913.
16. Assembly *Journal*, 4:301–9, appendix.
17. *New York World*, August 12, 1913.
18. *New York Times*, August 12, 1913.
19. *New York Times*, August 12, 1913.
20. *New York Times*, August 12, 1913.
21. Assembly *Journal*, 4:98.
22. *New York Times*, August 12, 1913.
23. *New York Times*, August 12, 1913.
24. *New York Times*, August 13, 1913.
25. *New York Times*, August 13, 1913.
26. *New York Times*, August 13, 1913.
27. *New York World*, August 14, 1913.
28. *New-York Tribune*, November 2, 1913.
29. *New York World*, November 2, 1913.
30. *New York World*, August 13, 1913.
31. *New York World*, August 14, 1913.
32. *New York Times*, August 13, 1913.
33. *The Sun*, August 13, 1913.
34. *New York Times*, August 13, 1913.
35. *New York Times*, August 10, 1913.
36. *New York Times*, August 14, 1913.
37. *New York Times*, August 14, 1913.
38. *New York Times*, August 13, 1913.
39. Assembly *Journal*, 4:112.

CHAPTER 19

1. Friedman, 165.
2. Slayton, 144.
3. Friedman, 166.
4. Forrest and Malcolm, 414.
5. Brown, 304.
6. Friedman, 166.
7. Friedman, 166.
8. Editorial, *North American*, August 20, 1913.
9. Sulzer, *Public Papers*, 1487–88.
10. *The Nation*, August 21, 1913, 158.
11. *Syracuse Journal*, quoted in Friedman, 167.
12. *World's Work*, October 13, 1913, 615.
13. *New York Times*, August 17, 1913.
14. Louisville *Courier-Journal*, editorial, August 23, 1913.
15. Baltimore *Sun*, editorial, August 23, 1913.
16. Friedman, 170.
17. *New York Times*, editorial, August 18, 1913.
18. *Harper's Weekly*, August 30, 1913, 3.
19. Sulzer, *Public Papers*, 1488.
20. *New York World*, editorial, August 14, 1913.
21. Springfield *Republican*, August 23, 1913.
22. *New York World*, September 5, 1913.
23. Friedman, 173.
24. *New York Times*, September 14, 1913.
25. *New York Times*, September 17, 1913.
26. Friedman, 174.
27. *New York World*, August 19, 1913.
28. *New York World*, August 19, 1913.
29. *New York World*, August 19, 1913.
30. *New York World*, August 4, 1913.
31. *New York World*, September 8, 1913.
32. *New York World*, August 16, 1913; August 22, 1913.

33 *New York Times*, September 8, 1913.
34 *New York World*, August 25, 1913.
35 *New York World*, August 16, 1913.
36 *New York World*, August 29, 1913.
37 Assembly *Journal*, 4:148.
38 Smith, 131.
39 Assembly *Journal*, 4:134; Senate *Journal*, 2:156–58.
40 *New York Times*, September 16, 1913.
41 *New York Times*, September 18, 1913.
42 *New York Times*, September 18, 1913.
43 *New York Times*, September 18, 1913.

CHAPTER 20

1 *New York World*, August 14, 1913.
2 *New York World*, August 16, 1913.
3 *New York World*, August 16, 1913.
4 *New-York Tribune*, August 16, 1913.
5 *New York World*, August 17, 1913.
6 *New York World*, August 16, 1913.
7 *New York World*, August 14, 1913.
8 *New York World*, August 14, 1913.
9 *New York World*, August 16, 1913.
10 *New-York Tribune*, August 16, 1913.
11 *New-York Tribune*, August 15, 1913.
12 *The People ex rel. Joseph G. Robin, Realtor, v. Patrick Hayes, Warden of New York Penitentiary, respondent Appellate* (163 App Div 725-30).
13 *New York Times*, August 17, 1913.
14 *New York World*, August 20, 1913.
15 *New York Times*, August 21, 1913.
16 Assembly *Journal*, 4:123.
17 *New York Times*, September 14, 1913.
18 Brown, 302.

CHAPTER 21

1 Brown, 302.
2 *New York Times*, January 2, 1913.
3 Friedman, 192.
4 *Proceedings of the Court for the Trial of Impeachments: The People of the State of New York by the Assembly Thereof Against William Sulzer, As Governor (Held at the Capitol in the City of Albany, New York, September 18, 1913, to October 17, 1913)*, Vols. 1–2 (Albany: J. B. Lyon Co., 1913), 57.
5 *Proceedings*, 1:81.
6 *Proceedings*, 1:81.
7 *Proceedings*, 1:177.
8 *Proceedings*, 1:188.
9 *Proceedings*, 1:212.
10 *Proceedings*, 1:233.
11 *Proceedings*, 1:387.
12 *Proceedings*, 1:303.
13 *Proceedings*, 1:305.
14 *Proceedings*, 1:315.
15 *Proceedings*, 1:437.
16 *Proceedings*, 2:1470.
17 Friedman, 199.
18 *Proceedings*, 1:562.
19 *Proceedings*, 1:566.
20 *New York Times*, October 13, 1913.
21 *Proceedings*, 1:902.
22 *Proceedings*, 1:601; 1:738.
23 *Proceedings*, 1:489–90.
24 *Proceedings*, 1:494.
25 *Proceedings*, 1:673.
26 *Proceedings*, 1:665.
27 *Proceedings*, 1:702.
28 *World's Work*, September 1921, 479.
29 *New York Times*, January 2, 1913.
30 *Proceedings*, 1:718.
31 *Proceedings*, 1:808–9.
32 *Proceedings*, 1:818–19.
33 *Proceedings*, 1:963.
34 *Proceedings*, 1:950.
35 *New York World*, October 2, 1913.
36 *New York Times*, December 3, 1928.
37 *New York Times*, October 21, 1913.
38 *Proceedings*, 2:1041.
39 The Department of Efficiency and Economy later confirmed that

Sulzer called the Ryan residence in New York City on October 8, 1912 (*New-York Tribune*, November 2, 1913).
40. *New York Times*, October 27, 1913.
41. *Proceedings* Vol. II 1106.
42. Friedman, 208.
43. *Proceedings*, 2:1112.
44. *Proceedings*, 2:1081–82.
45. *Proceedings*, 2:1092.
46. *Proceedings*, 2:1094–95.
47. Friedman, 210.
48. *Proceedings*, 2:1124.
49. *Proceedings*, 2:1160.
50. *New York World*, September 22, 1913.
51. *New York World*, September 22, 1913.
52. *New York World*, September 27, 1913.
53. *New York World*, September 27, 1913.
54. *Proceedings* 2:1295
55. *Proceedings*, 2:1302.
56. *Proceedings*, 2:1316.
57. *Proceedings*, 2:1382.
58. *Proceedings*, 2:1394.
59. *Proceedings*, 2:1395.
60. *Proceedings*, 2:1396.
61. *Proceedings*, 2:1399.
62. *Proceedings*, 2:1400.
63. *Proceedings*, 2:1402.
64. *Proceedings*, 2:1403–4.
65. *Proceedings*, 2:1410.
66. *Proceedings*, 2:1423.
67. *Proceedings*, 2:1437.
68. *Proceedings*, 2:1439.
69. *Proceedings*, 2:1446.
70. *Proceedings*, 2:1447.
71. *Proceedings*, 2:1449.
72. *Proceedings*, 2:1449.
73. *Proceedings*, 2:1454.
74. *Proceedings*, 2:1465.
75. *Proceedings*, 2:1492.
76. *Proceedings*, 2:1498.
77. *Proceedings*, 2:1496–525.
78. *Proceedings*, 2:1501.
79. *Proceedings*, 2:1508.
80. *Proceedings*, 2:1509–10.
82. *Proceedings*, 2:1509–10.
82. *Proceedings*, 2:1515.
83. *Proceedings*, 2:1522.
84. *Proceedings*, 2:1535.
85. *New York World*, October 13.
86. Friedman, 231.
87. *New York World*, October 13.

CHAPTER 22

1. Brown, 304.
2. Brown, 304.
3. Brown, 304.
4. Brown, 304–5.
5. *Proceedings*, 2:1625.
6. *Proceedings*, 2:1625.
7. Brown, 305.
8. Brown, 310.
9. *Proceedings*, 2:1685.
10. Brown, 310.
11. Friedman, 232.
12. *Proceedings*, 2:1685.
13. *Proceedings*, 2:1654.
14. Brown, 310.
15. Brown, 311.
16. *New York World*, October 4, 1913.
17. Friedman, 216.
18. *New York World*, editorial, October 9, 1913.
19. Brown, 303–4.
20. *New York World*, October 9, 1913.
21. *New York Times*, October 9, 1913.
22. Thomas, 452.
23. *New York Times*, October 21, 1913.
24. *New York Times*, October 21, 1913.
25. *New York World*, October 1, 1913.
26. *New York World*, October 2, 1913.
27. *Proceedings*, 2:1689.
28. *Proceedings*, 2:1721–22.
29. *Proceedings*, 2:1734.
30. *Proceedings*, 2:1621.

CHAPTER 23

1. Allen, 265.
2. Allen, 265.
3. Allen, 266.
4. *New York Times*, October 18, 1913.
5. *New York World*, October 18, 1913.
6. *New-York Tribune*, October 16, 1913.
7. *New-York Tribune*, October 16, 1913.
8. *New-York Tribune*, October 21, 1913.
9. *New-York Tribune*, October 21, 1913.
10. Allen, 267.
11. *New-York Tribune*, November 6, 1913.
12. *New York World*, November 7, 1913.
13. *New York World*, November 7, 1913.
14. *New York Times*, July 16, 1912.
15. Meyers, 356–59.
16. Meyers, 358–60.
17. Slayton, 161.

CHAPTER 24

1. Bernard Hirschhorn, *Democracy Reformed: Richard Spencer Childs and His Fight for Better Government*, Contributions in American History 174 (Greenwood Publishing Group, 1997), 5.
2. *New York Times*, April 17, 1918.
3. *New York Times*, April 17, 1918.
4. Hirschhorn, 5.
5. *New York Times*, April 17, 1918.
6. *New York Times*, April 17, 1918.
7. *New York Times*, April 17, 1918.
8. *New York Times*, April 19, 1918.
9. *New York Times*, May 17, 1918.
10. *New York Times*, May 23, 1918.
11. *New York Times*, May 17, 1918.
12. *New York Times*, May 17, 1918.
13. *New York Times*, May 17, 1918.
14. *New York Times*, May 17, 1918.
15. *New York Times*, May 23, 1918.
16. *New York Times*, July 12, 1918.
17. *New York Times*, July 12, 1918.
18. *New York Times*, September 14, 1918.
19. *New York Times*, September 16, 1918.
20. *New York Times*, September 16, 1918.
21. *New York Times*, September 15, 1918.
22. *New York Times*, April 18, 1919.
23. *New York Times*, April 22, 1919.
24. *New York Times*, April 21, 1920.
25. *New York Times*, January 1, 1922.
26. Hirschhorn, 5.

CHAPTER 25

1. Allen, *299*.
   New York Press, October 28, 1998.
3. *New York Times*, November 7, 1941.

BIBLIOGRAPHY

PRINT

Allen, Oliver. *The Tiger: The Rise and Fall of Tammany Hall.* New York: Addison-Wesley, 1993.
Angle, Paul McClelland. *Crossroads: 1913.* New York: Rand McNally, 1963.
Asbury, Herbert. *All around the Town.* New York: Basic Books, 2003.
Bergan, Francis. *The History of the New York Court of Appeals, 1847 to 1931.* New York: Columbia University Press, 1985.
Betts, Charles Henry. *The Naked Truth: Vital Issues before the Country Clearly Analyzed and Discussed.* New York: Lyons Republican Company, 1913.
Black, Conrad. *Franklin Delano Roosevelt: Champion of Freedom.* New York: Public Affairs, 2003.
Boller, Paul F. *Presidential Campaigns.* New York: Oxford University Press, 1996.
Brackett, Edgar T. *Arguments of Edgar T. Brackett: Of Counsel for the Managers for the Assembly on the Impeachment Trial of William Sulzer.* Albany, 1913.
Brands, H.W. *Traitor to His Class: The Privileged Life and Radical Presidency of Franklin Delano Roosevelt.* New York, Random House, 2008.
Brown, Roscoe C. E. *History of the State of New York: Political and Governmental.* Volume 4: *1896 to 1920.* Syracuse: Syracuse Press, 1922.
Chace, James. *1912: Wilson, Roosevelt, Taft & Debs — The Election That Changed the Country.* New York: Simon & Schuster, 2004.
Chester, Alden, and E. Melvin Williams. *Courts and Lawyers of New York: A History 1609–1925.* New York: American Historical Society, 1925.
Columbia University, The Faculty of Political Science. *Studies in History, Economics, and Public Law.* 11 vols. New York: Columbia University, 1899.
Connable, Alfred, and Edward Silberfarb. *Tigers of Tammany: Nine Men Who Ran New York.* New York: Holt, Rinehart, and Winston, 1967.
Dix, John A. *Speeches and Occasional Addresses.* New York: D. Appleton and Company, 1864.

Dix, Morgan. *Memoirs of John Adams Dix.* New York: Harper & Brothers, 1883.
Dougherty, J. Hampden. *Constitutional History of the State of New York.* New York: Neale Publishing Company, 1915.
Downy, Kristen. *The Woman behind the New Deal: The Life of Frances Perkins, FDR's Secretary of Labor and His Moral Conscience.* New York: Doubleday, 2009.
Dunne, John R. *New York's Impeachment Law and the Trial of Governor Sulzer: A Case for Reform.* Albany, 1986.
Grossman, Mark. *Political Corruption in America: An Encyclopedia of Scandals, Power and Greed.* Chicago: ABC-CLIO, 2003.
Facts on File. *The World Almanac and Book of Facts.* New York: Newspaper Enterprise Association, 1906.
Finan, Christopher M. *Alfred E. Smith: The Happy Warrior.* New York: Hill and Wang, 2002.
Fitch, Charles Elliott. *Encyclopedia of Biography of New York: A Life Record of Men and Women of the Past.* New York: American Historical Society, 1916.
Forrest, Jay W., and James Malcolm. *Tammany's Treason: Impeachment of Governor William Sulzer (The Complete Story Written from behind the Scenes, Showing How Tammany Plays the Game, How Men Are Bought, Sold and Delivered).* Albany: Fort Orange Press, 1913.
Friedman, Jacob Alexis. *The Impeachment of Governor William Sulzer.* New York: Columbia University Press, 1939.
Gover, William C. *The Tammany Hall Democracy of the City of New York.* New York: Martin Brown, 1875.
Hirschhorn, Bernard. *Democracy Reformed: Richard Spencer Childs and His Fight for Better Government.* Contributions in American History 174. New York: Greenwood Publishing, 1997.
Jenkins, John Stilwell. *History of Political Parties in the State of New York.* Auburn, NY: Alden & Markham, 1846.
Kennedy, William. *O Albany! Improbably City of Political Wizards, Fearless Ethnics, Spectacular Aristocrats, Splendid Nobodies, and Underrated Scoundrels.* New York: Penguin, 1983.
Klein, Milton M. *The Empire State: A History of New York.* Ithaca, NY: Cornell University Press, 2001.
LaCerra, Charles. *Franklin Delano Roosevelt and Tammany Hall of New York.* Lanham, MD: University Press of America, 1997.
LaFevre, Benjamin. *Campaign of 1884: Biographies of S. Grover Cleveland and Thomas A. Hendricks.* Chicago and New York: Baird & Dillon, 1884.
Lerner, Michael A. *Dry Manhattan: Prohibition in New York City.* Cambridge, MA: Harvard University Press, 2007.
Long, Kim. *The Almanac of Political Corruption, Scandals & Dirty Politics.* New York: Delacorte Press, 2007.
Luce, Henry Robinson. *Time,* Volume 3: *1923.* New York: Briton Hadden, 1924.
Luce, Henry Robinson. *Time,* Volume 4: *1924.* New York: Briton Hadden, 1924.
Marshall, Louis. *Arguments during the Impeachment Trial of Governor William Sulzer.* New York: J. B. Lyon Co., 1914.

McCombs, William Frank, and Louis Jay Land. *Making Woodrow Wilson President.* Charleston: Bibliobazaar, 1921.

McGuire, James K., and Martin Wilie Littleton. *The Democratic Party of the State of New York: A History of the Origin, Growth and Achievements of the Democratic Party of the State of New York, Including a History of Tammany Hall in Its Relation to State Politics.* New York: United States History Company, 1905.

Meyers, Gustavus. *The History of Tammany Hall.* New York: Boni & Liveright, 1917.

Mitgang, Herbert. *Once upon a Time in New York: Jimmy Walker, Franklin Roosevelt, and the Last Great Battle of the Jazz Age.* New York: Free Press, 2000.

Morgenthau, Henry, and French Strother. *All in a Life-Time.* New York: Doubleday, Page and Co., 1922.

Morris, Edmund. *Theodore Rex.* New York: Random House, 2001.

Murlin, Edgar L. *The New York Red Book: Containing the Portraits and Biographies of the United States Senators, Governor, State Officers and Members of the Legislature; Also with the Portraits of Judges and Court Reporters, the New Constitution of the State, Election and Populations Statistics, and General Facts of Interest.* Albany: J. B. Lyon Co., 1893, 1912–15.

Myers, L.T. *Great Leaders and National Issues of 1912.* New York: J. C. Winston, 1912.

Nasaw, David. *The Chief: The Life of William Randolph Hearst.* New York: Houghton Mifflin, 2000.

New York (State). Committee of Inquiry to Investigate Administration of State Government. *Report of the Committee of Inquiry to Governor William Sulzer.* New York: J. B. Lyon Co., 1913.

New York (State) Constitutional Convention. *Revised Record of the Constitutional Convention of the State of New York: April Sixth to September Tenth, 1915.* New York: J. B. Lyon Co., 1916.

New York (State) Court of Appeals. New York Supplement, Volume 149. New York: West Publishing Company, 1915.

New York (State) Legislature. Assembly, *Documents of the Assembly of the State of New York.* Vol. 136, Issue 35. 1913.

New York (State) Legislature. Assembly. *Journal of the Assembly of the State of New York.* Vol. 4. 1913.

New York (State) Legislature. Senate. *Documents of the Senate of the State of New York.* Vol. III, Issues 20–38. 1913.

New York (State) Legislature. Senate. *Journal of the Senate of the State of New York.* Vol. 2. 1913.

North, Simon Newton Dexter, Francis Graham Wickware, Albert Bushnell Hart, and William M. Schuyler. *The American Year Book.* New York: T. Nelson & Sons, 1914.

Platt, Thomas Collier. *The Autobiography of Thomas Collier Platt.* New York: Dodge, 1910.

Proceedings of the American Society of International Law at Its Annual Meeting. New York: Oxford University Press, 1912.

Proceedings of the Court for the Trial of Impeachments: The People of the State of New York by the Assembly Thereof Against William Sulzer, As Governor (Held at the Capitol in the City of Albany, New York, September 18, 1913, to October 17, 1913). Volumes 1 and 2. Albany: J. B. Lyon Co., 1913.

Rehnquist, William H. *Grand Inquests: The Historical Impeachments of Justice Samuel Chase and President Andrew Johnson*. New York: Quill, 1992.

Reichley, A. James, editor. *Elections American Style*. Washington, DC: Brookings, 1987.

Reynolds, John Francis. *The Demise of the American Convention System, 1880–1911*. Cambridge: Cambridge University Press, 2012.

Shannon, William V. *The American Irish: A Political and Social Portrait*. Boston: University of Massachusetts Press, 1989.

Slayton, Robert A. *Empire Statesman: The Rise and Redemption of Al Smith*. New York: Free Press, 2001.

Smith, Alfred E. *Up to Now*. Garden City, NY: Garden City Books, 1927.

Smith, Jean Edward. *FDR*. New York: Random House, 2008.

Sulzer, William. *Life and Speeches of William Sulzer*. Albany: Nabu Press, 2010.

Sulzer, William. *Miscellaneous Speeches (1898–1906)*. Ithaca, NY: Cornell University Digital.

Sulzer, William. *Public Papers of William Sulzer, Governor*. Albany: J. B. Lyon Co., 1914.

Sulzer, William. *Sulzer's Short Speeches*. Ed. George W. Blake. New York: J. S. Ogilvie, 1912.

Thomas, Samuel Bell. *The Boss, or the Governor: The Truth about the Greatest Political Conspiracy in the History of America*. New York: The Truth, 1914.

Von Drehle, Dave. *Triangle: The Fire That Changed America*. New York: Atlantic Monthly Press, 2003.

Weiss, Nancy Joan. *Charles Francis Murphy, 1858–1924: Respectability and Responsibility in Tammany Politics*. Smith College, 1868.

Wilson, Woodrow. *Congressional Government: A Study in American Politics*. New York: Houghton Mifflin, 1900.

Wilson, Woodrow. *A History of the American People*. 10 vols. New York: Harper & Brothers, 1901.

ONLINE

Alaska Mining Hall of Fame. http://alaskamininghalloffame.org/inductees/sulzer.php. Accessed February 11, 2010.

Congressional Biography Service. www.bioguide.Congress.gov. Accessed July 15, 2009.

C-SPAN Survey of Presidential Leadership. www.CSPAN.gov/http://www.c-span.org/PresidentialSurvey/presidential-leadership-survey.aspx. Accessed August 15, 2009.

Library of Congress. www.thomas.gov. Accessed July 22–23, 2009.

New York Elections — Governor. www.ourcampaigns.com/ContainerHistory.html?ContainerID=258. Accessed June 4, 2009.

United States Census Bureau. www.census.gov/popest/states/NST-ann-est.html. Accessed July 23, 2009.

United States Department of Labor, CPI Inflation Calculator. data.bls.gov/cgi-bin/cpicalc.pl. Accessed July–August 2009.

United States Senate. www.Senate.gov. Accessed July 23, 2009.